YOU'RE ABOUT TO MAKE
A TERRIBLE
MISTAKE!

YOU'RE ABOUT TO MAKE A TERRIBLE MISTAKE!

*How Biases Distort Decision-Making—
and What You Can Do to Fight Them*

OLIVIER SIBONY

Translated by Kate Deimling

Little, Brown Spark
New York Boston London

Little, Brown Spark
Hachette Book Group
1290 Avenue of the Americas, New York, NY 10104
littlebrownspark.com

First North American Edition: July 2020

Originally published in France as *VOUS ALLEZ COMMETTRE UNE TERRIBLE ERREUR!: Combattre les Biais Cognitifs pour Prendre de Meilleures Décisions* by Débats Publics. Translated from the 2019 edition, published by Flammarion.

Little Brown Spark is an imprint of Little, Brown and Company, a division of Hachette Book Group, Inc. The Little, Brown Spark name and logo are trademarks of Hachette Book Group, Inc.

The publisher is not responsible for websites (or their content) that are not owned by the publisher.

The Hachette Speakers Bureau provides a wide range of authors for speaking events. To find out more, go to hachettespeakersbureau.com or call (866) 376-6591.

10 9 8 7 6 5 4 3 2 1

ISBN 978-0-316-49498-4
LCCN 2020932931

LSC-C

Printed in the United States of America

For Anne-Lise

CONTENTS

YOU'RE ABOUT TO MAKE A TERRIBLE MISTAKE!

INTRODUCTION

You're About to Make a Terrible Mistake
(Unless You Read On)

Unless you've been living in a cave for at least a decade, you have heard about cognitive biases. Particularly since the publication of Daniel Kahneman's *Thinking, Fast and Slow,* terms like "overconfidence," "confirmation bias," "status quo bias," and "anchoring" have become part of daily conversations at the water cooler. Thanks to decades of research by cognitive psychologists and the behavioral economists they inspired, we are now familiar with a simple but crucially important idea: when we make judgments and choices—about what to buy, how to save, and so on—we are not always "rational." Or at least not "rational" in the narrow sense of economic theory, in which our decisions are supposed to optimize for some preexisting set of goals.

THE RATIONALITY OF BUSINESS DECISIONS

This is true, too, of business decisions. Just type "biases in business decisions" into your favorite search engine, and many millions of articles will confirm what experienced managers know: when executives make business decisions (even important strategic ones), their thought process does not remotely resemble the rational, thoughtful, analytical approach described in business textbooks.

My own discovery of this fact took place long before I'd heard of behavioral science, when I was a young business analyst freshly hired by McKinsey & Company. The first client I was assigned to work with was a midsize European company contemplating a large acquisition in the United States. The deal, if it went through, would more than double the size of the company and transform it into a global group. Yet after we spent several months researching and analyzing the opportunity, the answer was clear: the acquisition did not make sense. The strategic and operational benefits expected from the merger were limited. The integration would be challenging. Most importantly, the numbers did not add up: the price our client would have to pay was far too high for the acquisition to have any chance of creating value for his shareholders.

We presented our findings to the CEO. He did not disagree with any of our assumptions. Yet he dismissed our conclusion with an argument we had not anticipated. By modeling the acquisition price in U.S. dollars, he explained, we had missed a key consideration. Unlike us, when he thought about the deal, he converted all the numbers into his home currency. Furthermore, he was certain that the U.S. dollar would soon appreciate against that currency. When converted, the dollar-based cash flows from the newly acquired American company would be higher, and easily justify the acquisition price. The CEO was so sure of this that he planned to finance the acquisition with debt denominated in his home currency.

I was incredulous. Like everyone else in the room (including the CEO himself), I knew that this was the financial equivalent of committing one crime to cover up another. Finance 101 had taught me that CEOs are not foreign exchange traders, and that shareholders do not expect companies to take bets on currencies on their behalf. And this was a gamble: no one could know for sure which way exchange rates would move in the future. If, instead of appreciating, the dollar kept falling, the deal would go from bad to horrible. That was why, as a matter of policy, a large dollar-based asset should be evaluated (and financed) in dollars.

To a starry-eyed twentysomething, this was a shock. I had expected thorough analysis, careful consideration of multiple options, thoughtful debate, quantification of various scenarios. And here I was, watching a CEO who basically trusted his gut instinct and not much else knowingly take an unjustifiable risk.

Of course, many of my colleagues were more jaded. Their interpretations divided them into two camps. Most just shrugged and explained (albeit in more tactful terms) that the CEO was a raving lunatic. Wait and see, they said—he won't last. The others offered a diametrically opposite explanation: the man was a genius who could formulate strategic visions and perceive opportunities well beyond what we consultants were able to comprehend. His disregard for our myopic, bean-counting analytics was proof of his superior insight. Wait and see, they said—he'll be proven right.

I did not find either explanation particularly satisfactory. If he was crazy, why was he the CEO? And if he was a genius, gifted with powers of strategic divination, why did he need to ask us to apply our inferior methods, only to ignore our conclusions?

THE REVERSE ANNA KARENINA PRINCIPLE OF STRATEGY

The passage of time brought some answers. This CEO was certainly not a madman: before this deal, and even more so after it, he was regarded in his home country as one of the most respected business leaders of his generation.

He was also astoundingly successful. The acquisition turned out to be a great success (yes, the dollar did rise). Several big bets later, many of them equally risky, he had turned a near-bankrupt provincial company into a global industry leader. "See," some of my colleagues might have said, "he was a genius after all!"

If only it were that simple. During the following twenty-five years, as a consultant to CEOs and senior executives in multinational companies, I had a chance to observe many more strategic decisions like this one. I soon realized that the sharp contrast between the textbook decision-making process and the reality of how choices were made was not a quirk of my first client. It was the norm.

But another, equally important conclusion struck me too: although some of these unorthodox decisions had a happy ending, most did not. Errors in strategic decision-making are not exceptional at all. If you doubt it, just ask the people who observe them most closely: in a survey of some two thousand executives, only 28 percent said their company "generally" makes good strategic decisions. The majority (60 percent) felt bad decisions were just as frequent as good ones.

Indeed, our firm regularly produced voluminous reports warning business leaders against the risks of bad decisions. Along with other consulting firms and an army of academics, we felt compelled to blow the whistle on specific *types* of strategic decisions that proved especially perilous. But apparently no one listened. Watch out for overpaid acquisitions, we told executives—who immediately proceeded, like my first client, to buy bigger and more expensive companies, quite often destroying shareholder value in the process. Budget your investments carefully, we suggested, as plans are usually far too optimistic—and optimistic they remained. Don't let yourself be pulled into a price war, we wrote—but by the time our clients paid attention to this advice, they were deep in the trenches, under heavy fire. Don't let competitors "disrupt" you with new technologies, we warned—only to watch incumbent upon incumbent go out of business. Learn to cut your losses and stop reinvesting in a failing venture, we advised—and this advice, too, fell on deaf ears.

For each of these mistakes, there were, of course, a few specific examples, presented as cautionary tales. These were striking and memorable, even entertaining for readers given to Schadenfreude. (You will find more such stories—thirty-five of them, to be precise—in this book.)

But the individual stories were not the point. The point was that, when it comes to certain types of decisions, failures are much more frequent than successes. Of course, this is not an absolute, hard-and-fast rule: some acquirers did manage to create value through acquisitions, some incumbents did revitalize their core business before being disrupted, and so on. These successes gave some hope to those facing the same situation. But statistically speaking, they were the exception. Failure was the rule.

In short, when our clients made strategic decisions that turned out great, it was sometimes because they broke the rules and acted unconventionally, as my first client had. But when they failed, they rarely did so in a new, creative way. Instead, they made precisely the same poor decisions that others had made before them. It was just the reverse of Tolstoy's famous observation about families in *Anna Karenina*: as scholars of strategic differentiation have long theorized, every successful strategy is successful in its own way. But all strategic failures are alike.

THE BAD MAN THEORY OF FAILURE— AND WHY IT FAILS

The standard explanation for these failures remains the one most of my colleagues had offered on my first assignment: blame the bad, the incompetent, the crazy CEOs! Whenever a company runs into trouble, the stories we read in the business press put the blame squarely on the company's leadership. Books recounting these failures generally list the "inexcusable mistakes" of the people in charge and attribute them without hesitation to character flaws. The usual ones are straight out of the eight-hundred-year-old list of the seven deadly sins. Sloth (under the more business-friendly name "complacency"), pride (usually called "hubris"), and of course greed (no translation necessary) top the list. Wrath, envy, and even gluttony make cameo appearances.[*] That just leaves lust...well, for that, read the news.

Just as we lionize the leaders of successful companies (the

---

[*] Yes, gluttony. A *Fortune* cover story about J. C. Penney, which will be discussed in chapter 1, notes: "There were hints that the board was not as focused as it could be. Ackman had consistently complained about the chocolate-chip cookies served at Penney's board meetings....Other Penney directors also expressed concern about the caliber of cuisine served at their meetings."

Great Man Theory of leadership and success), we seem to unquestioningly embrace the Bad Man Theory of Failure. Good CEOs produce good results; bad results are the fault of bad CEOs. This explanation feels morally satisfying and provides justification for holding CEOs accountable (including, importantly, when they are generously compensated for successes). It also seems, at least superficially, logical: if CEOs, despite being copiously forewarned, repeat the mistakes that others have made, there must be something seriously wrong with them.

However, it does not require much digging to see the problems with this theory. First, defining good decisions and good decision makers by the results they will *eventually* achieve is circular, and therefore useless. If you are making decisions (or selecting people who will make them), you need a way to know what works (or who is good) *before* the results are in. In practice, as I learned from the divided opinions of my colleagues about my first client, there is no sure way, at the time a decision is made, of telling who is good and who isn't. Even knowing whether an individual decision is "good" or "bad" would, by this definition of "good," require an ability to read the future.

Second, if all companies tend to make the same mistakes, it is not at all logical to attribute those mistakes to the decision maker, who is different every time. Sure, incompetent decision makers might all make bad decisions. But wouldn't we expect them to make *different* bad decisions? If we observe one thousand identical errors, this seems to call for one explanation, not one thousand different ones.

Third and most importantly, calling these CEOs incompetent or crazy is blatantly absurd. Those who become the CEOs of large, established corporations have put in decades of hard work, consistently demonstrating an exceptional range of skills and establishing an impressive track record of success. Short of invoking some mysterious psychological transformation associated with the deleterious effects of supreme power ("whom the Gods would destroy, they first make mad"), it simply makes no sense to assume that so many leaders of large enterprises are mediocre strategists and bad decision makers.

If we rule out the Bad Man Theory of Failure, we're left with an intriguing problem. Bad decisions are not made by bad leaders. They are made by extremely successful, carefully selected, highly respected individuals. These leaders get advice from competent colleagues and advisors, have access to all the information they could hope for, and are generally incentivized in healthy and appropriate ways.

These aren't bad leaders. *These are good, even great, leaders who make predictable bad decisions.*

BEHAVIORAL SCIENCE TO THE RESCUE

To this puzzle, behavioral science brings a much-needed solution. Because humans do not conform to the economists' theoretical model of rational decision-making, they make mistakes. And not just any mistakes: systematic, non-random, predictable mistakes. These systematic deviations from economic rationality are the errors we have learned to call *biases*. No need to postulate mad decision makers: we should expect sane people, including CEOs, to make the same mistakes others have made before them!

This realization goes a long way toward explaining the popularity of behavioral science among leaders in business and government.

But so far, the most visible manifestations of this popularity have not concerned the decisions of CEOs. Instead, they have taken two forms you have certainly heard about—*unconscious-bias training* and *nudging.*

The "unconscious biases" that training aims to eradicate are those we bring to bear in our interactions with people, especially those who belong to minority groups. A growing number of organizations are aware of the problems posed by sexism, racism, and other biases, and train their employees to recognize and fight them. Training makes participants aware that, despite their good intentions, they are susceptible to these biases, and it usually exposes them to different images or models in order to change their unconscious associations. (Whether or not such mandatory training interventions are effective is a hotly debated topic, and not the focus of this book.)

In contrast to these attempts at making biases disappear, the second approach aims to use them productively. This is what the "Nudge" movement, launched by Richard Thaler and Cass R. Sunstein in their book of the same title, does.

The starting point is a debate as old as political science: if the choices of citizens produce outcomes that, as judged by the citizens themselves, are not optimal, what should government do? Some argue government should intervene actively. If, for instance, people don't save enough, they can be given tax incentives to do so; if they eat too much, taxes and bans can be put in place to deter them. Others, however, retort that adults should make their own choices, which may include making their own mistakes: so long as their choices do not harm others, it is not for government to tell them what to do and what not to do.

Thaler and Sunstein's great insight is that between these two views, the paternalistic and the libertarian, there is a third way, which they dubbed "libertarian paternalism." Choices can be presented in a way that gently "nudges" people toward the best behavior (again, as judged by themselves) without coercing them in any way. For instance, changing the order in which options are presented, and especially changing the option that will be selected by default if an individual does nothing, can make a large difference in many situations.

The UK government was the first to adopt nudging as a policy tool by creating the Behavioural Insights Team, more often referred to as the Nudge Unit. National, regional, and local government institutions (the Organisation for Economic Co-operation and Development counts more than two hundred) have created their own nudge units to assist policymakers in various areas, ranging from tax compliance to public health to waste disposal.

Businesses have adopted the "nudge" terminology as well, sometimes even setting up "corporate behavioral science units." Some, particularly in finance, have managed to exploit systematic anomalies in trading behavior to their advantage. For the most part, however, the methods businesses "discover" by applying behavioral economics are not new. As Thaler has written elsewhere, "Nudges are merely tools, and these tools existed long before Cass and I gave them a name." Indeed, exploiting other people's biases is one of the oldest ways to do business, legitimately or otherwise. When experts in "behavioral marketing" claim to analyze consumers' biases in order to influence them more effectively, this often leads them to rediscover well-known advertising techniques. And of course, Thaler notes wryly, "Swindlers did not need to read our book to know how to go about their business."

BEHAVIORAL STRATEGY

There is a third way of using behavioral science. Decision makers who adopt it do not aim to correct the biases of their own employees, as in unconscious-bias training. Nor do they attempt to exploit the biases of others, as with nudges and their corporate equivalents. They want to tackle biases in *their own strategic decisions*.

Once you think about it, this makes a lot of sense. If you believe your strategic decisions make a difference, and if you accept that biases in decisions result in errors, then your own biases might produce strategic errors. Even if you are a competent, careful, and hardworking executive, you might end up making avoidable, predictable mistakes. This is precisely the mysterious problem of bad decisions by good leaders that we discussed above. Except it is not "them"—it's you. And it is not mysterious—it is behavioral.

In academia, a new stream of strategy research, appropriately called *behavioral strategy*, focuses on this topic. In the words of some of its leaders, it aims "to bring realistic assumptions about human cognition, emotions, and social behavior to the strategic management of organizations." Keywords like *cognition, psychology, behavior*, and *emotion* now appear frequently in scholarly strategy journals. (In 2016, they appeared in more than one-fifth of papers in *Strategic Management Journal*.) Practitioner-oriented publications also reflect the growing interest in this topic. And surveys of decision makers show that many of them feel the need to tackle the bias problem to improve the quality of their decisions: a McKinsey survey of some eight hundred corporate board directors found that "reducing decision biases" was the number one aspiration of "high-impact" boards.

In short, many business leaders now realize that they should do something about biases in their own strategic decisions. But do what, exactly? Answering that question is the focus of this book.

THREE CORE IDEAS

Here is a very short overview of the answer. It can be summarized in three core ideas, each developed in one of the three parts of this book.

First idea: our biases lead us astray, but not in random directions. There is method to our madness. We may be irrational, but we are *predictably* irrational, as Dan Ariely memorably put it. In the strategic decisions of organizations, combinations of biases result in recurring patterns of strategic error that we can learn to recognize. These patterns explain the frequency with which we observe bad outcomes of certain types of strategic decisions, those where failure is not the exception but the rule. The first part of this book presents nine such patterns, *nine decision traps* into which our biases drive us.

Second idea: the way to deal with our biases is not *to try to overcome them.* Contrary to much of the advice that you may have read on the topic, you will generally not be able to overcome your own biases. Moreover, you don't need to. Consider a question that skeptics of behavioral science have often raised: how do humans achieve so much, despite their limitations? Or: "If we're so stupid, how did we get to the moon?" The answer, of course, is that "we," individual humans, did not land on the moon. A large and sophisticated organization, NASA, did. We have cognitive limitations that we may not be able to overcome, but organizations can make up for our shortcomings. They can produce choices that are less biased and more rational than our individual decisions would be. As I will show in part 2, this requires two key ingredients: collaboration and process. *Collaboration* is needed because many people are more likely to detect biases than a lonely decision maker is. Good *process* is required to act on their insights.

Third idea: while organizations can overcome individual biases, this does not just happen by chance. Left to their own devices, groups and organizations do little to curb individual biases. Often, they even exacerbate them. Fighting the effects of biases requires thinking critically about how decisions are made, or "deciding how to decide." A wise leader, therefore, does not see herself as someone who simply makes sound decisions; because she realizes she can never, on her own, be an optimal decision maker, she views herself as a *decision architect* in charge of designing her organization's decision-making processes.

In part 3, I will present three principles that decision architects use to design effective strategic decision processes. I will illustrate them with forty practical techniques implemented in organizations around the world, from start-ups to multinational corporations. These techniques are by no means "forty habits" that you should adopt by Monday morning. My hope in presenting this list is to prompt you to select the ones that may work for your organization or team, but also to encourage you to invent your own.

My essential aim in writing this book is to inspire you to view yourself as the architect of the decision processes on your team, in your department, or in your company. If, before your next important decision, you give some thought to deciding how you will decide, you will be on the right track. And you will, perhaps, avoid making a terrible mistake.

PART 1

THE NINE TRAPS

1

"TOO GOOD NOT TO BE TRUE"

The Storytelling Trap

> This story is completely true, because I made up the
> whole thing.
>
> —Boris Vian, *Froth on the Daydream*

In 1975, in the wake of the first oil shock, the French government launched an advertising campaign to encourage energy savings. Its tagline: "In France, we don't have oil, but we do have ideas." That same year, two men approached Elf Aquitaine, the French state-owned oil major. The two had no prior experience in the oil industry but claimed to be inventors of a revolutionary method for discovering oil underground without drilling. Their method, they explained, would allow a specially equipped airplane to "sniff" oil from a high altitude.

The so-called technology was, of course, a fraud—and not even a particularly sophisticated one. The con artists had fabricated, ahead of time, the images that the miraculous machine would produce during test runs. When the trials took place, they simply used a remote control to make images of oil reserves appear on the screen.

The story may seem preposterous, but the leaders of Elf Aquitaine—from the scientists in the R&D department to the CEO—bought it. When the time came to commit large sums of money to test the new process, they convinced the prime minister and the president of France to sign off. Remarkably, the scam went on for more than four years and cost the company roughly one billion francs. From 1977 to 1979, the amounts paid to the con men even surpassed the dividends that Elf Aquitaine paid the French state, its controlling shareholder.

This story is so incredible that when a younger audience hears it today, their reaction (especially if they're not French) is, at best, condescending pity, and, at worst, sarcastic attacks on the intelligence (or integrity) of the French leaders. How could such an obvious scam fool the top management of one of the biggest French companies, not to mention the entire French government? How could anyone be so foolish as to believe in oil-sniffing airplanes? Serious businesspeople would never fall for such a ridiculous story!

Or would they? Fast-forward thirty years to 2004. The place: California. A start-up called Terralliance is raising money. Its founder, Erlend Olson, has no experience in the oil industry: he is a former NASA engineer. What is his pitch? You guessed it! He wants to perfect a technology for detecting oil from airplanes.

The same scam takes place again, only the set and the actors have changed. This time the investors are Goldman Sachs, the venture capital firm Kleiner Perkins, and other big-name investment firms. The "inventor" has the rugged charm of a Texas cowboy. The rustic Boeing 707 that Elf Aquitaine purchased has made way for Sukhoi jets, bought surplus from the Russian army. History repeats itself so neatly that approximately the same amount of money, adjusted for inflation, is invested: half a billion dollars. Needless to say, the results are just as disappointing as they were the first time around: "sniffing" oil from airplanes, apparently, is quite difficult.

When smart, experienced professionals, highly skilled in their field, make large, consequential decisions, they can still be strangely blind. This is not because they decide to throw caution to the wind and take wild risks—in both oil "sniffing" cases, the investors did a considerable amount of due diligence. But while they thought they were critically examining the facts, they had already reached a conclusion. They were under the spell of storytelling.

THE STORYTELLING TRAP

The storytelling trap can derail our thinking about all kinds of managerial decisions, including ordinary ones. Consider the following case, adapted from a real (and typical) story.

You are the head of sales in a company that operates in an intensely competitive market for business services. You've just had a troubling call from Wayne, one of your highest-performing sales representatives. He told you that, twice in a row, your most formidable competitor, Grizzly, won business against your company. In both cases, Grizzly quoted a price that was much lower than yours. Wayne has also heard that two of your best salespeople have just resigned: the word is they're going to work for Grizzly. On top of that, he told you that there are rumors circulating that Grizzly is aggressively pitching some of your oldest, most loyal clients. Before hanging up, Wayne suggested that at the next management meeting you review your pricing levels, which, based on his day-to-day interactions with customers, seem increasingly unsustainable.

This call is cause for concern. But as an experienced professional, you do not lose your cool. You know, of course, that you must check the information that was just shared with you.

Right away, you call another sales rep, Schmidt, in whom you have complete confidence. Has he also noticed an atmosphere of unusually intense competition? As a matter of fact, Schmidt was planning on bringing this up with you! Without hesitating, he confirms that Grizzly has been especially aggressive recently. Schmidt just renewed a contract with one of his most loyal clients, despite a quote from Grizzly that was 15 percent lower than his. Schmidt only managed to keep the client thanks to his strong, longstanding personal relationship with the company's president. However, he adds, another contract is up for renewal soon. That one will be harder to keep if the price differential between Grizzly's offer and yours is this large.

You thank Schmidt for his time and hang up. Your next call is to the head of the human resources department: you want to check Wayne's report of salespeople who joined the competition. HR does indeed confirm that both departing sales reps, in exit interviews, said that they were going to Grizzly, drawn by the promise of higher performance-based bonuses.

Taken together, this information is starting to worry you. The first warning could have been just an insignificant incident, but you took the time to verify it. Could Wayne be right? Do you need to consider price cuts? At the very least, you'll put the question on the agenda of the next executive committee meeting. You have not decided to start a price war—yet. But the question is now on the table, with potentially devastating consequences.

To understand what brought you to this point, let's retrace your reasoning to Wayne's phone call. Whether purposely or not, what Wayne did is the essence of storytelling: he constructed a story by giving meaning to isolated facts. Yet the story he told is not at all self-evident.

Let's consider the same facts critically. Two salespeople have quit? Given the historical attrition rate of your sales force, maybe there is nothing unusual about this. The fact that they're leaving you for your largest competitor is not unusual, either: where would they be more likely to go? Then, both Wayne and Schmidt sound the alarm by complaining about the aggressiveness of the competition. When they manage to renew contracts and keep their clients, they take all the credit for it, attributing it to their strong relationships. Coming from sales reps, this is hardly surprising. Most importantly, how many deals are we really talking about? Wayne failed in his attempt to win two new clients, but did not lose any. Schmidt kept an existing client and is managing your expectations about an upcoming renegotiation. All in all, so far, you have not lost (or won) a single contract! If this information is considered without the distorting lens of the first story, it really doesn't add up to much.

So how did you get to the point of seriously considering a price cut? The storytelling trap was laid. You believed that you were objectively *checking* the facts Wayne presented, but you were actually *seeking to corroborate* what he said. To really check Wayne's story, for instance, you could have asked: How many new clients did all your other sales reps sign in recent weeks? Are you actually losing market share? Does the low price offered by Grizzly to one of your clients truly correspond to the same scope of work?

Asking these questions (and many others) would have helped you spot the only issue that might justify a price cut: a significant erosion of your company's value proposition relative to your competitors. If such a problem existed, you might want to cut prices. But those are not the questions you asked. Your definition of the problem was shaped by Wayne's initial story. Instead of searching for data that could *disprove* that story, you instinctively went looking for information that would *confirm* it.

It is easy to see how the same way of thinking can lead others astray—including the management of the French oil company and the American venture capital investors. When someone tells us a good story, our natural tendency is to search first and foremost for elements that corroborate it—and, of course, to find them. We think we're doing rigorous *fact-checking*. Checking the facts is essential, of course: Wayne's information, for instance, could have been factually incorrect. But one can draw a false conclusion from accurate facts. Fact-checking is not the same as story-checking.

The power of storytelling is based on our insatiable need for stories. As Nassim Taleb notes in *The Black Swan*, "Our minds are wonderful explanation machines, capable of making sense out of almost anything, capable of mounting explanations for all manner of phenomena." Neither Wayne, faced with some isolated facts, nor you, once those clues were in your hands, could imagine that the pattern they produced could be a fluke; that, taken together, they could mean nothing at all. Our first impulse is to see them as elements of a coherent narrative. The idea that they could be a mere coincidence does not occur to us spontaneously.

CONFIRMATION BIAS

The mental mechanism that makes us fall into this trap has a familiar name: *confirmation bias*. It's one of the more universal sources of reasoning errors.

Confirmation bias is especially powerful in politics. We have long known that people's susceptibility to political arguments depends on their preexisting opinions: when they watch the same debate between candidates, supporters of each side think that their champion has "won." Each side is more receptive to its own candidate's arguments and less attentive to the points the opponent scores— a phenomenon also known as *myside bias*. The same phenomenon occurs when individuals on opposite sides of the political fence are presented with identical facts and arguments on topics about which they already have firm opinions. It is even stronger when the two sides can choose the information sources they expose themselves to: doing so makes it even easier for them to ignore the data that inconveniently contradicts their positions.

The impact of confirmation bias on political opinions has become exponentially larger with the rise of social media. By design, social media overexposes its members to their friends' posts, which tend to match and therefore bolster each user's existing opinions. This is the now-familiar "echo chamber" or "filter bubble" phenomenon. Furthermore, social media often spreads incorrect or misleading information, now famously known as "fake news." There is little doubt that, under the influence of confirmation bias, many social media users take fake news at face value when it supports their preexisting beliefs. And confirmation bias does not just affect political opinions: even our reading of scientific facts is susceptible to it. Whether the subject is climate change, vaccines, or GMOs, we tend to uncritically accept accounts that confirm our opinions, while immediately searching for reasons to ignore those that challenge them.

You might think that this is a matter of education and intelligence, and that only obtuse, distracted, or blindly partisan readers fall into these traps. Surprisingly, this is not the case: myside bias has little to do with intelligence. For example, when Americans are presented with a study showing that a German car is dangerous, 78 percent of them think it should be banned on American roads. But if they're given identical data suggesting that a Ford Explorer is deemed dangerous in Germany, only 51 percent think that the German government should act. This is a blatant example of myside bias: national preference colors the way respondents interpret the same facts. Troublingly, the outcome of this experiment doesn't vary based on the intelligence of its subjects. The most intelligent subjects give the same response as those with a lower IQ. Intelligence does not guard against confirmation bias.

Obviously, not all people are equally naive or credulous. Some studies have reported a negative correlation between the inclination to believe the most ridiculous fake news stories and traits such as scientific curiosity or strong critical thinking skills. But whatever our critical thinking abilities may be, we all buy more easily into a good story that bolsters our opinions than one that troubles or challenges us.

Confirmation bias even slips into judgments that we think (and hope) are completely objective. For instance, a series of studies conducted by Itiel Dror, a cognitive neuroscience researcher at University College London, showed that forensic scientists— made famous by television shows like *CSI*—are also subject to confirmation bias.

In one of his most striking studies, Dror showed fingerprint examiners pairs of "latent" and "exemplar" prints (taken, respectively, from a crime scene and a fingerprint database) and asked them if the two were a match. In fact, the experts had seen these pairs of prints some months earlier in the course of their day-to-day work. But since they could not recognize these pairs among the hundreds that they examine every year, they believed they were dealing with new prints from new cases. The "evidence" was presented along with information that could bias the examiner—for example, "the suspect confessed" or, on the contrary, "the suspect has a solid alibi." In a significant proportion of cases, the experts contradicted their own previous readings of the data in order to provide a conclusion that was compatible with the "biasing" information supplied. Even if we are very competent and well-intentioned, we can be the victims of our biases without realizing it.

CHAMPION BIAS AND EXPERIENCE BIAS

For confirmation bias to be activated, there must be a plausible hypothesis, such as the ones Dror provided in his fingerprint experiments. And in order for the hypothesis to be plausible, its author must be believable.

In the example where you stepped into the shoes of the head of sales who received Wayne's phone call, one of the things that led you to believe Wayne's story was your confidence in him. If you had received the same call from one of your weakest salespeople, you might have written it off as the whining of an underperformer. Of course, we trust some people more than others, and what we know about the bearer of a message affects its believability. But we often underestimate how easily a story with a credible source can win us over. When the reputation of the messenger outweighs the value of the information he bears, when the project champion is more important than the project, we fall for *champion bias.*

And who is the champion in whom we have the most confidence? Ourselves! Faced with a situation we need to make sense of, the story that is immediately available to our mind, the one that we will then try to confirm, comes from our memory, our experience of apparently analogous situations. This is *experience bias.*

Champion bias and experience bias were both at work in the story of J. C. Penney. In 2011, this middle-market retailer, which operated some 1,100 department stores, was searching for a new CEO to breathe life into the aging company. Its board of directors found itself a "champion," a savior with the perfect résumé: Ron Johnson. A true retailer, Johnson had successfully transformed merchandising at Target. But most of all, he was credited (along with Steve Jobs, of course) with creating and developing the Apple Stores, which revolutionized electronics retailing and became one of the most stunning successes in the history of retail. What better leader could J. C. Penney find to spearhead its reinvention? No one doubted that Johnson would produce results just as spectacular as those he had achieved at Apple.

Johnson suggested a strategy that was a radical break from tradition, and he implemented it with rare vigor. In essence, he took inspiration from the strategy that had made the Apple Stores success-ful: an innovative store design, offering a new in-store experience in order to attract a new consumer target. But he applied it even more energetically to J. C. Penney, because he was now transforming an existing company instead of creating one from scratch.

Johnson's zeal for change knew no bounds, and his Apple inspiration was evident. Conscious that brand power played a key role in the Apple Stores' success, Johnson struck costly exclusive agreements with major brands and began reorganizing stores around brands, not departments. Remembering that Apple had spent extravagantly to create a luxurious setting for its products, Johnson invested large sums in redesigning J. C. Penney stores and rebranding them "jcp." Mirroring Apple's inflexible policy of fixed prices, with no sales or discounts, Johnson broke with Penney's practice of nonstop promotions and ubiquitous rebate coupons, replacing them with everyday low prices and modest monthly sales. Fearing that J. C. Penney's staff would not implement these changes energetically enough, Johnson replaced a large portion of its management team, often with former Apple executives.

Surprisingly, none of these changes were tested on a small scale or with focus groups before they were implemented across the company. Why? Because, as Johnson explained, Apple disdained tests, and that never stopped it from being wildly successful. Did anyone harbor doubts about this radical break in strategy? "I don't like negativity," Johnson would reply. "Skepticism takes the oxygen out of innovation."

To say that the results of this strategy were disastrous would be an understatement. Regular J. C. Penney customers no longer recognized the store or found coupons to draw them there. Other customers, whom Johnson wanted to wow with the new "jcp," were not impressed. By the end of 2012, sales were down 25 percent, and Penney's annual losses were approaching $1 billion, despite 20,000 layoffs to reduce costs. The stock price was down 55 percent.

Johnson's first full year at the helm would also be his last.

Seventeen months after his arrival, the board of directors finally ended the experiment. It rehired Johnson's predecessor, who tried as best he could to undo everything Johnson had done.

The board of directors had believed in its champion, and the champion trusted his experience. Both believed in a great story. What business story is more irresistible than the promise of a savior who can repeat his amazing success by once again breaking all the rules? Once sold on that story, the board (and the CEO himself) ignored all the signs that the strategy was failing. On the contrary, everywhere they looked, they found reasons to confirm their initial beliefs. Confirmation bias and the power of storytelling were at work.

ALL BIASED

Of course, we all believe that, had we been J. C. Penney board members, we wouldn't have bought Johnson's story. His mistakes— like those of the leaders of Elf Aquitaine in the oil-sniffing plane scandal—seem ridiculous. How incompetent, how arrogant these people must have been!

No wonder we react this way: after a shipwreck, we blame the captain. The financial press consistently attributes the failures of large corporations to their leaders' mistakes. Business books are full of these kinds of stories, usually centered on the leader's character flaws: pride, personal ambition, delusions of grandeur, bullheadedness, inability to listen to others, and, of course, greed.

How reassuring it is to blame every disaster on an individual's faults! This way, we can keep on thinking that we would not have made the same mistakes in their shoes. It also lets us conclude that such errors must be highly unusual. Unfortunately, both conclusions are false.

First of all, let's state the obvious: the leaders we discuss here are not stupid. Far from it! Before these failures, and sometimes still afterward, they were regarded as highly skilled executives, and much more than that: business wizards, visionary strategists, role models for their peers. The bosses of Elf Aquitaine, pure products of the French meritocracy, were certainly not considered naive, and neither were the Goldman Sachs or Kleiner Perkins investors. As for Ron Johnson, an article on his departure from Apple described him as "humble and imaginative," "a mastermind," and "an industry icon." As evidence of his reputation, it's worth noting that J. C. Penney's stock price shot up by 17 percent when his arrival was announced.

More importantly, while these stories are spectacular, the mistakes they illustrate are far from exceptional. As we shall see in the following chapters, there are many types of decisions for which error and irrationality are not the exception but the rule. In other words, these examples—like those that follow—are not chosen because they are out of the ordinary but, on the contrary, because they are all too ordinary. They represent archetypes of recurring errors that push leaders in predictable but wrong directions.

Instead of dismissing these examples as exceptions, we should ask ourselves a simple question: how could widely admired decision makers, surrounded by carefully selected teams, heading time-tested organizations, have fallen into traps that seem very crude to us? The simple answer is that when we are in the grip of a great story, confirmation bias can become irresistible. As we will see, the same reasoning applies to the biases we will discover in the coming chapters.

"JUST GIVE ME THE FACTS"

Many executives believe themselves immune to the dangers of storytelling. The antidote, they say, is simple: put your trust in facts, not stories. "Facts and figures!" What trap could they possibly fall into?

The very same one, it turns out. Even when we believe that we're making a decision on the basis of facts alone, we are already telling ourselves a story. We cannot consider objective facts without finding, consciously or not, a story that makes sense of them. One illustration of this danger comes from those who should be, both by method and by temperament, obsessed with the facts and immunized against confirmation bias: scientists.

In the past couple of decades, a growing number of published scientific results have turned out to be impossible to replicate. Particularly in medicine and experimental psychology, a "replication crisis" is raging. One of the most cited articles on the issue is simply titled "Why Most Published Research Findings Are False." Of course, explanations for the phenomenon are many, but confirmation bias plays an essential role.

In theory, the scientific method should guard against the risk of confirmation bias. If, for example, we are testing a new drug, our experiment should not aim to confirm the hypothesis that the treatment works. Instead, we should test the "null hypothesis" that the drug has *no effect*. When the results allow for *rejecting* this null hypothesis with sufficient probability, the alternative hypothesis—that the drug has an effect—is plausible, and the conclusion of the study is positive. On paper, the process of scientific discovery goes against our natural instincts: it seeks to *disprove* an initial hypothesis.

In practice, however, things are more complicated. A research project is a long effort, during which researchers make many decisions. As they define their research questions, conduct their experiments, decide which "outlier" data points to exclude, choose statistical analysis techniques, and select which results to submit for publication, researchers face many methodological questions and may have a choice among several acceptable answers. Leaving aside cases of scientific fraud (which are rare), these choices are the holes through which confirmation bias slips in. With the best intentions, and in complete good faith, a researcher can influence her results in the direction of her desired hypothesis. If these influences are subtle enough, they may remain undetected in the peer-review process. This is one of the reasons why scientific journals can end up publishing "false positives," studies that are technically solid and pass all the required tests of statistical significance but turn out to be impossible for other researchers to replicate.

The authors of a 2014 piece in *Psychology, Public Policy, and Law,* for instance, had to add an erratum to a published article: a mistake in statistical analysis had led them to overestimate their results. And what was the subject of their article? The effect of cognitive biases, especially confirmation bias, on the court testimony of mental health experts! As the authors noted in their correction, their mistake "ironically demonstrates the very point of the article: that cognitive biases can easily lead to error—even by people who are highly attuned to and motivated to avoid bias."

Ironic indeed...but telling: however hard we try to be "objective," our interpretations of facts and figures are always subject to our biases. We can only view them through the prism of a story we are unconsciously trying to confirm.

THE ILLUSION MACHINE

Let's return to the two stories of the oil-sniffing airplanes. Confirmation bias and the power of storytelling help explain how so many smart, experienced people managed to get things so totally wrong. While the details of the 1975 scam and the 2004 pipe dream differ, both featured skillful "inventors" who targeted their victims with a tailor-made story.

In 1975, France was reeling from the first oil crisis. The "inventors" promised Elf Aquitaine, and the country, nothing less than a new kind of energy independence. France had Airbus planes and a world-leading nuclear program, and it was working on the TGV, an innovative high-speed train. The country still believed in its superior technological prowess and its unique destiny. It did not seem implausible at all that France could invent a process no one else in the world had yet discovered or even dared to envision—a revolutionary technology that would restore the country to its past glory. For good measure, the crooks, aware that the chairman of Elf Aquitaine was a former minister of defense, dangled the possibility of military applications of their technology: if you can see oil through the ground, why couldn't you spot strategic submarines at sea?

The so-called inventors had no engineering skills, but they excelled at one thing: building a story that appealed to their audience. For those people, at that time, and in that context, it was irresistible. As the chairman of Elf Aquitaine confessed in the aftermath of the scandal, "A general atmosphere of faith had taken hold of everyone, and, for that reason, those who had doubts kept them to themselves."

This, of course, does not excuse him or his coworkers. In a scathing report, the magistrates who investigated the case wrote that "none of these considerations should have prevented the relevant individuals

from exercising vigilance and critical thinking." "Instead of systematically seeking to challenge the inventors and their process," the report
continued, "…all of their statements were accepted without examination or verification." Management emphasized "major campaigns
of aerial exploration…and declined to conduct one-off missions
designed to test the instruments and hold them up to scrutiny." The
experts Elf Aquitaine sent "were on a mission to learn and understand,
not to question the process systematically." The magistrates writing
this report had probably never heard the term "confirmation bias," but
their description sums up its essence: seeking proof that confirms the
initial hypothesis while neglecting to seek disconfirming evidence.

The same skill for adapting a story to its target audience is evident
in the 2004 remake. This time, the inventors promised "a revolution" to create "the Google of the oil and gas industry." This was just
the kind of story ambitious investors in the early 2000s dreamed of:
disruptive technologies that could revolutionize entire industries—
preferably the largest ones. Viewed in this light, every weakness
became a strength, every red flag a green light. Should investors be
concerned that Olson knew nothing about oil? On the contrary—
everyone knows that breakthrough innovations never come from
industry insiders but instead from disruptive entrepreneurs with a
fresh outlook! What about the fact that just about all the experts
were highly skeptical? A good sign—Terralliance would be able to
take this conservative, lethargic sector by storm!

When you want to believe a great story, everything goes. After losing
part of his fortune in the venture, one of the disillusioned investors said:
"It didn't make sense to me that you could acquire that kind of data with
a satellite. But I left the meeting saying, 'Shit, I'd better think about
this.' The real story, to boil it down, is as old as mankind: a charismatic
individual with a compelling story you just want to believe."

THE STORYTELLING TRAP IN THIRTY SECONDS

- **Storytelling** makes us construct a coherent story from a selection of facts. But this is never the only possible story, and it can lead us into error.
  - ▶ *A pattern of facts that are consistent with the beginning of a price war may have a different explanation—or be a mere coincidence.*
- **Confirmation bias** makes us ignore or discount information that contradicts our initial beliefs.
  - ▶ *In politics: myside bias, or politically motivated reasoning*
  - ▶ *On social media: the "filter bubble"*
- Confirmation bias also affects **smart people and apparently "objective" judgments.**
  - ▶ *Even fingerprint analysis is subject to confirmation bias.*
  - ▶ *Confirmation bias contributes to the "replication crisis" in scientific research.*
- Confirmation bias fuels **champion bias** when it supports our confidence in a "hero"...
  - ▶ *J. C. Penney's board of directors had complete faith in Ron Johnson.*
- ...and **experience bias** when it makes us believe in the relevance of our own experience.
  - ▶ *Ron Johnson thought he could replicate his Apple Stores success at J. C. Penney.*
- It's especially powerful when the story is one that we **want to hear.**
  - ▶ *Both stories of oil-detecting airplanes were tailor-made for their audience.*

2

"STEVE JOBS WAS SUCH A GENIUS"

The Imitation Trap

The people who are crazy enough to think they can change the world are the ones who do.

—Apple advertisement

Years after his premature death, Steve Jobs continues to be universally revered. This veneration is sustained by hundreds of books that promise to teach us anything and everything we need to know about Apple's founder: his innovation secrets, his design principles, his presentation techniques, his leadership style, his "zen," his secret habits, even his style of dress.

While the cult of Steve Jobs is unique in its scope, revering business leaders and raising them to the rank of quasi-divine models is nothing new. Jack Welch, head of General Electric from 1981 to 2001, and Warren Buffett, the idol of investors, were among the first to acquire a cult following. Other business legends include Alfred P. Sloan (General Motors), Bill Gates (Microsoft), Larry Page (Google), and recently Elon Musk (SpaceX and Tesla). All these charismatic individuals have been, or are, presented to us as models.

The need for models is understandable. For any executive, questioning oneself by comparing one's methods to those of other leaders is a good instinct. However, in our quest for models, we too often commit three mistakes. First, we attribute all of a company's success to a single person. Then, we see all the aspects of this person's behavior as reasons for his or her success. Finally, we're too quick to think we should imitate the model.

APPLE IS SUCCESSFUL BECAUSE STEVE JOBS IS A GENIUS: THE ATTRIBUTION ERROR

We have already seen how we instinctively create meaning through stories. To stick with the example of Apple, the story that we've heard hundreds of times—success beyond belief, following a fall and then a stunning comeback—nicely matches the structure of a heroic tale.

There is one problem, though: the hero in this tale is Steve Jobs, but the success is Apple's. This, after all, is one of the largest companies in the world by market capitalization. While it's certain that Jobs played a decisive role in its history, it's also fair to say that many of Apple's 60,000 employees (as of 2011, the year Jobs died) contributed in some way. Apple's continuing performance after Steve Jobs's death confirms this. Even if we focus only on the "creative" aspect of the Apple miracle—that is, the repeated invention of revolutionary products—Steve Jobs is certainly not the only individual who should get credit.

So why do the stories of Apple and Steve Jobs merge in our minds? Because the story we desperately want to hear is the story of a hero. The best stories are stories of archetypal characters.

Then we attribute all the results to these archetypes. We underestimate the role of other players on the team; the effects of the environment and the competitors; and, of course, the impact of plain old luck, whether good or bad.

The previous chapter showed how Ron Johnson became the hero of a success story: the story of the Apple Stores' creation. Other computer manufacturers—including, for instance, Gateway—had tried to create their own store network before. All had failed spectacularly. "Nobody believed a computer maker would make a good computer retailer," one financial analyst wrote. The Apple Stores proved the naysayers wrong. With revenues of $9 billion in less than ten years, they became a source of inspiration for the entire retail industry.

With their premium locations, unique design, elite customer service, and technological innovations (letting people avoid standing in line at the cash register, for example), the Apple Stores turned the industry's conventional wisdom on its head. And despite Jobs's influence, the concept was clearly Johnson's brainchild. Johnson acquired a reputation as a kind of King Midas of retail: "Anything Ron Johnson touches just turns to gold," one industry expert opined. "He understands retail in a way that I've never met in anyone."

Yet an entirely different reading of the story is possible. By attributing the Apple Stores' success to their innovative design (and therefore to their designer), we're too quick to forget a sizable factor: three of the most successful product launches in consumer history. A quick look at the stores' revenue growth is enough to set the record straight. The opening of the first stores in 2001 coincided with the launch of the iPod, a revolutionary innovation at the time. Sales really took off in 2008, when revenue jumped by

50 percent, following the iPhone launch. They were then flat for a year and suddenly rocketed from $6.5 to $9 billion in 2010, the year the iPad came on the market.

In other words, the cause-and-effect relationship between the design of the Apple Stores and their success is tenuous at best. Customers who spent the night waiting in line in front of Apple Stores weren't coming to admire the marble floors or the blond wood decor. They were there to get their hands on the new products they couldn't find elsewhere. A thought experiment in counterfactual thinking may be helpful here. Let's imagine that a less inspired version of Ron Johnson had been hired and had developed "basic" Apple Stores, resembling traditional electronics retailers like, say, Best Buy. Would they have been less successful? It seems likely. Would they still have ranked as one of the biggest successes in the history of distribution? Given the insatiable demand for Apple products that were available in priority in the Apple Stores, it's almost certain.

The value of this observation lies not in its originality but in its very obviousness. It is hardly a new insight to say that a store's success owes a lot to the merchandise it carries. And, to be fair to Ron Johnson, he was perfectly aware of this. His eagerness to radically reinvent J. C. Penney's product range, at the risk of driving away the store's traditional customer base, can only be explained in this light. However, as you read the story of J. C. Penney in the previous chapter, did that occur to you? You probably thought that it was foolish of Johnson to try to replicate at J. C. Penney his success with the Apple Stores. But did you think, *It's not even clear that this success had much to do with him*?

If this thought didn't pop into your head, you're not alone. The media, the stock market, and certainly the J. C. Penney board of directors didn't seem to doubt that Johnson had played a decisive role. Invariably, and so naturally that we don't even notice it, our first impulse is to attribute success (or failure) to individuals, to their choices, to their personality, but not to the circumstances. This is our first mistake: the *attribution error*.

STEVE JOBS IS A GENIUS, SO EVERYTHING HE DOES IS BRILLIANT: THE HALO EFFECT

The second mistake occurs when our admiration for a model leads us to study his or her life, decisions, and methods, and to find meaning in them. The American psychologist Edward Lee Thorndike described this mistake in 1920 and called it the *halo effect*. Once we have an impression of a person, we judge all that person's other characteristics in the "halo" of our first impression. For instance, tall men are considered to be better leaders (and, all else being equal, they receive higher salaries). Another example is the way in which voters judge candidates partly on their appearance: a politician must "look the part." In essence, we use information that is readily available (height or appearance) to avoid making much more difficult evaluations (for instance, of leadership ability or skills).

In his book *The Halo Effect*, Phil Rosenzweig showed how this effect applies not only to people but also to companies. In the case of companies, the most available characteristics are top-of-mind brand awareness and financial performance. So it shouldn't come as a surprise that we seek models among companies whose products are familiar to us (how many inches away are you right now from the closest Apple logo?). It is just as predictable that we will seek inspiration in the companies that perform most spectacularly on the stock market.

This second aspect has turned many corporations besides Apple into objects of study and imitation. The best example is General Electric (GE) during the era of its star CEO, Jack Welch. Named "manager of the century" by *Fortune* magazine in 1999, Jack Welch presided over an unprecedented creation of shareholder value: GE's total return to shareholders during his tenure was about 5,200 percent, far more than other large American companies constituting the S&P 500 index were able to deliver over the same period. As with Apple today, this success led to an endless urge for imitation. Indeed, Jack Welch himself encouraged GE managers to copy each other by sharing "best practices" inside the corporation. If best practices could be transferred from one division of this diversified conglomerate to the next, why couldn't they be applied elsewhere?

The answer to this question isn't so obvious. Imitating "best practices" looks like common sense. By seeking inspiration from the outside, we hope to fight complacency and the *"not invented here* syndrome," which leads companies to reject ideas generated elsewhere. This would be fine if the practices, methods, and approaches we chose were the right ones. Unfortunately, they usually aren't.

The reason is the halo effect. Typically, we *first* identify a successful company and *only then* choose one of its practices to emulate, on the theory that it contributes to the company's overall success. But it's not so easy to identify which of Apple's or GE's practices "explain" their success. Of all the things these companies do (or don't do), which ones, if any, should be considered recipes for superior performance? From *In Search of Excellence* to *Built to*

Last, countless management books have tried to answer this question. By studying the "best-run" or most "visionary" companies, they strive to isolate decisive factors (preferably under the control of managers, of course) that would account for their results. Sadly, the search for universal rules of success in business has so far been fruitless.

Of all of General Electric's management practices, surely none attracted more attention than its systematic use of "forced ranking" starting in the 1980s. This system for evaluating employee performance required each manager to put employees into one of three categories: the top 20 percent, the middle 70 percent, or the lowest-performing 10 percent. As Jack Welch explained, low performers "are given a chance to improve, and if they don't in a year or so, you move them out. And that's the way it goes."

Many companies tried to adopt this system. Not only did GE's success win respect, but the logic of forced ranking seemed unassailable. Who could doubt that the quality of talent is essential to a company's success? Who wouldn't want to constantly raise this quality? Who could dispute the fact that getting rid of the lowest-performing employees would mechanically raise the average quality of people?

Yet most of the companies that adopted forced ranking quickly gave it up. The percentage of American corporations using it fell from 49 percent in 2009 to 14 percent in 2011. Many cited its negative consequences on team spirit, motivation, and creativity, as well as the political jockeying and favoritism that it encourages. Even GE abandoned the system and now uses more nuanced methods of performance evaluation. Apparently there were more varied and complex reasons for GE's success than forced ranking.

But that's not all. Suppose we can identify with certainty the practices that explain the success of Apple or General Electric. There still remains the task of distinguishing which ones are applicable to a given situation and which are not.

Let's take another look at the story of J. C. Penney. We saw that Ron Johnson cited Steve Jobs's famous aversion to market research when refusing to test his new pricing strategy. Many leaders similarly rely on their intuition before launching a product. "Consumers only ask for what they are already familiar with," they explain. So, they argue, anyone who truly wants to innovate must place creativity and self-confidence ahead of public opinion.

This reasoning makes sense—for breakthrough innovations. Indeed, if a company aspires to *radically* change consumer behavior, there is reason to doubt the predictive power of market studies (at least in their most conventional form). But it's astonishing that this argument is so often cited as justification for refusing to test incremental innovations, such as product line extensions, or any new product that simply replaces an existing one. Everyone can tell the difference between introducing the first iPad and launching a new flavor of cookie, but it's so much more tempting to identify with a radical innovator...

An additional problem arises from the search for best practices. It distracts companies from what might give them a real advantage: differentiation. Since a good strategy must be different, imitating a competitor's practices can never make for good strategy.

More specifically, what is loosely called "best practices" includes practices of two distinct types. Some are *operational* tools—methods and approaches that have proved effective in a number of other companies. In IT, marketing, manufacturing, logistics, and many other areas, these practices can clearly improve operational performance. But on their own they cannot give you a lasting strategic advantage. The reason for this is simple: your competitors can imitate them, too. To rely on such approaches to win is to confuse strategy with operational effectiveness—a common and dangerous mistake.

The other type of best practices concerns *strategic* positioning. When you study a competitor's strategy and call it a "best practice," the underlying assumption is that there is a single generic strategy to win in your industry. Therefore, success can only be achieved if you target the same customer segments, use the same sales channels, and adopt the same pricing policies. Airlines, food retailers, and mobile phone operators have often followed this pattern of strategic imitation. The result is competition without differentiation, which focuses customers on price and destroys value for all the players in the industry. Imitating the strategies of others, however effective they may be for them, is a dead end.

Models can be useful. Idol worship, less so. Sometimes we need to leave best practices to those who invented them.

WHAT STEVE JOBS DID WAS BRILLIANT, SO I SHOULD IMITATE HIM: SURVIVORSHIP BIAS

It is especially important to think twice before emulating others when we think they're geniuses. This is the third mistake we make when looking for models. When I state that "Steve Jobs was a genius" and conclude "so I should imitate him," I've forgotten to mention the second premise of the syllogism: "I'm a genius, too." The current Formula One champion, for instance, is surely a driving wizard, but when you're behind the wheel, you wouldn't dream of emulating his "best practices." You know that only a wizard can do it! The logical fallacy is obvious in this example, but it too often escapes us when we're talking about the methods of a supposed business wizard.

Take, for instance, the undisputed wizard of investing, Warren Buffett. Buffett has delivered outstanding performance for half a century and has become the third-wealthiest person in the world, with a net worth of over $80 billion in 2020. Investors are especially likely to study Buffett's investment strategies, because they seem simple and because he expresses them in a folksy, no-nonsense style: stick to what you understand; beware of the fads and fashions that lead to bubbles; don't hesitate to keep holdings for ten, twenty, or even thirty years if they still have appreciation potential; do not overdiversify. The tens of thousands of Berkshire Hathaway shareholders who make the annual pilgrimage to Omaha, Nebraska, to hear the "Oracle of Omaha" all hope to understand his investment principles and apply them themselves.

Yet a mountain of evidence shows that trying to beat the market is a losing battle. It is highly unlikely that even one of the Omaha pilgrims will ever approach Buffett's performance. Indeed, Buffett himself cautions them against trying: the sage doubts that money managers can justify their fees and advises individual investors to buy index funds instead. In investing as in other fields, geniuses, if they exist, are by definition exceptional. We should not try to imitate them, because we will never manage to equal their accomplishments.

Of course, this message is not one we want to hear! Our eagerness to emulate geniuses is fueled by our tendency to overestimate our abilities, as chapter 4 will show. No amount of reasoning or statistical evidence will ever really convince us that we can't be exceptional, too. After all, would Steve Jobs, Jack Welch, or Warren

Buffett have been so incredibly successful if they had heeded this kind of warning? Isn't the very existence of these men, and so many other great figures, proof that exceptional performance is within our reach, if we just have enough talent and drive? Isn't it true, as an ad for Apple once planted in our minds, that "the people who are crazy enough to think they can change the world are the ones who do"?

Of course. And if we're seeking inspiration, we'll surely find it in these extraordinary figures. But if we're looking for practical lessons from them, we're making a serious reasoning error.

The models whose success we admire are, by definition, those who have succeeded. But out of all the people who were "crazy enough to think they can change the world," the vast majority *did not* manage to do it. For this very reason, we've never heard of them. We forget this when we focus only on the winners. We look only at the survivors, not at all those who took the same risks, adopted the same behaviors, and failed. This logical error is *survivorship bias*. We shouldn't draw any conclusions from a sample that is composed only of survivors. Yet we do, because they are the only ones we see.

Our quest for models may inspire us, but it can also lead us astray. We would benefit from restraining our aspirations and learning from people who are similar to us, from decision makers whose success is less flashy, instead of a few idols the whole world is striving to copy.

Better yet, why shouldn't we study *worst practices*? After all, everyone agrees that we learn from our mistakes even more than from our successes. Studying companies that collapsed may hold more lessons than focusing on those that succeed. Learning from their mistakes might be a good way to avoid making them ourselves.

THE IMITATION TRAP IN THIRTY SECONDS

- **Attribution error** leads us to attribute success (or failure) to a single person, and to underestimate the role played by circumstances and chance.

  ▶ *The success of the Apple Stores was attributed to Ron Johnson, not to Apple's product introductions.*

- The **halo effect** causes us to get an overall impression based on a few salient characteristics.

  ▶ *Steve Jobs's remarkable success makes us think that all his practices are worthy of emulation.*

  ▶ *We try to imitate the practices of successful companies even when they are unrelated to their performance.*

  ▶ *We don't challenge these practices enough to learn whether they are really applicable to us.*

- **Survivorship bias** consists of focusing on successful cases while forgetting about the losers, and it makes us think that risk-tasking is the reason for success.

  ▶ *Those "crazy enough to think they can change the world" sometimes do—but most of them fail.*

3

"I'VE SEEN THIS BEFORE"

The Intuition Trap

Don't trust anyone blindly, not even yourself.

—Stendhal

In 1994, Quaker Oats, then a prosperous, independent company, outbid several other prospective buyers to acquire Snapple, a brand of tea-based drinks. The price: $1.7 billion. Quaker's CEO, William Smithburg, was sure that this high price was justified by massive synergies. He had acquired Gatorade a decade earlier and made it into a superstar brand, and he was confident that Quaker could use its marketing power to repeat this feat with Snapple.

The acquisition turned out to be disastrous. Three years later, Quaker resold Snapple for less than one-fifth of the price it had paid. The mistake cost Smithburg his job and Quaker its independence, eventually (it was acquired by PepsiCo in 2000). Among investment bankers, to call a deal "a Snapple" has become shorthand for a gross strategic mistake. Yet Smithburg, one of the most experienced and admired executives in his industry, was confident in his intuition.

Whether they call it "gut feeling," "business instinct," or "vision," most executives don't hesitate to affirm that they rely on their intuition to make strategic decisions. Paradoxically, our rationality-obsessed world glorifies this ability and those who possess it. The clichés of conquerors on their mountaintops or inventors sitting under their trees is one of inspiration, not perspiration. And when we read the stories of successful entrepreneurs, outstanding CEOs, or great political leaders, they are much more likely to be celebrated for their vision and intuition than for their rationality or discipline.

The reality is that intuition does play a role, and often an important one, in our decisions. But we have to learn to tame and direct it. We need to know when it helps us and when, on the contrary, it leads us astray. And we should admit that when it comes to *strategic* decisions, it is, unfortunately, a poor guide.

TWO VIEWS ON INTUITION

The most important scholar of intuition may be the psychologist Gary Klein, a pioneer of what has become known as the "naturalistic decision-making" research tradition. Naturalistic decision-making researchers study real professionals in real situations. They observe military commanders, police officers, chess grand masters, and nurses in neonatal intensive care units. Evidently these decision makers do not apply the standard "rational" model of decision-making. They don't have time to analyze the situation, define the possible options, compare pros and cons against an established list of criteria, and finally choose the best course of action. So what guides them? In a word, intuition.

In one of his books, Klein recounts the story of a firefighter squad chief who somehow sensed that a house on fire was going to collapse. Seconds after he ordered his men to evacuate, the floor of the house caved in. When asked how he had made this excellent decision, the fire chief was unable to explain it. He even wondered if he had some kind of extrasensory perception.

What went on in the fire chief's head? Where did his lifesaving intuition come from? Of course, Klein does not believe in his subject's paranormal explanation. There is nothing magical about intuition. Napoleon once wrote, "On the battlefield, inspiration is usually nothing but recollection," and most researchers today share this opinion. According to them, intuition is based on the rapid recognition of a situation that has already been experienced and memorized, even if the lessons from that experience haven't been consciously formulated. Klein calls this the *recognition-primed decision model*.

The fire chief's story provides a perfect illustration. Upon entering the house, he perceived objective signals. In particular, he noticed the very high temperature in the room, but he heard no sound. As any firefighter knows, fires are loud. If this had been a kitchen fire, as the chief had originally expected, he would have heard noise coming from the kitchen. Conversely, if the fire in the kitchen were too small to be heard, the heat would have been less intense. The signals that he perceived were inconsistent with the scenario that he had in mind. What happened later explained these contradictory signals: the fire was not a small kitchen fire but a huge blaze in the basement. It soon consumed the floor on which the chief and his men had been standing.

The fire chief's decision was based on the recognition of a known situation (or, more precisely, on its nonrecognition, because the signals were inconsistent with his initial hypothesis). Thanks to his experience, the chief detected this inconsistency. Instantly, and without conscious reasoning, he drew the conclusion that this was not a plain kitchen fire.

This ability to draw on experience to instantly recognize weak signals allows professionals in many areas to make decisions in the blink of an eye. Malcolm Gladwell's book *Blink* is devoted to the subject. Its main point: we're all capable, if we would only listen to our gut, of making brilliant decisions based on the strength of our intuition.

What a great pitch this is! We all want to believe in the strength of our intuition. And heroes like the firefighter are such wonderful role models—so much more inspiring than methodical, nitpicky managers. If these great men and women who put their life on the line are trusting their intuition, why shouldn't we have faith in ours, too?

To understand why matters are somewhat more complicated, let's leave Gary Klein and his naturalistic decision-making colleagues behind for a moment. While they were developing their theories by observing extreme situations, another school of thought, the "heuristics and biases" tradition of cognitive psychology, was focusing on laboratory experiments. And this different approach to decision-making was producing radically opposing conclusions.

In a seminal 1969 experiment, Daniel Kahneman and his colleague Amos Tversky, the founders of the heuristics and biases movement, used seasoned statisticians as their subjects. The task they assigned them seemed quite simple: to determine the optimum sample size required for a study. The problem is technical but consequential: too large a sample creates unnecessary expense; too small a sample might produce inconclusive findings. Of course, the statisticians knew what formulas they should use to determine the optimum sample size. But, as experts who had used these formulas dozens of times, they tended to skip the calculations and just make rough estimates based on their experience with similar studies. Isn't that what experience is all about? Just like the firefighter, we might expect them to get to the correct answer, only faster.

Except they didn't. Kahneman and Tversky found that these experienced statisticians suggested seriously inappropriate sample sizes. By trusting their judgment, they overestimated the relevance of their experience and their ability to build on it. And they did this with complete self-confidence. Many later studies in other fields came to similar conclusions. The bottom line, for researchers in the heuristics and biases camp, is that we should be wary of self-assured experts who place too much faith in their intuition.

WHEN CAN WE TRUST OUR GUT?

The two viewpoints—the naturalistic decision-making view and the heuristics and biases one—seem irreconcilably different. Yet, in an unusual example of "adversarial collaboration," Gary Klein and Daniel Kahneman decided in 2009 to look beyond their theoretical differences and join forces to study the role of intuition in decision-making. The key question, they decided, was not *whether* the naturalistic decision-making researchers or the heuristics and biases ones were right. It was *when*. And surprisingly, once the question was reframed in this way, the two psychologists ended up on common ground. The subtitle of their joint article says it all: "A Failure to Disagree."

When, then, can we trust our intuition? Whenever, Kahneman and Klein agreed, two conditions are met. First, we must find ourselves in an environment of "high validity," in which the same causes generally tend to produce the same effects. Second, we must have had "adequate opportunities for learning the environment" through "prolonged practice and feedback that is both rapid and unequivocal." In other words, since our intuition is nothing but the recognition of situations that we have experienced before, we should trust it when such situations can truly be recognized, and when we have truly learned the right responses to them.

In light of these criteria, we can better understand the apparently contradictory results of studies on the value of expertise conducted in different settings. As surprising as it may seem at first glance, firefighters or intensive care unit nurses work in relatively high-validity environments. This does not mean that the environment is without uncertainty or risk. It means that the environment provides valid cues about a situation. Observing buildings on fire or emergency room patients provides reliable information about what will soon happen to them. Firefighters and nurses who have observed them for years, and who have seen what happened immediately after the fire or the emergency, have learned many lessons—more, perhaps, than they consciously realize. The same is true of test pilots, chess players, or even accountants: these are regular environments, providing quick and unambiguous feedback about the quality of most (if not all) decisions. Learning is possible.

Contrast this with the tasks facing psychiatrists, judges, or stock market investors. "Experts" in these fields may also think that they can trust their intuition. But these environments are complex and largely unpredictable. Feedback, if there is any, is ambiguous and delayed. True expertise is thus impossible to acquire.

Perhaps the most extreme case of an environment in which expertise cannot develop is the challenge of forecasting political, strategic, and economic events. Psychologist Philip E. Tetlock compiled forecasts made by almost three hundred experts on political and economic trends over a twenty-year period—82,361 forecasts in all. He then evaluated each prediction: when a pundit had predicted a recession, did it happen? When a political commentator had foreseen an electoral landslide, did it take place? Tetlock concluded that forecasts by experts were less good than if they had answered at random, and less good than those of amateurs who were asked the same questions. In these fields of extremely low validity, the intuition of experts is totally worthless.

The practical question then becomes: In which category do our decisions fall? When making business decisions, should we rely on our intuition, as firefighters and chess players do, or try to keep it at bay, as psychiatrists and traders should?

Unfortunately, there is no hard-and-fast rule. We must apply Kahneman and Klein's framework *to each and every decision*. There is no such thing as general-purpose intuition. There are situations in which intuition is useful for making management decisions, but that can only be true if we've encountered a sufficient number of similar situations to develop real expertise. In reality, this is not often the case.

For instance, what about hiring decisions? Does your intuition have anything valuable to offer when you select candidates? Perhaps, if you have hired many candidates for the same type of position, and if you have been able to learn the results of your hiring decisions. An HR manager who has hired hundreds of people for the same entry-level position over the years and who has tracked the hires' subsequent job performance may have developed good intuitive judgment. But this situation is the exception, not the rule. Many interviewers are not full-time recruiting professionals but managers hiring their future colleagues. Even HR professionals are unlikely to be tasked with filling the same positions over and over again, making it difficult for them to acquire the kind of experience necessary to trust their intuition. Furthermore, few organizations bother to systematically keep track of the quality of their past hiring (and nonhiring) decisions.

In this context, Kahneman and Klein's conditions are not met, and intuition will be an unreliable guide. This is confirmed by decades of empirical work on personnel selection. Traditional, "unstructured" hiring interviews, in which an interviewer forms an overall, intuitive impression of the candidate, do a very poor job of predicting the success of those hired. In many cases, simple tests would give better results.

Yet our confidence in the value of intuition remains undiminished: we are convinced that, in the course of a short interview, we can evaluate a candidate's skills, strengths, weaknesses, motivation, and fit with the corporate culture. When applying for a job, we would be shocked if a company hired us without an interview. This is why the overwhelming majority of organizations continue to rely on unstructured interviews and to make hiring decisions largely on the basis of interviewer intuition. Three leading researchers who have observed the "embarrassingly poor validity" of this personnel selection tool can only describe its continuing popularity as the "persistence of an illusion."

Another prime example of intuition-based decision-making is the launch of new products in consumer goods and luxury products companies. Some executives pride themselves on their irreplaceable expertise in this field. As the president of one such company put it, "I have a thousand cases of product launches in my head when I evaluate whether a product is worthy of our brand. Who could decide this better than I can?" Indeed, in this leader's case, the conditions for intuitive expertise were met. The president's extensive experience in the same company, in an industry in which the success of new products can be instantly measured, was invaluable. If his judgment—including his aesthetic judgment— about proposed new products was so often right, it was not just, as he would put it, because he has "good taste." His successful track record was the result of decades of hard work, during which he had acquired intuitive expertise about what worked (and what didn't) in a relatively high-validity environment.

So it made perfect sense for the president to be the final arbiter on all product launch decisions…until he was replaced by a younger executive. The newcomer was brilliant but didn't have the same industry experience. His gut feeling was therefore much less reliable. Unfortunately, his confidence in the value of his own intuition was just as complete as his predecessor's.

As these examples suggest, the question isn't whether or not "hiring" and "launching new products" are areas in which intuition is useful; it is whether or not a decision maker's intuition, based on her experience, is suited to making the specific decision at hand. Experienced executives tend to believe that their intuition is precious, and they're often right. But only the wisest among them are able to recognize when to listen to it—and when not to.

One experienced dealmaker, for instance, describes how valuable his intuition is in negotiation situations. His extensive negotiating experience allows him to "feel out" the other party, to perceive fatigue or weakness, to accurately detect the moment when he should push his advantage or make a tactical retreat. But while he relies on his intuition to manage the human aspect of negotiations, he is careful not to use it when making decisions about the deal itself. Should we bid for this asset? What is our maximum price? What are the essential conditions that must be met? These are questions that shouldn't be answered by relying on intuition. Even for someone who has brokered dozens of deals, judging what made them succeed or fail is not easy. The conditions for intuitive expertise are not met. Dealmaking benefits from intuition. Deciding which deals to make doesn't.

This brings us back to the case of William Smithburg and his acquisition of Snapple. His intuition was based on a single experience: the acquisition and subsequent success of Gatorade. It was tempting to see this acquisition as a successful case that would be easy to replicate. But intuition overlooked what analysis revealed to outside observers: Snapple, unlike Gatorade when it was purchased by Quaker, was already losing market share. Its distribution model was very different from Quaker's and would be difficult to integrate into the company. The production methods for tea-based drinks were also different from those Quaker knew. And Snapple's brand positioning as a natural, slightly offbeat product was difficult for a corporation like Quaker to maintain. For an outside observer, all these differences with Gatorade were significant. But Smithburg, confident in his intuition, only saw the similarities.

INTUITION, A POOR GUIDE TO STRATEGIC DECISION-MAKING

The moral of this story goes beyond Smithburg's case. Let's revisit Kahneman and Klein's conditions for knowing when a decision maker's intuition is relevant: prolonged practice with clear feedback in a high-validity environment. Were these conditions met when Smithburg decided to acquire Snapple? And, in general, can they be met when any *strategic* decision is on the table?

One defining characteristic of strategic decisions is that they are relatively rare. There is, thus, little chance that an executive facing a strategic decision has made many decisions of the same type in the past. When you embark on a radical restructuring, launch a breakthrough innovation, or attempt an acquisition that will change your company's course, these are often things you have not done before. Sometimes, as in the case of Smithburg with Gatorade, you have done them exactly once, and it is easy to overestimate the true relevance of your limited experience.

Another essential characteristic of strategic decisions is that they aim to shape the long-term trajectory of the company as a whole. This makes their effects difficult to read. The results you see are not simply the effects of your strategic decisions. They combine with countless other effects—economic downturns and upturns, new market trends, unforeseen competitive moves, changed circumstances, and so on. Except for some undisputed successes or egregious mistakes, feedback on your past strategic decisions is seldom unambiguous and never quick. In other words, even if you do have experience with strategic decisions, this experience does not allow for real learning.

True strategic decisions aren't just a poor fit with Kahneman and Klein's framework. They are the *exact opposite* of it. Strategic decisions take place in a low-validity environment, in which the decision makers have had limited practice, with delayed, unclear feedback. If we searched for a textbook example of conditions in which expert intuition *cannot* develop, we couldn't find a better one.

Yet most executives give credence to their "gut feeling" when making a strategic decision. For many of us, particularly if we have been successful before, the intensity of our subjective belief is our compass: "If I have any doubts, I hold back, but when I'm really sure, I go for it."

When we do this, we forget that the CEOs, statisticians, and traders who were led astray by their intuition also had great confidence in their gut feelings, and that, in general, our confidence in our own judgment is almost always too great. That is the subject of the next chapter.

THE INTUITION TRAP IN THIRTY SECONDS

- **Naturalistic decision-making** emphasizes the value of intuition in real, often extreme, situations.

  ▶ *The firefighter can "feel" when the house is going to collapse.*

- On the contrary, **heuristics and biases** researchers, who study decisions in the laboratory, generally conclude that intuition leads us astray.

  ▶ *The "expertise" of political forecasters does not lead to better forecasts.*

- Kahneman and Klein worked together to resolve their disagreement and identified the **two necessary conditions** for the development of real expertise: **a high-validity (predictable) environment; and prolonged practice with quick, clear feedback.**

  ▶ *Expert intuition can thus be developed by firefighters, pilots, or chess players...*

  ▶ *...but not by psychiatrists, judges, or traders.*

- **"Should I trust my intuition?"** is a question to ask **on a decision-by-decision basis.** The answer depends on whether the two conditions are met, not on how confident we are in our intuition.

  ▶ *Smithburg was convinced that his intuition about Snapple was right.*

- Generally, **the more strategic a decision is, the less helpful intuition will be:** strategic decisions are rare, their environment is low-validity, and feedback is ambiguous.

4

"JUST DO IT"

The Overconfidence Trap

We place absolute confidence in the *Titanic*. We believe that the boat is unsinkable.

—Philip A. S. Franklin, vice president of
International Mercantile Marine Co.,
owner of the White Star Line

In the early 2000s, the U.S. market for video rentals was a large, profitable industry. It accommodated all kinds of players, from mom-and-pop corner stores to regional chains. But it had its eight-hundred-pound gorilla: Blockbuster. With its 9,100 stores, the chain, led by John Antioco, generated revenue of about $3 billion.

Meanwhile a fledgling start-up, founded in 1997, had begun competing on an entirely different business model. For a flat monthly subscription fee, its customers could go online to create a "queue" of DVDs on the company's website and have them shipped for free to their mailbox. Once they mailed back the DVDs they had watched, they would automatically receive the next DVDs in their queue. It wasn't a high-tech model, but it met consumer needs: with a centralized video library, movies were less frequently out of stock, and advice on selecting a title was more relevant. Above all, while the video stores imposed stiff penalties on customers who returned their videos late, the monthly fee model, like an all-inclusive phone plan, acted as a no-surprises guarantee. By early 2000, the start-up had signed three hundred thousand subscribers. Its name: Netflix.

By the time the dot-com bubble burst that spring, Netflix was not yet profitable, and the company was in dire need of financing. Its CEO, Reed Hastings, and his close associates paid Blockbuster a visit and made John Antioco a straightforward offer: Blockbuster would acquire 49 percent of Netflix, and turn it into its internet arm, under the brand Blockbuster.com. Blockbuster stores would also sell Netflix's subscription service. It would be a seamless "click-and-mortar" company, along the lines of what many retailers are still trying to accomplish today. The price tag Hastings put on his company was $50 million.

How did John Antioco and his team respond? "They just about laughed us out of their office," Netflix's leaders later related. For Antioco, Netflix was not at all a threat. Of course, the start-up had developed a small customer base on the web. But this was the era of dial-up internet, long before broadband became standard. The concept of streaming movies was still unimaginable for most people. Furthermore, Antioco probably reasoned that if Blockbuster ever wanted to imitate Netflix with a monthly subscription model, nothing would stop him from doing it all on his own.

We all know how this story ends. Netflix reached 1 million subscribers in 2002 (the year it went public) and 5.6 million by 2006—still with its low-tech, rent-by-mail model. Only later would the rise of streaming give it a decisive boost. By early 2020, Netflix had 167 million subscribers. Its market capitalization was over $150 billion, several hundred times its introduction price (and three *thousand* times the price Antioco could have paid).

As for Blockbuster, it did try to launch its own subscription service in 2004. It was too little, too late. The company filed for bankruptcy in 2010. David had conquered Goliath.

It is easy to criticize Antioco's lack of vision, or Blockbuster's inability to change its business model. But Blockbuster is not the only incumbent that let a start-up disrupt its industry and threaten its survival. Why did this Goliath so seriously overestimate his own powers, while underestimating David's? If he hadn't, perhaps he would have taken the deal that was offered to him. At the very least, he might have taken advantage of the intervening years, before broadband internet became widely available, to enter this area. Admittedly, even if he had, there is no guarantee that Blockbuster would have been able to maintain its lead amid the tumult of technological change. But the story would certainly have been different.

EXCESSIVE SELF-CONFIDENCE

Do you remember how you felt about the oil-sniffing planes in chapter 1? If you're like most people, your initial reaction to the Blockbuster-Netflix story is probably quite similar. "Blockbuster's leaders were not thinking clearly," we earnestly declare. "Had we been in their shoes, we never would have made such a mistake."

There is reason to believe that this reaction reflects our own overconfidence, which is ironically the same error that John Antioco made when underestimating Reed Hastings.[*]

In general, we significantly overestimate ourselves relative to others (a form of overconfidence sometimes referred to as *over-placement*). Simply put, when it comes to a wide range of important traits, we all believe we are better than most.

For instance, 88 percent of Americans believe they drive more safely than 50 percent of their fellow drivers (60 percent even claim to be in the top 20 percent). Similarly, about 95 percent of MBA students believe that they're in the top 50 percent of their class, even though they regularly receive grades allowing them to compare their achievements with those of their classmates. Their professors are subject to the same bias, as a mischievous academic found when he asked his colleagues if they're part of the top 50 percent of professors: 94 percent are sure they are. Ask yourself whether you are better or worse at your job than the majority of your coworkers: most likely, you believe you are above the median. In light of these numbers, it is hardly surprising that most of us think we would have been better strategists than the leaders of Blockbuster.

OPTIMISTIC PREDICTIONS AND THE PLANNING FALLACY

In addition to having excessive confidence in our own abilities, we are often overconfident about the future. This excessive optimism takes several forms.

---

[*]   This reaction also reveals our tendency to judge a past decision in light of information that only became available after the fact. This is *hindsight bias*, which will be discussed in chapter 6.

The first form is the simplest: our theoretically "objective" forecasts about events that are out of our control are often exaggeratedly bullish. The typical example is economic forecasts: one study of thirty-three countries showed that economic growth forecasts produced by official budget agencies are generally too optimistic, even more so for the medium term (three years) than for the short term.

A second kind of optimism, called the *planning fallacy*, specifically concerns estimates of the time and budget we will require to complete a project. Anyone who has had their kitchen renovated knows the problem; but on a bigger scale, it can reach epic proportions. The construction of the Sydney Opera House, begun in 1958, was supposed to cost 7 million Australian dollars. It cost 102 million and took sixteen years. And this is not a unique case—far from it. The impressive Getty Center in Los Angeles opened its doors in 1998, ten years later than originally planned, after eating up $1.3 billion, nearly four times more than its initial budget. The next-generation nuclear power plant in Flamanville, France, should have been completed in 2012 at a cost of 3.5 billion euros; as of 2019, it was scheduled to open in 2023 and to cost 12.4 billion euros. Similar or worse delays and overruns are expected on two other sites piloting the same technology in Olkiluoto, Finland, and Hinkley Point, in the UK. A global study of 258 transportation infrastructure projects—railroads, tunnels, bridges—showed that 86 percent of them went over their original budget. And, of course, aerospace and defense projects are notorious for their astronomical overruns: the F-35 Joint Strike Fighter program is on track to exceed initial cost estimates by tens, if not hundreds, of billions of dollars.

Perhaps you're not surprised by these examples. In truth, we have gotten used to seeing the costs of publicly financed projects spiral out of control. Even if we're not dyed-in-the-wool cynics, we have an explanation at the ready: the companies submitting bids overpromise to win the contract, expecting (correctly) that they will be able to renegotiate later. Meanwhile, the buyers have to convince their own stakeholders to sign on, which makes them prone to minimizing the costs and risks as well. Bent Flyvbjerg, the Oxford University researcher who compiled most of these statistics on megaprojects, confirms that this "Machiavellian explanation" is part of the problem: "underestimation cannot be explained by error and seems to be best explained by strategic misrepresentation, i.e., lying."

However, the planning fallacy, which leads a project's advocates to underestimate its time frame and costs, is not limited to publicly financed projects. Entirely private projects have delays and overruns, too. Even individuals succumb to the planning fallacy: students who need to finish a paper or authors who commit to turn in a manuscript by a certain date almost always underestimate how long it will take.

This suggests that the planning fallacy has many causes besides the "strategic" or "Machiavellian" one. When we make a plan, we don't necessarily imagine all the reasons it could fail. We overlook the fact that success requires the alignment of many favorable circumstances, while a single glitch can derail everything. Above all, we focus on our plan as seen "from the inside"; that is, we don't consider the universe of similar projects that took place in the past, ask ourselves what schedules and budgets they anticipated and whether they experienced delays and overruns. In chapter 15, we will return to the technique of using an "outside view" to address the planning fallacy.

OVERPRECISION

There is a third kind of overconfidence, quite distinct from the previous varieties: expressing our predictions (whether or not they are optimistic) too precisely. We can overestimate our *ability* to predict the future, even when our prediction is pessimistic.

Of course, any prediction is uncertain. This is why it is not enough to make predictions: we must also have an idea of the level of confidence that we can place in them. This is particularly important when we make quantitative predictions. In principle, a good practice would be to use a "confidence interval": if, for instance, we want to be 90 percent confident in our forecast, we will offer not a point prediction but a range, chosen so that we are 90 percent sure the real outcome will fall within it.

This is exactly what subjects are asked to do in the classic over-precision test, originally designed by Marc Alpert and Howard Raiffa and popularized by J. Edward Russo and Paul Schoemaker. The test subjects are given ten general knowledge questions. For managers, these may be questions linked to their field of activity, while in the popular version of the test, subjects have to estimate the length of the Nile, the year of Mozart's birth, or the gestation period of an African elephant. For each question, the respondents must answer with an interval, making it large enough for them to be "90 percent certain" that it contains the correct answer. For instance, you might be "90 percent sure" that Mozart was born between 1700 and 1750.

You would be wrong (little Wolfgang was born in 1756). And you wouldn't be alone. Almost all people who take this test choose confidence intervals that are too narrow; 99 percent of the two-thousand-plus people tested by Russo and Schoemaker did.

If we were good judges of the precision of our own estimates, we would obtain nine correct answers out of ten, or eight at the very least.* But on average, depending on the version of the test, subjects only get three to six questions right. Simply put, when we're 90 percent sure, we're wrong at least half of the time.

It is worth pointing out that, in this experimental situation, nothing stops a respondent from choosing a very large interval. There is no penalty for answering that Mozart was born between 1600 and 1850, something that we can be 90 percent certain of (and even a good deal more). In a real situation, however, this kind of estimate would immediately discredit its author. Companies may acknowledge the uncertainty and volatility of the business environment, but very few of them reward executives for acknowledging the uncertainty of their own judgments. As a result, most executives continue to express predictions as if the future were perfectly predictable. When they forecast revenue growth or quarterly earnings, they are expected to confidently give specific predictions. How would a manager who wants to look competent *not* be guilty of overprecision?

"ALONE IN THE WORLD": HOW WE UNDERESTIMATE OUR COMPETITORS

Our overconfidence in our own abilities, our exaggerated faith in our predictions, and organizational pressure to appear self-confident all produce another widespread problem: underestimating our

---

* Someone who provides ten answers with a confidence interval of 90 percent should have at least eight correct answers in 94 percent of cases.

competitors. "Underestimating" is actually an understatement, because usually we simply ignore them, failing to take their behavior and reactions into account at all.

If you are, or ever have been, a senior leader of any company, try this quick evaluation. You have surely been the recipient, or the provider, of many plans—marketing plans, sales plans, strategic plans, and so on. What percentage of these plans predicted some kind of gain—of customers, of market share, or of something else? Surely most of them. How many of these same plans predicted your competitors' reaction to this hoped-for gain? Probably none. Most plans do, of course, take stock of the competition—but usually as an element of context, a backdrop to the proposed action plan. The section in a strategic plan that reviews competitors is usually the first, and is often called the "competitive landscape." As the term suggests, the plans assume that the landscape is just waiting to be invaded without resistance. When has a landscape ever fought back?

The simple fact we so conveniently forget is that, at the very moment when we are presenting a project intended to beat our competitors, those same competitors are coming up with a plan to do the exact same thing to us. And they also don't stop to think that *we* will defend *our* market share. Richard Rumelt, a professor at UCLA and author of the excellent book *Good Strategy/Bad Strategy*, notes that when executives consider a strategy problem, it is totally predictable that they will not think about competitors. "Half of what alert participants learn in a strategy exercise is to consider the competition even when no one tells you to do it in advance."

It would be an exaggeration to attribute this state of affairs solely to decision makers' overconfidence. Many factors contribute to our neglect of competitors. First, your real, immediate objective when presenting a plan is not to beat the competition—it is to secure resources internally. If others are promising the moon, why shouldn't you? Second, trying to predict your competitors' reaction is a difficult exercise and will produce uncertain results. Is it really worth the effort? Moreover, if you really studied the probable reaction of your competitors, you might reach a conclusion no one wants to hear: the plan is bad, either because you don't have any advantage over your competitors or because their likely reaction will cause it to fail!

Consider, for instance, a story told by A. G. Lafley, former CEO of Procter & Gamble, about its attempt to enter the bleach business. P&G's reasoning was simple: by throwing its considerable marketing and sales muscle behind a good product, called Vibrant, it would easily carve out a place in the bleach category at the expense of Clorox, the undisputed market leader. Of course, P&G's managers suspected that Clorox would respond. But imagine their surprise upon discovering that in the city they had chosen as their test market, Clorox had delivered a gallon of free bleach to the doorstep of every single house! This preemptive strike, which was obviously expensive, was nevertheless predictable if you put yourself in Clorox's place. For Clorox, letting P&G invade their turf, the core business from which they derived most of their profits, was unthinkable. Clorox spared no expense in sending P&G a crystal clear message. P&G soon gave up the idea, and Lafley learned a memorable lesson: "Head-on, World War I–like assaults on walled cities generally end with a lot of casualties."

POOR DECISION MAKERS BUT EXCELLENT LEADERS?

This last example illustrates the practical problem that over-confidence poses to managers. As a rule, products are launched every day on the basis of overoptimistic plans. If we adopted a coldly realistic vision of the environment, our competition, and the countless variables that can threaten the success of any of our projects, we would do nothing—or very little. This would surely be the worst of all strategies. The "paralysis by analysis" that cripples many companies surely causes more damage than optimism. Optimism at least moves us to action, even if we may need to change course subsequently.

So let's make it clear: yes, optimism is valuable, even essential! This is why organizations intentionally and unapologetically encourage it. In most managerial situations, we operate in a state of intentional confusion between ambition and realism, goals and predictions, wishes and beliefs.

The clearest example of this confusion is the ritual of establishing an annual budget. The budget is both a tool for engagement and an exercise in prediction. The manager to whom you have given a goal wants to meet it, and if you trust her, you believe she will. This tension between predictions and goals is part and parcel of the exercise. In theory, it allows for negotiating a number that both parties find realistic. Her target is your forecast.

The troubles start when this tension increases, which is unfortunately frequent. For example, if you think this manager's objective seems compromised, what will you say? Do you tell her that you believe this objective is still realistic—a forecast you still *believe* in? Or do you still demand she meet it—that is, treat it as a target you *wish* her to achieve, without necessarily believing in its realism? This may be a question you'd rather not answer. Sincerely or not, it is in your best interest to keep up the confusion between prediction and objective, between beliefs and desires, in order to maintain your subordinate's motivation. A cold, realistic analyst might declare the original goal definitively out of reach: a rational judgment, perhaps, but often a counterproductive one.

Where do our beliefs stop and our desires start? No experienced leader wants to answer this question directly. It can be very useful for an effective leader to be an optimistic planner.

DARWINIAN OPTIMISM

There is another reason why optimism is bad for decisions but good for leaders: leaders are optimists. First of all, because we value this quality in and of itself: optimism, ambition, and boldness are all qualities we associate with inspiring leaders. But also for a less obvious reason: evaluating success on results rewards optimists.

Why are we subject to cognitive biases? Why do we make systematic errors in our reasoning, like those caused by excessive confidence and optimism? Specifically, how did evolution select for these biases? If the systematic mistakes produced by cognitive biases were detrimental to our adaptation and survival, natural selection would have eliminated the biased individuals, making biases rarer. Yet biases are universal. This suggests that for our distant ancestors, these biases, or rather the heuristics of which they are the occasional flip side, weren't handicaps but assets. It is not hard to imagine how natural selection favors the optimistic, the enterprising, and the risk takers over the timid, the conservative, and the prudent.

Selecting for optimistic biases in organizations is just as inevitable. Wherever leaders are selected through some kind of meritocracy, this selection mechanism will resemble the Darwinian process that selected for optimistic biases. Quite logically, aspiring leaders will want to obtain visible, even spectacular, results. And what is the best way, whether in a company, a political party, or a lab, to obtain such results? To take risks, of course—and to get lucky! The cautious and timid who settle for regular, acceptable results may enjoy long, respectable careers. They are indispensable, but they will seldom shine. Risk takers, on the contrary, will often crash and burn; but a few of them will end up on top.

The bottom line is that our leaders are the optimists who succeeded, not the cautious (or the unlucky). And so much the better! But we shouldn't be surprised, then, if these optimists, once they get to the top, often place too much faith in their own abilities, in the value of their intuition, or in the quality of their own predictions. After all, they've been amazingly successful . . . so far.

WHEN SHOULD WE BE OPTIMISTIC?

Since we have a visceral need for optimism, especially when we are in a leadership position, how can we know where productive optimism stops and overconfidence begins? What is the difference between a bold, optimistic leader and a fool wearing rose-colored glasses?

This question has no easy answer, but one guiding principle can help. To borrow a simple but essential distinction from Phil Rosenzweig, we must distinguish between the aspects of the future we can influence and those that we cannot. In one case, we are creating the future; in the other, we are merely predicting it. For the former, optimism is indispensable. For the latter, it may be deadly.

Let's take the example of a product launch. It is healthy to be optimistic about the aspects of the project that we can influence: the production costs that we must meet, the price point at which we will position ourselves in relation to the market average, even the market share we aim for. By setting these kinds of goals with deliberate optimism, we are accomplishing a managerial act: defining our ambitions and encouraging our teams to do their very best.

If, on the contrary, we are optimistic, consciously or not, about factors that we do not control, the problem is very different. When discussing the size of the market, the reaction of our competitors, changes in market prices, input costs, exchange rates, and countless other uncontrollable variables, we must forecast the future as neutrally as possible. Optimism about things we do not manage is nothing but self-deception.

The difficulty lies in the fact that the question is not always posed in such clear terms. For instance, when a product is launched and a sales forecast is made, planners do not always explicitly separate the controllable from the noncontrollable elements. Often, they display managerial optimism about the overall objective.

That is how, too often, sensible leaders end up unwittingly endorsing overoptimistic plans about things they can't control. It is the age-old mistake of dictators who end up toppled because they believed their own propaganda.

THE OVERCONFIDENCE TRAP IN THIRTY SECONDS

Overconfidence takes many forms:

- We **overestimate ourselves** (relative to others or in the absolute).
    - ▶ *Eighty-eight percent of drivers think they're in the top 50 percent.*
- We are too optimistic about our projects (**planning fallacy**).
    - ▶ *Eighty-six percent of megaprojects have delays and cost overruns.*
    - ▶ *Misaligned incentives are not the only cause: we are overoptimistic about our own private, individual projects.*
- We are too confident in the accuracy of our predictions (**overprecision**).
    - ▶ *When we are "90 percent sure," we are at least 50 percent wrong.*
- We underestimate our competitors...
    - ▶ *Netflix said of Blockbuster: "They just about laughed us out of their office."*
- ...and even sometimes totally forget to anticipate their reactions.
    - ▶ *Procter & Gamble did not anticipate Clorox's predictable response.*
- Companies, like evolution, favor optimists, because **optimism is essential to success:** leaders are optimists who have succeeded.
- Optimism is useful until we start to **believe our own propaganda:** it's healthy to be optimistic about what we can control, not about what we can't.

5

"WHY ROCK THE BOAT?"

The Inertia Trap

If we want things to stay as they are, things will have
to change. D'you understand?

Giuseppe di Lampedusa, *The Leopard*

In 1997, Polaroid was a world leader in photography, admired for
its technological mastery, marketing skills, and dominant market
share. It had booked revenues of $2.3 billion in the previous year.
The stock market had confidence in its recently arrived CEO,
Gary DiCamillo, and his new strategic plan. The stock price had
increased by almost 50 percent since his arrival. Four years later,
Polaroid filed for bankruptcy.

The story looks like yet another example of "death by digital disruption." But there are important differences between Polaroid's
story and Blockbuster's. Neither DiCamillo nor his predecessors
underestimated the importance of digital photography. As early as
1990, I. MacAllister Booth, the company's long-serving CEO, who
had spent almost his entire career at Polaroid, told shareholders
that "we intend to be a major player in the powerful emerging
trends in electronic imaging." In 1996, Polaroid's digital business

exceeded $100 million in revenue and was growing fast. Its flagship digital camera, the PDC-2000, was considered the best product in the category. DiCamillo was fully aware of the importance of this technological revolution. Of the three major themes his strategic plan covered, digital was the first. Polaroid's shipwreck didn't happen because the captain didn't see the iceberg. It happened because the ship was just too hard to turn.

The problem is widespread: organizations don't always do what their leaders decide. When they face disruption in their market, companies change much, much slower than the words at the top. The focus of their people's energies and the allocation of their financial resources does not mirror the boss's stated strategy. This inertia has its roots in a combination of cognitive biases and organizational factors. And sometimes, as for Polaroid, it is deadly.

ARRANGING YOUR TROOPS ON THE BATTLEFIELD

The notion that a company's allocation of resources does not reflect its leader's intentions requires some explanation. After all, companies, like governments and countries, have priorities, strategic plans, budgets, and other instruments that are supposed to help the captain steer the ship. In theory, companies first set strategic goals and then allocate the financial and human resources required to reach them. These processes consume considerable amounts of time and energy, as anyone who has prepared plans and budgets in a large company can attest.

But do these procedures help companies allocate their resources *differently* from one year to the next? Hardly at all. After spending weeks every year in marathon budget meetings, most companies end up allocating their resources almost exactly as they did the previous year, regardless of the changes in their environment.

This surprising conclusion is the key finding of a McKinsey study on resource allocation in multibusiness companies. The consultants studied the annual reports of 1,600 diversified American corporations over fifteen years. Their question was a simple one: how much do these diversified companies reallocate resources across their business units? They found that the amount of capital received by a given business unit in a given year, when measured as a percentage of the total corporate capital expenditures, was almost entirely predicted by the amount it had received in the previous year. The correlation between these two numbers was 92 percent. For one-third of the companies studied, it was as high as 99 percent. Instead of suffering through marathon budget sessions, the executives in charge might as well have been playing golf: the results would have been essentially the same. However energetic and sincere their efforts to reallocate resources were, they hit a wall of inertia.

This doesn't mean that budget figures are simply copied and pasted from one fiscal year to the next. Some years budgets go up; some years they go down. But this doesn't change the general pattern of allocation. If, for instance, business conditions require an overall reduction in capital expenditures, all units tend to cut spending by the same percentage. Sometimes top management singles out a strategic priority that gets special treatment and escapes the general inertia. But that is the exception, not the rule. The net result is a complete disconnect between the strategic priorities stated by senior management and the actual allocation of financial resources. Companies simply don't put their money where their strategy is.

THE AGILE AND THE SLEEPY

One might be tempted to find justification for this absence of resource reallocation. Acquiring and divesting, surfing trends, chasing opportunities: isn't that a job description for financial portfolio managers, rather than corporate strategists? Doesn't a consistent allocation of resources reflect the consistency and perseverance that are essential to the success of a multiyear corporate strategy?

This objection is somewhat paradoxical. The corporations that so consistently fail to reallocate their resources are the same whose leaders note, in their letters to shareholders, how volatile and uncertain their business environment has become, and how crucial it is for them to be quick in seizing new opportunities (the trendy word is "agile"). This is hardly compatible with resource allocations that are set in stone. Of course, each year's budget cannot be a blank slate. But when every year, for fifteen years in a row, what corporations do is 90 percent identical to what they did the previous year, that does not suggest much agility.

Moreover, whether or not such agility pays off is an empirical question with an unambiguous answer: it does. The authors of the McKinsey study sorted their sample of companies into three groups according to the degree of their year-to-year capital reallocation. Not surprisingly, the "high reallocators" outperformed the "low reallocators." Over a fifteen-year period, companies in the former group had 30 percent higher total return to shareholders. They were also less likely to go bankrupt or to be acquired. Low reallocators, it turns out, are not keeping a steady hand on the helm. They are asleep at the wheel.

ANCHORING

Like the overconfidence trap, the inertia trap has its roots in cognitive biases, and its effects are amplified by organizational dynamics. The main bias behind resource allocation inertia is *anchoring*: when we need to estimate or establish a numerical value, we tend to use an available figure as an "anchor," and then we insufficiently adjust it.

Surprisingly, anchors influence us even when they bear no relationship to the estimated value, and even when they're patently absurd. Following the seminal experiments of Kahneman and Tversky in the 1970s, two German researchers named Thomas Mussweiler and Fritz Strack demonstrated this effect with remarkable creativity. In one of their experiments, they divided their subjects into two groups, asking one group whether Mahatma Gandhi was over or under 140 years old when he died, and the other whether he was over or under 9 years old when he died. Obviously, no one had trouble answering these questions. But when the respondents were then asked to estimate Gandhi's age at death, these clearly ridiculous "anchors" made a difference: the group anchored on 140 thought, on average, that Gandhi had died at age 67, whereas the group anchored on 9 believed he had died at age 50. (Actually, Gandhi died at age 78.)

Like many cognitive bias experiments, this story often elicits a defensive reaction at first. Would I ever fall into such a crude trap, you might ask, especially if it concerned an important decision on a subject I know something about? Aren't such manipulations possible only when the subjects don't know anything about the answer, and don't really care?

To address this objection, the researchers came up with other experiments that placed their guinea pigs into realistic professional situations. One of them involves judges, whose decisions are not supposed to be made lightly. The experimenters submitted a detailed file about a shoplifting case to a panel of experienced judges and asked them what sentence they would give the thief. But the file lacked an important piece of information: the sentence sought by the prosecution. The judges were asked to produce this number themselves by throwing two dice and writing down the result, which would represent the number of months on probation sought by the prosecution. Producing the number this way could leave no doubt in their minds that it was randomly generated. The judges were also told that the reason this number was determined at random was to ensure it did *not* influence their sentencing decisions. Nevertheless, it did: the judges who rolled a three issued a sentence of five months on average, whereas those who rolled a nine sentenced the defendant to eight months![*]

The lesson from these experiments (and many others) is clear. However hard we may try to dissociate ourselves from numbers we are exposed to, we remain subject to anchoring. Even when the anchor number clearly bears no relationship to the question asked, it influences our judgment.

If arbitrary, irrelevant numbers can so easily bias us, how then can we expect to distance ourselves from relevant ones? When reviewing a budget, for instance, how would we not be heavily influenced by the previous year's budget, full of numbers that we ourselves approved? Once we understand the power of anchoring, corporate inertia in resource allocation is no longer a mystery. It is its absence that would be surprising.

---

[*] In order to make the results easier to interpret, the dice were loaded, so that all the judges rolled either a three or a nine.

THE POLITICS OF INERTIA

The effects of anchoring are amplified by human and organizational dynamics that any experienced manager will recognize. Building a strategic plan or developing a budget entails constant negotiation between players in the organization. In any negotiation, anchoring matters: whatever number serves as the starting point is the anchor. In a budget discussion, these starting points are known and highly visible. The head of the business unit that had a marketing budget of 100 last year will perhaps request 110 this year, but rarely 200. With the same anchor in mind, you may ask her to make do with 90, but you won't suggest 40. Anchoring implicitly establishes negotiating boundaries.

Another form of social pressure exacerbates the importance of historical anchors. Executives' personal credibility is a function of their ability to defend their unit or department by maintaining and increasing its financial resources. Their prestige in the eyes of their peers and subordinates depends on it. These peers and subordinates, too, treat last year's number as the reference point.

If we look at this situation not from the point of view of the managers but from that of the CEO who is trying to reallocate resources, the problem is no simpler. As one of them pointed out, "I should be taking from the rich and giving to the poor, but I'm not Robin Hood!" As a general rule, a CEO would do well to take resources away from mature business units in order to fund those with more growth potential. But the "rich" managers who head the cash-rich business units do not see matters in this light. They have no wish to see their budgets cut to subsidize the "poor"; indeed, they usually have plenty of ideas for spending the money allocated to them. Better yet, they can easily explain how difficult it would be for their units, if they were forced to make do with less, to generate the cash flow the corporation is counting on. In this negotiation game, yesterday's winners have the advantage.

Finally, let's recall that the players in all this wheeling and dealing were involved in the same negotiation last year. Radically changing resource allocation means questioning one's own judgment. Will it look like the decisions we made last year were wrong? Of course, we all think we're capable of doing this and being "agile" in our resource allocations. When C-level executives are asked if their company "admits mistakes and kills unsuccessful initiatives in a timely manner," 80 percent say it does. But when we go a step down in the hierarchy and ask the same question of non-C-level executives, 52 percent say it does not. Whom would you trust?

All these reasons explain why serious resource reallocation is so difficult. One thing, however, does make it happen: a fresh pair of eyes. Companies reallocate markedly more resources in the year following the arrival of a new CEO. This is even more true when the CEO is an outsider, and therefore more capable of resisting anchoring and social pressures from within the organization. Not surprisingly, these new CEOs tend to get good results—all the more so when their resource reallocation efforts are quick and decisive.

SUNK COSTS AND ESCALATION OF COMMITMENT

Inertia consists, strictly speaking, in doing nothing. But sometimes we do worse, and increase, rather than just maintain, the resources committed to a losing course of action. This pattern is the *escalation of commitment*.

The most tragic example of escalation of commitment is the

situation of a nation mired in a war it cannot win. In July 1965, writing about the Vietnam War, George Ball, the undersecretary of state, predicted such a situation in a memorandum to President Lyndon Johnson: "Once we suffer large casualties, we will have started a well-nigh irreversible process. Our involvement will be so great that we cannot—without national humiliation—stop short of achieving our complete objectives." Alas, this dire prediction came true: between 1964 and 1968, the number of American ground troops in Vietnam rose from 23,000 to 536,000.

Tragically, the inescapable logic of escalation persists as history repeats itself. In 2006, George Bush stated: "I'm going to make you this promise: I'm not going to allow the sacrifice of 2,527 troops who have died in Iraq *to be in vain* by pulling out before the job is done." Five years later, whether the "job" could be considered done or not, the American death toll had risen to nearly 4,500. And in August 2017, justifying his decision to send fresh troops to Afghanistan, Donald Trump—despite his initial hostility to continuing this war—found it essential to attain an "honorable and enduring outcome worthy of *the tremendous sacrifices that have been made*, especially the sacrifices of lives."

The logic is always the same: the higher the losses, the more essential it becomes to convince oneself that they "have not been in vain." In a perfect illustration of what economists call the *sunk-cost fallacy*, future escalation is "justified" by the losses that have already been suffered. The logical fallacy should be obvious: the decision to commit new resources should not consider irrecoverable losses, costs (or lives) that can never be recouped. The only valid question concerns the future, the expected "return on investment": does the expected outcome justify the additional resources we commit today?

But it is quite difficult to reason in this way, as we see in our daily decisions. If you have ever ordered too much food and felt compelled to eat it all, forced yourself to finish reading a book you found boring, or gone to the theater with a bad cold because you had already paid for the ticket, you have been influenced by sunk costs.

In business, the most striking examples of escalation of commitment are found in companies that try desperately to save failing initiatives. A spectacular case is Saturn, the division created by General Motors in 1983 to compete against Japanese imports. The original idea was to create a "different kind of company" making "a different kind of car." Saturn's products and methods would not be subject to the rules of the giant company (and its sluggish bureaucracy). Not everything went according to plan—to say the least: by 2004, over *twenty years* after its launch, Saturn had swallowed up more than $15 billion and, according to industry analysts, had never made one cent of profit. So what did management decide to do? They recommitted $3 billion to transforming Saturn into an "ordinary" division of GM! The division was no more successful than the semi-independent company had been. Only in 2008, as part of GM's government bailout, was Saturn put up for sale. By then, of course, there were no buyers. It was finally shut down in 2010.

The case of Saturn is extreme: few companies can afford to lose some $20 billion over twenty-seven years of consistent failure. But GM's reluctance to get rid of a failing business and its limitless faith in successive turnaround plans are far from unusual. In fact, large companies divest businesses much less often than one would expect. A study of two thousand companies over seventeen years showed that they executed, on average, only one divestment every five years. The total value of divestments was one-twentieth of the amount they spent on acquisitions.

As these examples show, suffering irrecoverable costs alone does not cause escalation of commitment. We must also convince ourselves that we are not headed down a dead-end path but rather the road to a glorious future. When sending additional troops to a war zone, military leaders are sure that *this time*, given the necessary resources, victory is within reach. Investors who reinvest in a stock after it has collapsed firmly believe that *now* it will rise again. The leaders of GM were persuaded with every new turn-around plan that *this time* a new strategy, a new president, or more favorable market conditions would finally put Saturn back on the right track.

By now, you've recognized it: this is the same overconfidence we encountered in the previous chapter. Escalation of commitment is not only a form of inertia. It is also, at the same time, grounded in unreasonable optimism. This perverse combination of concern over sunk costs and excessive confidence in future plans is what makes it so difficult to combat.

INERTIA IN DISRUPTION

The case that opened this chapter—Polaroid in 1997—illustrates a familiar pattern: powerful, profitable incumbents failing to over-come inertia and reallocate their resources when confronted with a major change in their environment. Record companies destabilized by digital music, telecom operators squeezed between tech giants and nimble app providers, software developers faced with cloud computing, brick-and-mortar stores threatened by e-commerce:

all companies disrupted by the digital revolution face a version of the same dilemma.

The choice these companies must make boils down to a simple question. Should they embrace the new technology and compete with their existing core business, making it obsolete before someone else does? In the short term, the new business will inevitably face stiffer competition and generate less profit than the mature business it replaces. On the other hand, in the long run, there is little doubt that the new technologies will replace the old.

In hindsight, the answer seems obvious. But in the moment, it is far murkier. Any leader will find many reasons to hesitate. Are we sure that our traditional activity is hopelessly condemned? Can't we promote, for instance, "hybrid" technologies that offer the best of both worlds? Of all the emerging technologies, which one should we bet on? How can we develop it profitably, given our big-company cost structure? Finally, what is the optimal pace—not too quick, not too slow—to transition to a new technology?

Another Netflix anecdote illustrates how crucial timing is in such situations. We saw in the previous chapter that Blockbuster responded too late to the simultaneous emergence of DVDs and the internet. Netflix took advantage of this first transition. But the second transition (the real one, one might say) took place a few years later, with the advent of broadband internet, enabling movie streaming to replace DVDs.

Reed Hastings, Netflix's cofounder, had learned from his competitors' mistakes. He was keen to make sure that Netflix didn't act like an incumbent, neglecting the emerging streaming business to protect its core mail-order business. In 2011, he came up with a radical solution: breaking Netflix into two companies. One would focus on streaming, while the other (called Qwikster) would manage the legacy business of sending DVDs by mail. Two businesses, led by distinct, competing teams: a sure way, he thought, of fighting on two fronts, optimizing both for growth and profitability.

The plan backfired. Consumers thought the scheme was needlessly complicated (why should they have to manage two accounts?). They also saw it for what it was: a way to make them pay twice for what they considered a single service. It took only a few weeks for Reed Hastings to realize his gaffe and abandon the idea of breaking up the company. But in just one quarter, Netflix had lost 800,000 American subscribers. Admitting his mistake, Hastings later acknowledged that he had acted too quickly: the future was certainly in streaming, not DVD rentals...but the future wasn't here yet.

It's not easy to know how long to support a profitable business, even when you know that it's doomed. Some, like Hastings, may start too soon. But if there's a guiding principle, it's that Blockbuster's inertia is the rule, and Netflix's rush is the exception. Almost always, when a traditional business is faced with "disruptive technologies," to use Clayton Christensen's now-familiar term, it delays reallocating its resources to face it. The vast majority of companies do not overreact. They dither until it's too late.

That seems to be exactly what happened at Polaroid, despite the strategic foresight of its successive leaders. When he took up his job as CEO, DiCamillo found a company that was marginally profitable but very sure of itself. Its marketing department blithely produced reports proclaiming it had 100 percent market share: it defined its market as instant cameras in the United States. Its laboratories were overflowing with new ideas.

DiCamillo immediately perceived the problem with this business culture. As soon as he arrived, he reorganized Polaroid to bring the labs closer to the market. As he told his troops, "We're not in the business to get the most patents. We're not in the business to write the most research papers. And we're not in the business to see how many inventions we can come up with." It was a strong—and new—message. DiCamillo restructured the company and let 2,500 people go, a quarter of the workforce. Clearly, he didn't underestimate either the urgency of the situation or the importance of taking the company in a new direction to face it.

But the organization's inertia was inescapable. What did Polaroid's laboratories and their remarkable researchers work on? Developing digital products, but mostly extending their range of instant cameras with new, more affordable models, some of which were quite successful. Polaroid's economic model also encouraged inertia: using a classic "razor and blades" business model, Polaroid sold cameras at a low price and made its profit on film cartridges. This model is impossible to reproduce in the digital world, where there are no more consumables. To make the transition to digital, Polaroid would have needed to undergo a drastic (and high-risk) transformation: radically reduce its cost base, actively cannibalize its core business (or sell parts of it), and massively reinvest in digital technologies.

Like Polaroid, many companies do too little, too late in response to changing environments, and never manage to adequately re-allocate their resources. To cite the authors of a landmark study on exit decisions, cognitive biases "cause companies to ignore danger signs, to refrain from adjusting goals in the face of new information, and to throw good money after bad."

STATUS QUO BIAS

There's another factor that deters companies from exiting underperforming business and more generally leads them to inertia: it's simply that the question of exit may not even be asked. We're all subject to *status quo bias:* it's easier for us not to decide than to decide.

Imagine that you have just inherited a large sum of money. You have the choice of investing this capital in various ways—stocks, bonds, and so forth. Of course, your choice depends on your preferences (especially your risk appetite) and on what you think of the various options that are offered to you. Not all people will respond in the same way, and this is to be expected. But what if your inheritance was already invested in a portfolio consisting of one of these assets? In a seminal experiment on status quo bias, the economists William Samuelson and Richard Zeckhauser tested that proposition. A large proportion of their subjects chose to keep the portfolio as it was when they received it rather than reallocate it according to their own preferences. The comfort of nondecision won out over their supposedly rational preferences.[*]

We find the preference for the status quo in countless situations where there is a "default choice." Whether we are choosing the color of our car, allocating funds inside a retirement plan, or even giving consent to organ donations, we tend not to choose, and thus adopt the default option. "In the real world, the first decision is to recognize that there is a decision," Samuelson and Zeckhauser write, but "such a recognition may not occur."

---

[*] Transaction costs to change the composition of the portfolio might have been a rational reason to favor inertia, but the subjects were told these costs were zero.

Companies, like people, are subject to status quo bias. As a rule, in the annual budget process, headquarters reviews the budget of each unit separately. It does not explicitly engage in a reallocation exercise involving all the units. Because of this approach, the "default" choice is to modify resource allocation only marginally. The small number of divestitures is also a manifestation of status quo bias: for a corporation, the default choice is to keep units, not sell them.

In addition to anchoring, sunk costs, and status quo bias, another bias plays a role in reallocation decisions (or, rather, in *non*-reallocation decisions): loss aversion. It is discussed in the next chapter.

THE INERTIA TRAP IN THIRTY SECONDS

- **Anchoring** encourages us to base an estimate or forecast on a number that comes to mind, even if it is irrelevant to the matter at hand.
  - ▶ *Even absurd anchors influence us: Gandhi's age, judges rolling the dice…*
  - ▶ *So do relevant numbers, such as last year's budget when discussing this year's.*
- Anchoring plays a key role in **resource allocation inertia.**
  - ▶ *If this year's budgets are 90 percent identical to last year's, why have long budget meetings?*
- The **battle for resources** within organizations aggravates the problem.
  - ▶ *The "rich" don't want to give to the "poor"; the CEO "isn't Robin Hood."*
- A more extreme version of inertia is **escalation of commitment**—doubling down on losing endeavors.
  - ▶ *The troops who died at the beginning of the war must not have died "in vain."*
  - ▶ *GM continued to bail out Saturn for twenty-seven years.*
- Inertia contributes to the pattern of **under-reaction to disruption** that plagues incumbents.
  - ▶ *Polaroid saw the digital revolution coming, but didn't reallocate its resources quickly enough.*
- In general, it is easier not to decide than to decide: this is **status quo bias.**

6

"I WANT YOU TO TAKE RISKS"

The Risk Perception Trap

Don't play for safety—it's the most dangerous thing
in the world.

—Hugh Walpole

Suppose that you are offered an investment that requires an irrecoverable capital outlay of $100 million. If successful, the investment will soon produce profits of $400 million. If it fails, there will be no revenue, and the $100 million will be lost. What is the probability of success you demand—or the maximum probability of failure you can tolerate—in order to give this project the green light?

This, in simplified terms, is a problem that businesses deal with every day. This particular hypothetical has a risk profile that is similar, for instance, to a risky R&D investment: if things go well, the bet could pay off big-time; if they don't, you lose everything.

So, how much risk should you tolerate? It's up to you! All we can say for sure is that, with a loss probability of 75 percent, the expected gain would be zero: a 25 percent chance of making $400 million and a 75 percent chance of earning nothing produce an expected value of $100 million, canceling out the initial investment exactly. Therefore, accepting any loss probability over 75 percent would be irrational. Suppose, for instance, that the loss probability is 95 percent: obviously, you would not want to pay $100 million to have only one chance in twenty of making $400 million.

Provided it is under 75 percent, the probability of loss you choose to tolerate is up to you, and reflects your personal level of risk appetite (or risk aversion). Suppose Dave answers 50 percent and Terry 25 percent. Brave Dave is prepared to risk the same loss for a much smaller probability of gain. Wary Terry is the more risk averse of the two.

A research team from McKinsey posed this problem to eight hundred executives at large companies. On average, the maximum loss probability they said they would tolerate was around 18 percent. Barely one-third would accept a loss probability of more than 20 percent. This reflects a severe aversion to risk: to accept a bet that can earn four times the initial investment, they demand more than an 80 percent chance of success. Few bookies would earn a living if gamblers were this risk averse.

Of course, managers aren't gamblers but stewards of corporate resources. Caution is certainly appropriate, especially when an investment of $100 million is at stake. For a medium-sized company, losing such an amount could be a fatal risk. To measure the significance of this factor, the same question was asked of another sample of managers, this time with an investment of $10 million instead of $100 million (and a potential upside of $40 million).

We might expect risk aversion to be lower in this scenario. Imagine your company is not making a one-off, bet-the-farm decision but can afford to invest in a *portfolio* of research projects that present this sort of risk profile. You would do well, then, to accept a higher loss probability. For example, suppose you invest in ten projects with a loss probability of 50 percent. The most likely scenario is that five of the projects will be successful: the company will then have doubled its initial investment, which is an excellent return.

Oddly enough, however, the managers' answers hardly change at all when the amount of the investment is divided by ten. It's not the sum itself that turns off these decision makers. It's the possibility of loss, whatever the amount.

If you are used to making these kinds of decisions in a corporate setting, you won't be surprised. No one wants to be the one signing his name on the dotted line when an investment has a one-in-two chance of failing. Besides, as the previous chapters have shown, it is sensible to assume that the costs have been underestimated and that the predicted profits (and the probability that they will materialize) are exaggeratedly optimistic.

But this behavior is nonetheless disturbing. When the same decision makers are asked, in the same questionnaire, to describe their company's attitude toward taking risks, 45 percent of them reply that the company is *too* risk averse (only 16 percent think the opposite). And 50 percent of them (vs. 20 percent) think that their company does not invest enough. Basically, they wish their company would take more risks. But given their reaction to our hypothetical investment, they're not likely to be the ones to resolve this problem.

DO AS I SAY, NOT AS I DO

What we see here is a deep contradiction. On the one hand, any corporation (especially a large one) has, in theory, a healthy appetite for risk. On the other hand, its individual managers are considerably risk averse. This poses a real problem: exaggerated risk aversion can be just as harmful as unreasonable optimism.

One troubling manifestation of risk aversion is the reluctance of large companies to reinvest the cash they generate. As of 2018, publicly listed American companies were hoarding some $1.7 trillion in cash. This suggests that they did not find enough attractive projects in which to invest. This might be understandable for aging companies in declining industries. But almost half of this reserve of unused cash was in the high-tech sector. Apple alone sat on some $245 billion in cash (more than the federal corporate income taxes paid by all corporations that year). And what does Apple, a company universally admired for its innovation capabilities, buy with this extra cash? Its own stock. Since 2012, Apple has been running the largest share repurchase program in history. Clayton Christensen and Derek van Bever, who study the way large companies let innovators disrupt their businesses, observe that "despite historically low interest rates, corporations are sitting on massive amounts of cash and failing to invest in innovations that might foster growth."

It is puzzling to see these juggernauts apparently short on new projects, considering their access to all the resources they might need: cash, of course, but also talent, brands, patents, distribution networks, and so on. Meanwhile, entrepreneurs without any of those resources manage to create innovative businesses. Some, like WhatsApp, are then acquired by large companies (in this case, by

Facebook, for $19 billion). Other "unicorns," like Spotify or Uber, raise billions in private capital before eventually going public. One thing all these transformational innovators have in common is that they were not born inside existing corporations.

Ask the CEO of a large company about this paradox, and his reply will probably be a variation on this theme: "I would gladly approve more risky projects, but no one proposes them to me!" Innovative and risky initiatives, CEOs say, probably get killed or self-censored at lower levels of the organization, because they never reach the top. Some CEOs are even puzzled by the simplified investment proposal described at the beginning of this chapter: no one, they say, would dare pitch such a risky proposal to them!

Many business leaders try to remedy this problem by urging their troops to be more entrepreneurial. "Take more risks!" is a frequent motto in large corporations. To make it happen, some companies launch idea competitions, create divisions dedicated to radical innovation, or set up internal venture capital funds. The need for such approaches shows how difficult it is for a mature organization to support risky projects.

The reasons for this difficulty are to be found in our individual and collective attitudes to risk. To understand them, we must review three distinct biases. In combination, they produce the irrational levels of risk aversion we observe across corporations.

LOSS AVERSION

The first and most important of these biases is what Kahneman and Tversky called *loss aversion*. Loss aversion is not the same thing as risk aversion. It's a much more basic phenomenon: losses and disadvantages count for more than gains and advantages of the same size. The pain of losing a dollar is more intense than the pleasure of winning one.

The simplest way to measure your loss aversion is to ask you to answer the following question: "We're going to flip a fair coin. If it's tails, you lose $100. How much would you have to win if it's heads in order to agree to play this game?" In theory, for a perfectly rational agent, $101 should be enough. But, for most individuals, the acceptable answer is around $200, reflecting a "loss aversion coefficient" of 2. When the amount of money at stake increases, so too does the loss aversion coefficient, which can approach infinity. Unless you are incredibly rich, with a high roller's passion for gambling, no potential gain would make you agree to a game of heads or tails in which you can lose $1 million.

Loss aversion has countless practical consequences. For instance, it underpins sales techniques we are all familiar with. Instead of offering the consumer a benefit, it is often more effective to talk about avoiding a loss: "don't miss out on this unique opportunity"; "tomorrow, it will be too late." Perhaps you have noticed that the title of this book applies the same principle: promising to help you avoid a "terrible mistake" (a loss) is more persuasive than offering you a benefit. (Would you have picked up this book if it were titled *How to Make Better Decisions?*)

But the importance of loss aversion goes further. Daniel Kahneman sees it as "certainly the most significant contribution of psychology to behavioral economics." For example, in a negotiation, each party is more willing to make a concession to avoid a loss than to achieve an equivalent gain. And the fact that change is so difficult to achieve can be seen as a consequence of loss aversion, too: When a change makes winners and losers, the losers feel the losses much more acutely than the winners feel the gains. That helps explain why a minority so often takes action to block a plan that a majority supports.

UNCERTAINTY AVERSION

A second phenomenon contributes to abnormal levels of risk aversion: a risky investment is never presented in the clear terms of our introductory problem, with its artificial simplicity. The business world is not a casino, where we know the exact odds of winning when we throw the dice. In practice, we can never know the probability of a project's success or failure with any precision. Moreover, whenever the person proposing a project estimates its probability of success, we suspect him (often correctly) of being too optimistic.

As for the return on our investment, it is just as uncertain. We can sometimes be quite sure of losing 100 percent of our investment in case of failure, but we never precisely know the expected profit in case of success. It's often a challenge even to estimate how long it will take to determine whether the project has been a success or a failure.

Finally, countless other factors come into play when you decide whether to make a risky investment. Are you familiar with the subject? How much confidence do you have in the team in charge? How much control can you have over the project's implementation? Is there a way to divide the project into multiple phases to limit the initial cash outlay?

In the real world, an investment hardly ever looks like a clean gamble. When we make an investment decision, we do not just face risks. We face what economist Frank Knight called *uncertainty*: risks we cannot quantify. And if there is one thing we hate almost as much as loss, it's uncertainty. Economists call this *uncertainty aversion* or *ambiguity aversion*. "Better the devil you know than the devil you don't," as the saying goes. And many experiments confirm that we are willing to pay to avoid uncertainty. We'd much rather take a quantified risk than an unknown one.

HINDSIGHT BIAS

There is a third reason for avoiding risk. In order to understand it, think of an event in recent news (or even in your personal life) that surprised you when it happened. As you reflect on it now, can you identify reasons why you should have expected it? Surely the answer is yes. Even when something takes us by surprise, we soon come up with ways to explain it quite easily. The same pundits who confidently declared that Donald Trump could never get elected had many eloquent arguments, the very next day, to explain why his election was understandable, logical, even inevitable. When Saudi oil installations were hit by drone attacks in 2019, many observers wondered how such attacks had not been anticipated— even though they had never imagined the possibility themselves.

This gap between our perception of an event's likelihood before and after it happens is what psychologist Baruch Fischhoff has called *hindsight bias*. Fischhoff discovered it by asking volunteers to estimate the probability of political events—for instance, various potential consequences of Nixon's historic trip to China in 1972. Later, once these events had (or had not) taken place, Fischhoff asked the same volunteers to recall what probability they had assigned to them. Of course, very few remembered their precise answers. But the majority were mistaken in the same direction. When an event had taken place, they overestimated the probability that they had previously assigned to it: "I knew that would happen." When, on the contrary, the event had not taken place, they forgot how plausible it had seemed to them at the time: "I knew that wouldn't happen."

Hindsight bias is everywhere, even in history textbooks. We have all learned to analyze "the causes of World War I" or "the consequences of the Treaty of Versailles." But historians who make logical connections between causes and effects choose them carefully from the potentially infinite set of facts at their disposal. The "causes" often go completely unnoticed in the moment.

A team of historians and artificial intelligence experts recently provided support for this view by training machine learning algorithms to predict, based solely on contemporary information, whether events will later be seen as historic. Their conclusion: historical significance is extremely difficult to predict. The world is simply too messy and random for that. It is only in hindsight that historians can single out the facts that fit their narrative, leaving out all others. This is why it is possible for multiple, equally plausible interpretations of history to coexist; or for a new, "revisionist" theory to appear.

This is also why it is so irresistible, in hindsight, to see contingent events as inevitable. We have all learned that in 1940, as England faced an imminent and mortal threat from Nazi Germany, the country "needed" to choose an inflexible warrior as prime minister. And it's hard for us to imagine that this prime minister could have been anyone other than Winston Churchill. What we often forget is that, just a few days before the king sent for Churchill, no one in the House of Commons would have bet one shilling on his chances. It took an extraordinary turn of events for a parliamentary debate about the Norwegian campaign, a military disaster of which Churchill was the primary architect, to paradoxically result in his being named prime minister. Churchill biographer Martin Gilbert was once asked what he had learned from the thirty thousand pages he had written about the great man. Gilbert's answer: "I learned what a close thing it was."

All this is true not just of History with a capital *H* but also of our own personal history: when we try to explain an accident or a failure, we are often victims of hindsight bias. Recall our hypothetical investment decision: if $100 million is lost on this risky investment, no one will remember that taking the risk made perfect sense at the time. On the contrary, everyone will think of a thousand reasons why failure was inevitable. Even if an unexpected difficulty was to blame, they will ask why it had not been anticipated. After all, it's rare that an event happens totally out of the blue; and whoever runs a project is expected to consider all possible contingencies. Basically, everyone will think, like the subjects of Fischhoff's experiment, "I knew it would happen."

Managers who can propose entrepreneurial endeavors know this. They are fully aware that their initiative will be judged in hindsight, once the results are known. Why, then, should they ever champion a risky project? Richard Thaler, who won the Nobel Prize in economics in 2017, sees this as a practically unsolvable problem. "One of the toughest problems a CEO faces is convincing managers that they should take on risky projects if the expected gains are high enough," he writes.

Loss aversion, uncertainty aversion, and hindsight bias conspire to produce an exaggerated aversion to risk. This helps explain why companies take fewer risks than they could, fewer than they rationally should, and fewer than their leaders themselves say they'd like to.*

HOW TO LOSE EVERYTHING
WITHOUT TAKING ANY RISKS

But how can we reconcile our observations about the costs of exaggerated risk aversion with our equally valid observations about the large number of mistakes caused by excessive optimism? Why didn't risk aversion dissuade the leaders of J. C. Penney or Quaker from rushing into their risky ventures? When entrepreneurs stake their finances and their time on projects that are inherently risky, why don't they seem to be subject to the same levels of risk aversion as the managers discussed above? In other words, how can the timid, risk-averse behaviors we have just analyzed coexist with the bold, overconfident risk-taking discussed in chapter 4?

The paradox is easily resolved. Even if you are risk averse, you can still make risky decisions *if you don't realize they're risky*. This is how corporations place big bets: most often, they are not aware of how risky they are.

If you are in a position to observe how decisions are made within organizations, recall the most recent time a risky endeavor was discussed in your presence. Was the inherent irreducible riskiness of the project recognized and discussed? Did the person

---

* In addition to these timeless explanations, there are, of course, additional factors that contribute to the historically low levels of reinvestment in large corporations we have observed in recent years, including the macroeconomic context and changes in the tax code.

proposing it attempt to quantify the odds of failure (or success)? In other words, did the decision seem to have anything in common with a roll of the dice?

Your answer to all these questions is probably a resounding "no," and for good reason. Decision makers accept, in principle, that the future is uncertain and that investments are risky. But they do not view themselves as gamblers who place bets based on statistical odds of success they can calculate. To them, "risk" has a different meaning. A risk is an inconvenience to be minimized, a challenge that it is their responsibility to meet. As soon as a manager mentions a risk, she is expected to list the measures taken (or proposed) to mitigate it. "Risk" is not what it means to decision theorists—that is, something uncontrollable: it is something to be controlled.*

This helps explain how mistakes of overconfidence take place. When a company takes a risky path, it's almost never because it *consciously* decides to bet on a high-risk, high-return project. On the contrary, it's usually because it has close to 100 percent confidence in an exaggeratedly optimistic outlook.

The process that produces this illusion is a direct consequence of the biases discussed in chapter 4. The project may be risky, but the *forecast* associated with it is subject to overconfidence. Invariably, projections for sales, profits, time to completion, and so on will be overoptimistic. Just as importantly, overprecision will lead the decision makers to overstate the degree of confidence they have in these plans.

A typical example is a revenue projection that includes a "base

---

*   One exception to this concerns financial institutions, where risk is usually
      treated as a technical business variable.

scenario" and a "pessimistic scenario" (a precaution intended to show just how reasonable the project champion is). It is a safe bet that the "base scenario" is in fact optimistic and that the "pessimistic scenario" is far from being a "worst case." The goal, for the plan's author, is to present the project as almost certain to produce a satisfactory outcome. This is a smart play in terms of corporate politics: plans that are promoted with unshakable confidence and can pass as "safe bets" have the best chance of being approved.

These organizational dynamics explain how corporations can be both overconfident and risk averse. These two biases, which should produce opposite effects, do not cancel each other. Daniel Kahneman and Dan Lovallo described this paradox in an article entitled "Timid Choices and Bold Forecasts": you are risk averse in your *choices*; but choices seem very easy when they are based on overconfident, overprecise *forecasts*.

Of course, not everyone in an organization can make a bold forecast believable. Investment procedures are designed to challenge project advocates and to pressure-test the realism of their plans. Large companies subject investment proposals to multiple layers of hierarchical and functional scrutiny. At every stage, the proposal is critically analyzed to weed out any trace of exaggerated optimism.

It makes sense, in this light, that the boldest, riskiest projects are also often the largest. If a project advocate occupies a position near the top of her organization's hierarchy, her proposals, forecasts, and assumptions will be subject to less scrutiny. In the most extreme cases, it is the CEO who champions a project, such as a large acquisition or a radical transformation. It is not surprising that the stories of Snapple and J. C. Penney fall into these two categories.

Conversely, smaller-scale projects championed by more junior employees must surmount numerous hierarchical obstacles and survive many layers of scrutiny before being approved. Remember the CEOs who were astonished that no one ever proposes risky projects to them? They should probably blame the rigorous, effective application of their company's policies and procedures. By demanding a level of confidence in a project that is difficult to demonstrate, they effectively dissuade employees from entrepreneurial initiatives.

It would be more rational to do the exact opposite. A single large high-risk project, even if it has a big upside, puts the company in danger. Risk-taking in smaller projects, on the other hand, should be tolerated, even encouraged: a diversified portfolio of high-risk, high-return projects would be an extremely rational choice. Unfortunately, optimism more easily carries the day when the project is big, while risk aversion takes over when it's small. The conjunction of timid choices and bold forecasts thus explains how the same company can sit on piles of cash for want of exciting opportunities and still occasionally make wild gambles.

"They did not know it was impossible, so they did it," Mark Twain is often quoted as saying. This quotation is often used to encourage people to take risks. But it beautifully reveals what usually causes us to do so: not courage but ignorance. Attempting the impossible is, of course, bad policy: by definition, success would be rare. But it would be wise to overcome our risk aversion and to more frequently attempt the difficult and risky, *in full awareness that we are doing so*. Investment professionals and venture capitalists for whom risk is a daily companion have developed methods and cultures that can help us in this quest. The third part of this book will cover this topic in more detail.

THE RISK PERCEPTION TRAP IN THIRTY SECONDS

- Companies seem to take **too few risks:** They hoard cash, and their managers refuse to take on risky projects. At least three biases contribute to this.

- **Loss aversion:** We feel more pain over a loss than pleasure over a gain of the same amount.
  - ▶ *How much would you have to win to accept the risk of losing $100 on the flip of a fair coin?*

- **Uncertainty aversion**
  - ▶ *"Better the devil you know than the devil you don't."*

- **Hindsight bias:** "I knew it would happen."
  - ▶ *After the fact, history seems "inevitable."*
  - ▶ *...and when a project fails, the person who proposed it gets the blame.*

- Companies **overcome their risk aversion by denying the existence of risk.** Risky ideas are presented as sure things, which can be approved without the impression of taking a risk: **"Timid choices and bold forecasts."**

- This combination leads companies to **reject small risks while approving very large ones:** the exact opposite of what should happen!
  - ▶ *Very few companies develop a portfolio of small high-risk, high-return projects, as venture capitalists do.*
  - ▶ *Instead, they justify taking on large projects (for example, acquisitions, major transformations) by underestimating their difficulties.*

7

"THE LONG TERM IS A LONG WAY OFF"

The Time Horizon Trap

In the long run we are all dead.

—John Maynard Keynes

"Many companies have shied away from investing in the future growth of their companies. Too many companies have cut capital expenditure and even increased debt to boost dividends and increase share buybacks....When done for the wrong reasons and at the expense of capital investment, [returning cash to shareholders] can jeopardize a company's ability to generate sustainable long-term returns."

Who wrote these words to the CEOs of large U.S. corporations, warning them against the dangers of short-term thinking? Was it a political activist? An angry union leader? A governor worried about jobs being eliminated in his state? No, this letter, dated March 2014, bears the signature of Larry Fink, CEO of BlackRock, one of the largest investment funds in the world. *No, don't give me higher returns,* he is essentially saying. *Instead, I want you to invest in the businesses of tomorrow, in research and development, or in training your employees.*

Shareholders, investment firms, pension funds, and other financial players are often blamed for encouraging executives to focus on stock price and short-term results. Yet here a financial titan is worried about the failure of corporations to focus on the long term. A few months after Fink's letter, the *Harvard Business Review*, which isn't in the habit of criticizing capitalism, ran a cover story asking: "Are Investors Bad for Business?" Evidently, short-termism has become a cause for concern. Or rather, two: the critique of short-termism conflates two very distinct arguments.

THE TWO CRITIQUES OF SHORT-TERMISM

An example of the first and most widespread critique of short-termism can be found in the much-noted 2019 declaration of the Business Roundtable, an association of American chief executive officers. Signed by nearly two hundred CEOs, this statement on the "purpose of the corporation" aims to move away from the primacy of shareholder value creation and to reemphasize the goals of other stakeholders: "customers, employees, suppliers and communities."

Despite notable pockets of resistance, this critique has become increasingly accepted, at least in principle. Many executives have distanced themselves from the hard-line shareholder value–oriented vision of yesteryear, encapsulated in Milton Friedman's famous line: "The social responsibility of business is to increase its profits." In this respect, American corporations are catching up with those of continental Europe, where a broader vision of the purpose of the corporation and a more expansive list of its stakeholders have long been the standard (and, in many countries, are enshrined in law).

But the issue raised by this critique is not just one of time horizons: it's a larger issue about companies' role in society. The Business Roundtable promotes "An Economy That Serves All Americans." It's no surprise that there is tension between the quest for profit and its societal consequences, between shareholders' interests and the goals of other stakeholders. In fact, it's inevitable.

What may be more surprising is that short-termism is an issue *even if we consider companies' financial objectives alone*. This is the second form the critique of corporate short-termism is taking. Even if the sole purpose of corporations is assumed to be shareholder value creation, they are still at risk of making serious errors by prioritizing immediate gains over future profits. In his 2014 letter, Larry Fink was focused on this issue: he was worried that companies would be unable to maintain their profitability in the future if they did not make the necessary investments today.[*]

Striking a balance between different time horizons is not easy. One study showed that 80 percent of managers would be willing to give up an investment that creates long-term value if it meant missing an immediate profit target. Another study interviewed some 1,000 board members and C-suite executives at companies all over the world: 63 percent of them said the pressure to demonstrate short-term financial performance had increased over the previous five years. Yet almost nine out of ten were certain that

---

[*] Fink, who signed the 2019 Business Roundtable declaration, has since made clear that he is also concerned about the broader purpose of the corporation and about its multiple stakeholders. Indeed, as he explained in subsequent letters to shareholders, in the long term the two issues become one: companies that are unable to show that they make a positive contribution to society end up losing their license to operate, which cannot be good for their investors.

using a longer time horizon for their decisions would positively affect their companies' financial results and innovativeness.

This preference for short-term profits over long-term gains, sometimes called *managerial myopia*, is especially visible in publicly held companies. A study by researchers from Harvard and New York University demonstrates its extent. The researchers were able to compare accounting information from a sample of publicly traded companies with corresponding data from privately held companies of similar size in the same industries. They hypothesized that the short-termist pressure of the stock market would lead publicly traded companies to invest less than their privately held counterparts. And that is exactly what they found—to a surprising extent. All else being equal, private companies invest *twice as much* as public ones! Furthermore, when their revenues increased (a proxy for the presence of investment opportunities) or when the state corporate tax rate decreased (freeing up cash for investing), public companies were much slower than private ones to seize these opportunities.

TWO EASY SCAPEGOATS

As this comparison of managerial myopia between public and private firms suggests, it is very tempting to put the blame for short-termism on investors alone. Unpredictable and faceless, the financial markets are the perfect scapegoat. It is convenient for executives to explain that, if they obsess over their company's hourly stock price, it's because of fickle traders. Of course, this tyranny of the stock market requires willing accomplices: CEOs, whose compensation schemes tie bonuses to the stock price through stock options and other mechanisms. In this view, short-termism is what happens when myopic markets meet greedy executives.

The explanation seems compelling, but it is not fully satisfactory. It ignores a basic fact about the stock market: contrary to popular belief, it is *not* obsessed with the short term. In fact, stock prices mostly reflect expectations about the cash flows companies will generate in the distant future. Seventy to 80 percent of most companies' market value reflects the present value of expected cash flows that are more than five years out. In other words, the stock market is not at all short-termist. It looks ahead. It cares about the long-term value of a company, and that, to a very large extent, is what it measures.

The reason this simple point is easy to miss can be summarized in one word: *volatility*. Even though stock prices measure long-term value, this measurement varies every day. Expectations about future value are influenced by short-term news about a company and its environment. This process of continuous adjustment is often misunderstood as an obsession with short-term results. We read, for instance, that the market "punished" a bad quarterly result. But this is a simplification. What actually happened is that the market revised its long-term forecasts in light of a surprising quarterly result. When stock prices drop after unexpected bad news, it is because the stock market interprets this news as a reflection of underlying problems that will affect long-term results. If the market thinks these problems are severe—if, for instance, it loses confidence in a company's management—the market may appear to "overreact" to the news. That is what executives fear.

Shareholders and investors are quite capable of understanding a strategy oriented toward long-term results. If they weren't, Amazon would not have been able to fund its growth for so many years while delivering no (or very little) profit. Unicorns, which are typically unprofitable at the time of their IPO but promise stellar future results, would not exist. A public company does not trade on its short-term results—it trades on the story these results tell.

More and more big companies are attempting to change this story, and the conversation they are having with their investors, in an attempt to avoid excessive focus on the short term. Many, for instance, are reconsidering the practice of earnings guidance. Traditionally, companies give financial analysts "guidance" about the earnings per share target that management sets itself for a given quarter. Once committed, management is trapped by its own story: if it misses the target, it is either because it has failed to deliver on its plans or because its plans were unrealistic to start with. Both explanations are quite logically seen as cause for concern about management capabilities. They are warning signals that negatively affect the credibility of the company's long-term targets. In such cases, management can indeed expect to be "punished" by a drop in stock price. In order to avoid this short-term consequence, it will be tempted to cut discretionary spending in R&D or employee training, with possible negative consequences for long-term value creation.

Considering this serious disadvantage, it seems that providing earnings guidance is hardly worth it. Valuation multiples do not seem to be affected by the commitment to short-term targets; neither does share price volatility. Many companies, including Coca-Cola, Costco, Ford, Google, and Citigroup, have abandoned the practice. Unilever went even further: instead of announcing results on a quarterly basis, it now publishes them only twice a year, like its main European competitors.

What happened to these companies? Did investors desert them?

Did their stock price collapse? Not at all. Many did see a change in their investor base, but it was a positive one: they attract more investors focused on the intrinsic value of the company, and fewer speculators in search of a quick buck. By not talking so much about the short term, they attract shareholders who care about the long term. As Unilever CEO Paul Polman observed in 2014, "Our share price went down 8 percent when we announced the ending of guidance.... But that didn't bother me too much; my stance was that in the longer term, the company's true performance would be reflected in the share price anyway." In 2018, Warren Buffett and Jamie Dimon (chairman and CEO of JPMorgan Chase) wrote an op-ed in the *Wall Street Journal* suggesting that other public companies take the same route: "Reducing or even eliminating quarterly earnings guidance won't, by itself, eliminate all short-term performance pressures that U.S. public companies currently face, but it would be a step in the right direction."

What about the other easy scapegoat, CEOs and their compensation packages? Do executives' incentives play a role in managerial myopia? Clearly the answer to this question depends on the structure of these incentives. But stock options, which are often criticized, can actually be used to promote long-term thinking. Since stock prices take the long term into account, a CEO who sacrifices the future for immediate gains would decrease the value of her stock options. So, if the stock market is actually more long-term-minded than we give it credit for, the holders of stock options should be so, too.

The bottom line: short-termism is indeed real, but neither stock market pressure nor the self-interest of executives provides sufficient explanations for it. Besides, the dangers of short-termism extend far beyond the limited circle of public company CEOs. Are the heads of state-owned companies totally guiltless when it comes to preference for the short term? Aren't public agencies tempted, too, to postpone long-term infrastructure investments? (Think of maintenance investments in metropolitan transit authorities or much-needed works on highway systems.) Don't we frequently see political leaders put off essential reforms for fear of the immediate reactions of public opinion? Simply put, is anyone ever criticized for their excessive *long*-term thinking?

If the answer to these questions is obvious, it's because, once again, our search for scapegoats leads us astray. Executives are certainly too focused on the short term. But so are we all.

WE ARE ALL SHORT-TERM THINKERS: PRESENT BIAS

In a classic behavioral economics experiment, you are asked if you'd rather receive $100 today or $102 tomorrow. It's likely that you will choose $100 today. Common sense is on your side, as two proverbs with equivalents in many languages suggest. First of all, "time is money": $100 received today can earn interest until tomorrow. Second, "a bird in the hand is worth two in the bush": waiting for anything is risky, because a promise may not always be kept.

The choice between $100 today and $102 tomorrow is a question straight out of Economics 101. To compare a present value to a future value, we use a *discount rate*: an interest rate that reflects both time and risk. By choosing $100 today instead of $102 tomorrow, you have implicitly indicated that your discount rate is higher than 2 percent per day. In other words, for you to be willing to wait, your patience and risk-taking would have to be compensated at a higher rate. For example, if the $102 option were replaced by a promise of $150, you would quite probably choose to wait.

So far, so good. The problem is that we are not at all consistent in the discount rates that we apply. Let's use the same figures but change the dates. Would you rather receive $100 *in a year*, or $102 *in a year and a day*? For the vast majority of us, this is a no-brainer. If we're going to wait such a long time, what's one extra day? We might as well get $2 more!

This seems natural, even obvious. But it's actually illogical. If in the first situation you chose $100, but in the second you decided to wait to get $102, why does your discount rate change over time? To ask the question more simply, if you're willing to wait one more day to get $2 more, why don't you do it right now? Or, to make the paradox even more obvious: in exactly one year's time, won't the choice of the second situation be exactly the same as the first—a choice between today and tomorrow?

As this experiment shows, we are much less patient when one of the options involves the immediate present. We're much more likely to choose a bird in the hand when the decision is made today, and more likely to choose two in the bush when it takes place tomorrow. This tendency, called *present bias*, has been extensively demonstrated. For instance, in an experiment similar to the one described above, Richard Thaler asked subjects to choose between a payment of $15 right now and a larger payment in the future. How large would that payment need to be to justify the wait? The median answer was $100 if the payment was to be delayed by ten years and $20 if it was delayed by one month. The numbers may not seem absurd, but from an economist's perspective, they are: the implicit annual discount rate they reflect is 19 percent with a ten-year horizon, but 345 percent with a one-month horizon.

An even more obvious (and more familiar) illustration of present bias is the problem of self-control. It is hard for us to resist dessert, to stop smoking, or to wake up early to go to the gym—despite the future benefits we anticipate from these virtuous behaviors. It's much easier to make New Year's resolutions, to empty our cupboards of sweets and cigarettes, or to join a gym. By doing this, we are committing ourselves to make an effort *tomorrow* in order to reap the benefits *after tomorrow*. It's the same effort that we refuse to make *today* to get the same benefit *tomorrow*. We're completely capable of being patient…as long as we don't have to do it right away!

If we combine present bias with loss aversion, which we discussed in the previous chapter, we can start to understand the behavioral basis of short-termism. Recall that a "loss" weighs more than a gain of comparable size in our cost-benefit analysis. Add the fact that when making trade-offs between the present and the future, the present speaks much louder. It becomes clear that choosing *a loss today* in hopes of *a gain tomorrow* is a deeply unappealing proposition. Announcing that a short-term goal will be missed is framed as a loss; even when it can be explained by a long-term calculation, it is seen as a defeat. The loss of credibility and prestige it entails can seem unbearable.

Short-termism also contributes to the inertia trap described in chapter 5, in which inertia encourages us to put off difficult decisions. Choosing to stop the escalation of commitment is an example of this sort of difficult decision: to sell (or close) a failing business unit, to stop a project that is not bearing fruit, is to record a loss. Even though this immediate loss will result in future benefits (or in the avoidance of a larger loss), loss aversion and present bias make this decision irrationally difficult.

All this is human, all too human … so human that it's tempting, once again, to express the problem in terms of virtue and vice, heroes and villains. For instance, Bill George, the former CEO of Medtronic, writing about CEOs, says, "The good ones have the courage to look past the pressures from the outside world to capitulate for the short-term gain and go for the long term."

How simple it is, this opposition between "the good ones," who have "courage," and lesser mortals who "capitulate"! But addressing this issue will require more than moralistic pronouncements. The difficulty of managing time horizons is not only an evil of capitalism; nor is it only a moral failing of some CEOs. It's human nature.

THE TIME HORIZON TRAP IN THIRTY SECONDS

- Short-termism doesn't just mean putting shareholders' interests ahead of other stakeholders' interests; it's also the preference for immediate profit at the expense of future profit (**managerial myopia**).

  ▶ *Even investors are worried about it (BlackRock).*

  ▶ *Public companies are more short-term-focused than private ones.*

- However, stock market pressure is not a sufficient explanation: **share price also reflects the long term.**

  ▶ *Some companies work to shift their shareholder base toward long-term investors, for instance by abandoning earnings guidance.*

- The inconsistency in our preferences over time reflects **present bias.**

  ▶ *The time between today and tomorrow feels longer than the time between two days a year from now: our discount rates are not constant over time.*

- **Short-termism** is loss aversion plus present bias.

  ▶ *In order not to miss an earnings target (framed as a loss), many managers neglect investments that create long-term value.*

8

"EVERYONE'S DOING IT"

The Groupthink Trap

Worldly wisdom teaches that it is better for reputation to fail conventionally than to succeed unconventionally.

—John Maynard Keynes

In 1961, shortly after his inauguration, President Kennedy authorized a battalion of 1,400 CIA-trained Cuban expatriates to invade Cuba. Their landing at the Bay of Pigs turned into a fiasco, as nearly all the anti-Castro forces were killed or taken prisoner within days. It was a humiliating moment in American history.

Many historians would later show that this fiasco owed nothing to bad luck. The plan presented to the president was riddled with inconsistencies. It was based on unsound assumptions, notably the notion that the Cuban people would welcome the invaders as liberators. How did the president and his inner circle, who had a reputation for being picked from the best and the brightest of their generation, make such a disastrous decision? Or, as Kennedy himself asked, "How could we have been so stupid?"

The same question could be asked with regard to all the examples of terrible decisions we have discussed so far. Why didn't anyone sound the alarm and stop the runaway train? How did the boards of these companies fail to prevent overpriced acquisitions or notice red flags?

In order to understand this, we need to step away from cognitive science for a moment and take a detour through the world of social psychology. Leaders must take final responsibility, but in organizations, they do not decide alone. Making a really big mistake usually requires a team effort.

QUASHING DISAGREEMENT

In his memoirs, Arthur M. Schlesinger Jr., President Kennedy's special assistant, noted: "In the months after the Bay of Pigs I bitterly reproached myself for having kept so silent during those crucial discussions in the Cabinet Room. . . . I can only explain my failure to do more than raise a few timid questions by reporting that one's impulse to blow the whistle on this nonsense was simply *undone by the circumstances of the discussion.*" (Emphasis added.)

This lucid admission is a perfect illustration of *groupthink*. Irving L. Janis, the psychologist who popularized this term (invented by William Whyte many years earlier), based his study of group dynamics in part on the study of that decision. Schlesinger was one of JFK's closest advisors. He was convinced that the decision being made was a mistake, and aware of its potentially disastrous consequences. Yet this renowned intellectual could not find it in himself to "do more than raise a few timid objections." He silenced his doubts and sided with the prevailing opinion of the group and its leader.

The key to this phenomenon lies in what Schlesinger calls "the circumstances of the discussion." Strictly speaking, there is no such thing as groupthink: the group does not do any thinking; its members do. And groups do not always converge. We have all witnessed discussions in which participants are at odds with each other and debate vigorously, with the discussion sometimes degenerating into personal conflict. Yet in the Bay of Pigs decision, it seemed the group had its own way of thinking, and even of crushing the participants' independent thoughts. Where does this homogeneity come from? When, and why, does each individual adopt the opinion he perceives as the dominant one in the group?

This subject was first explored in the 1950s by psychologist Solomon E. Asch. In a series of famous experiments, Asch asked small groups of participants to accomplish an extremely simple task—comparing the length of several lines on a piece of paper—by answering out loud, one by one. The first participants to answer in each round were actually confederates of the experimenter, and they confidently, and unanimously, gave an incorrect answer. The last participant to answer was thus the only true "guinea pig." The choice was simple: he could either describe the reality that stared him in the face or conform to the opinion of the group, which had so far agreed on an obviously incorrect answer.

The results of this experiment still surprise us today. About three-quarters of the participants chose at least once to conform to the group opinion, even though they were perfectly aware of the conflict between what they were saying and the evidence of their senses. The power of groupthink was enough to make them yield to the collective point of view.

And that was in a group of perfect strangers, answering a

question that required no thinking or judgment, when the correct answer lay right before their eyes. Should we be surprised, then, that we are susceptible to group influence when we need to form an opinion on complex problems that may have several equally acceptable solutions? Is it at all surprising that we're even more impressionable when surrounded by colleagues whose viewpoints we respect, or by hierarchical superiors whose directions we usually follow?

As with other biases we have discussed, our intellectual "immune system" immediately raises many objections. We can think of many reasons why we—unlike these naive, suggestible subjects— would be immune to groupthink. Perhaps Asch's guinea pigs were especially impressionable. Or perhaps they chose to yield to the group's opinion simply out of convenience, to avoid an awkward moment: in an experiment with no real consequences, it wasn't worth the trouble to correct incompetent strangers. As for the Bay of Pigs decision, would it have been made the same way if President Kennedy and his advisors had not been egregiously misled by military advisors pursuing their own political goals?

If these or other objections are running through your mind right now, if you doubt the power of groupthink could ever sway you, here is another story that may lead you to reconsider. The scene takes place in 2014 at a meeting of the Coca-Cola Company board of directors. The company's management has proposed an equity compensation plan and is asking the board to approve it. The plan is rather generous—so generous, in fact, that at least one large shareholder, an activist investor, has publicly and vociferously spoken out against it. He believes the plan would dilute shareholder equity massively and frames the choice as one in which shareholders' interests must be defended against the greed of management—which is one of the roles of a public company board. Joined by other investment funds, he asks the board to reject the plan.

We may or may not agree with the activist investor. Coca-Cola's management, of course, doesn't. But it is the board's role to resolve this issue. It just so happens that one of the most eminent independent directors on Coca-Cola's board has often criticized stock options, even calling them "lottery tickets." He has done his calculations and disapproves of the proposed plan. He makes no bones about his opinion, which he has even expressed in a CNBC interview. Given all this, one might think he would vote against the plan. But when the time comes to vote, he doesn't—instead, he abstains. Asked sometime later to explain this vote, he answers characteristically bluntly: opposing a stock option plan "is a little bit like belching at the dinner table. I mean, you can't do it too often. If you do, you find you're eating in the kitchen pretty soon."

By now, you may have recognized this mystery director: it was Warren Buffett. Buffett, the "Oracle of Omaha" to whom people flock in hopes of learning from his wisdom, the greatest investor of all time! If any director had the clout to stand up to his board colleagues, it would be him. His interests as a shareholder (owning, at the time, roughly 9 percent of the Coca-Cola Company) were perfectly aligned with those of the other shareholders he was supposed to represent, not with those of management. Yet even though he was convinced the proposed plan was a bad one, Buffett refused to break the harmony of the group. His comments say it all: "I love Coke. I love the management, I love the directors. So I didn't want to vote no. It's kind of un-American to vote no at a Coke meeting."

If you thought good corporate governance was just a matter of having competent, strong-willed, independent directors on the board, this should give you pause. But one could still object that this was a situation of overt conflict, in which Buffett made a wise tactical choice. By not publicly censuring the company's management, he preserved a strong relationship that he could use later, more discreetly, to encourage tweaks to the equity compensation plan that would make it more acceptable. In this particular case, that is in fact what eventually happened. But that's not often how it works: "I've never yet heard at any of the 19 boards I was on," Buffett says, "anybody say in the meeting they were against [a compensation plan]." If that's the norm, it seems unlikely that shareholders can count on boards to exercise effective control over these plans.

Furthermore, groupthink affects us even when harmony reigns and there is no overt conflict. This is what a private equity fund found out when it reviewed the decision process of its investment committee, which approves acquisitions and divestments. In this case, the interests of all committee members are perfectly aligned: all have invested in the fund and receive carried interest compensation based on its performance. This should motivate them to make the right decisions! To be on the safe side, the committee has adopted a rule: to approve an investment, ten votes out of the twelve committee members are required. Agreement must be almost unanimous.

Yet when analyzing their past investments, the committee members found that they had sometimes been overly optimistic. This result astonished them. They had been afraid that requiring near-unanimous approval could have led them to be too cautious and to reject attractive investments. With such a prudent rule in place, how did they end up making risky choices?

The paradox is easily resolved if one considers the dynamics of the committee. As with any team, collective victory counts, but it's best to be the one who scores. In this case, the hero is the committee member who proposes an investment that is approved. Each committee member who votes today on a peer's proposal will tomorrow be submitting her own investment ideas for approval. If she challenges a colleague's opinion, she can fear retaliation against her own proposals. The trap of groupthink has been sprung.

Worse: as discussions with committee members revealed, the supermajority requirement didn't just fail to limit the effects of groupthink. It made them worse.

To understand why, put yourself in the shoes of a skeptical committee member. You know that if you are the first to start asking tough questions, others will probably follow (especially if you raise a valid point). By breaking the silence and the implied consensus it reflects, you are giving others license to speak up, too. And you know that it takes just two more people who share your doubts to kill the proposal! You also know that the colleague presenting this proposal has worked on it for weeks and staked part of his reputation on it. Do you really want to be remembered as the one who started this discussion?

In this group, and in many similar ones, it's almost irresistibly tempting to quash one's doubts about the proposed investment, just as the subjects in Solomon Asch's experiment quashed theirs about the length of the lines. Even experienced managers whose interests are all perfectly aligned may choose to preserve the harmony of the group rather than express a well-founded criticism.

TWO WAYS OF LOOKING AT GROUPTHINK

The vocabulary we use to describe groupthink often reflects moral judgment. We naturally think of individuals who yield to group-think as lacking the necessary courage to express their opinions.

It is true that groupthink is partly related to *social pressure*. We yield to the thinking of the majority out of a fear of retaliation. This retaliation is sometimes real, as in the case of the members of the investment committee who are thinking of how their next investment proposals will be received. More often, it is symbolic: if you oppose group consensus, you will encounter first a lack of understanding, then annoyance, and, finally, ostracism. This is wonderfully summed up in Warren Buffett's quip about "eating in the kitchen." Whatever form retaliation may take, those who fear it keep quiet in order to avoid it. And whether you regard this as a cowardly, cynical calculation or (as in the Warren Buffett example) as the hallmark of a realist who wisely picks his battles, the underlying mechanism is one of social pressure.

But there is another, perhaps more honorable reason to silence one's doubts in a group. We may change our mind as a result of a *rational adjustment* to the majority opinion. When many members of a group share the same view, it is entirely logical to suppose that they have good reasons for doing so, and therefore that their view is right. This commonsense reasoning was mathematically demonstrated by French mathematician and political philosopher Condorcet. In his "jury theorem," published in 1785, Condorcet showed that if several voters form their opinions independently of one another, and if each is more likely to be right than wrong, then the probability that the majority is right increases with the number of votes. In other words, under what seem to be fairly reasonable conditions, the larger the majority, the more likely it is to be correct.

In the case of a management team, it is very sensible to assume that every one of your colleagues is more likely to be right than wrong. (If that's not the case, you may want to start looking for another job.) This is true not only in general but also when it comes to specific questions: you will quite sensibly give more weight to a colleague's opinions when you believe this colleague is competent, knowledgeable, and well informed on the topic considered. Schlesinger could have legitimately thought that other participants in the meeting who approved of the Bay of Pigs invasion (and, of course, the generals who suggested it) had access to relevant information and to analyses he had not seen himself. Similarly, in the case of the private equity fund that thought its supermajority requirement was a safeguard against risky investments, the members of the investment committee are aware that the member who proposes a transaction is an expert on the relevant industry and has done due diligence on the target. It is quite sensible for a generalist who is now reading the proposal for the first time to defer to its author's judgment.

Under these conditions, it may be completely rational for the enthusiasm of the group to carry more weight than the doubts of one individual.* When you enter a meeting with a minority opinion and choose to keep quiet, this may simply be because you have become aware that your initial view was wrong. Adopting the majority opinion is not necessarily a sign of weakness: it can be a rational choice.

---

* It is possible to quantitatively determine the extent to which one should rationally change one's opinion in light of the opinions of others. We will return to this in chapter 15.

Which of these motivations is stronger? When an individual sides with the majority, is it social pressure or rational adjustment? The power of groupthink comes from the very fact that these two mechanisms are inextricably linked. A few people, perhaps, consciously choose to keep their doubts and questions to themselves. But most who embrace the majority view have *really* changed their minds. As the group consensus is revealed—and the corresponding social pressure increases—they become genuinely convinced by the arguments they hear. In the end, they haven't quashed their doubts: they have conquered them. They have a ready explanation for their change of heart. It is not cowardice: it is intellectual honesty.

CASCADES AND POLARIZATION

In its typical form, groupthink silences disagreement. The group converges toward one of the preexisting opinions. But in some cases groupthink can go further and *accentuate* the majority opinion.

To understand this, picture a management meeting in which people speak in turn about their position on an issue—for example, whether or not they are in favor of an investment proposal. All participants will engage in the "rational adjustment" we described above. If the first person to speak is in favor of the investment, then the second person will take this into consideration. Had she spoken first, she might have expressed some doubts. But hearing her colleague speak has made her more confident. She is now a bit more likely to approve of the plan without any reservations. Then comes the third person's turn. As he considers the favorable opinion shared by two of his colleagues, he also becomes more likely to vote for the plan. And so on: in a completely rational fashion, each person will adjust his or her judgment in order to take into account previously expressed opinions. This is an *information cascade*.

Information cascades have two essential consequences. If you have ever run a meeting, you are familiar with the first: the order in which people speak can change the outcome of a discussion. Information cascades give the first speakers disproportionate importance. Chapter 14 will return to this observation and consider its practical implications for those who want to establish quality dialogue.

The second consequence is more subtle: a group acting completely rationally can make an error that many of its participants would have been able to avoid if they were working alone. In order to understand this, let's go back to the simplified example of an investment decision. Each participant considers the conclusions of those who have spoken before. Those who speak first are all in favor. Let's assume that subsequent speakers decide that the reasons given by the early speakers in favor of the plan carry more weight than their own doubts about the proposal. The proposal ends up unanimously approved. Hurray!

Except…the unanimous decision may be a mistake. The tragedy of information cascades is that the logical decision of each individual can produce a disastrous result for the group. At each step in the cascade, some information is lost. Each speaker refrains from raising concerns and doubts that, if expressed and considered by all, would have changed the collective equation. *Private information*, held by only some members of the group, is not shared—or it is only partially shared, and therefore carries less weight in the discussion. So the discussion ends up focused on the shared information and viewpoints, supporting the group consensus. All in all, the group is less well informed than the sum of its members.

It's easy to see how information cascades not only lead a group to approve the majority opinion but make it more extreme. Many studies suggest that deliberating as a group produces two simultaneous effects. A group will often reach a *more extreme* conclusion than its average member would have been initially inclined to suggest. At the same time, the individual group members will be *more confident* in this conclusion than they would have been if they had not discussed it. This double amplification—of the result itself and of the group's degree of confidence in it—is *group polarization*.

Recent research suggests that this phenomenon is at play when the compensation committees of corporate boards discuss CEO compensation. For better or worse, most companies use benchmarking to set CEO compensation. The objective is to set a reference point: the average compensation package for CEOs of companies roughly the same size in the same industry.[*] The compensation committee then decides whether its own CEO deserves more, or less, than this reference point. To assess whether group polarization was taking place, the researchers analyzed the decision patterns of the committee members on other boards they'd served on. Some, they found, tended to pay CEOs above market price; others to pay below market price. Did this background influence their decisions in a subsequent board? Yes—and the deliberation amplified it! When the board members had previously voted to

---

[*] Setting CEO compensation by comparison with industry peers is a debatable practice, and not just because it is sensitive to group polarization. Evidently, most CEOs are eager to believe that their performance is above the median of their peer group, and many boards seem to agree with them. This practice is probably an important driver of the rise of executive compensation in recent decades.

pay CEOs above the market price, deliberation led to paying the CEO even more generously than they had historically done. Conversely, if the board had experience paying CEOs below the relevant reference point, members set a compensation level even lower than they had on those other boards. The deliberations of the compensation committee accentuated the original preferences of its members. They polarized the group.

Another phenomenon that often results from group polarization is escalation of commitment, which was mentioned in chapter 5. In general, it is not individuals who escalate commitment but teams or even entire organizations. Escalation of commitment is both more common and more powerful when it is decided in a group.

GROUPTHINK AND COMPANY CULTURE

Not surprisingly, all these group dynamics are exacerbated by cultural homogeneity. The respect granted to the judgment of one's peers is all the greater when one identifies with them, and the social pressure we feel to conform to their opinion is also increased by strong shared values. Homogeneity thus increases both engines of groupthink. Many empirical studies confirm that when group members identify with a common organizational culture they are more inclined to keep their doubts to themselves, to become polarized with an extreme opinion, and to stubbornly stay on a dead-end path.

The weight of group identity can be seen when groups of individuals in an organization make harmful decisions that they would not have made individually, a problem often described as a "toxic culture." One example is the crisis that started in 2016 and continued for several years at Wells Fargo, one of the largest banks in America. Bank employees were encouraged to boost their sales figures by "cross-selling" as many financial products and services as possible to their clients. Selling is hard, though: it is much easier to add savings accounts, credit cards, additional insurance, and other services to the accounts of existing clients without telling them about it! Wells Fargo employees created millions of fraudulent accounts, using fake emails, fake PINs, and fake addresses when convenient. Some even forged customers' signatures.

Clearly, just about everyone knows (and certainly every bank employee should know) that these are not acceptable practices. However, it seems that they became widespread at Wells Fargo: 3.5 million fake accounts were opened, and at least 5,300 employees had to leave the company. As of late 2018, the bank had paid about $3 billion in fines and settlement costs, and was still facing fines and penalties that could add up to several billion more. At this scale, we're not talking about a few bad apples but about a bad barrel: reports about Wells Fargo are full of employee comments describing its "toxic sales culture," "cutthroat corporate culture," and "culture problem."

But what exactly do we mean when we talk about "culture"? First, of course, that the bank put in place incentives to encourage its employees to sell more. Fortunately, not all employees who are given sales targets to meet break the law. For there to be a "toxic culture," incentives are not enough. Problems become rampant when each person can observe deviant behavior in his or her immediate environment. When many peers whom you respect adopt abnormal practices, especially if your boss does the same (or looks the other way), the abnormal becomes normal. Groupthink normalizes deviance. Breaking the rules becomes the rule. "If they're all doing it, why shouldn't I?"

People who are part of the same company culture, who observe deviant behavior, and who fall into line with groupthink: these are the ingredients for a company's downward spiral. And when groupthink strikes not just in a single company but in an entire industry—or when all the players in a market economy start thinking the same way—the downward spiral can take the form of a speculative bubble or systemic crisis.

This short inventory of the ravages of groupthink is not at all exhaustive. But it does illustrate the significant social dimension of big mistakes.

Perhaps you also noticed another essential component in all these errors: individual incentives that diverge from organizational goals. This is the subject of the next chapter.

THE GROUPTHINK TRAP IN THIRTY SECONDS

- **Groupthink** can lead the best-informed participants to keep their doubts to themselves.
  - ▶ *Kennedy and the Bay of Pigs invasion: "How could we have been so stupid?"*
  - ▶ *Warren Buffett: Voting no as a board member is "like belching at the dinner table."*
- Groupthink is **rational for the individual:** partly because of social pressure, and partly because it is logical to take other people's opinions into account.
- But it is **harmful to the group** because it deprives it of private information that would be useful.
- The group can also amplify the majority opinion: **group polarization.**
  - ▶ *Polarization also accentuates escalation of commitment.*
- **Homogeneity,** the presence of a **shared culture,** exacerbates groupthink.
  - ▶ *This can lead to an ethical downward spiral: "If they're all doing it, why shouldn't I?"*

9

"I'M NOT THINKING OF MYSELF, OF COURSE"

The Conflict of Interest Trap

It is difficult to get a man to understand something,
when his salary depends on his not understanding it!
—Upton Sinclair

The idea that personal interests can influence decisions is certainly not new. It's usually the first explanation that comes to mind when we hear about a mistake. Weren't the bankers who contributed to the 2008 financial crisis influenced by their compensation structure? Didn't the CEOs who made risky acquisitions care most of all about extending their empire and getting media attention? Aren't political leaders who put off difficult reforms mainly thinking of getting reelected?

The answers to all these questions seem obvious. Adam Smith, writing in 1776 about what were then called "joint-stock companies," observed that "the directors of such companies...being the managers rather of other people's money than of their own, it cannot well be expected that they should watch over it with the same anxious vigilance with which the partners in a private copartnery frequently watch over their own."

Smith's observation resonates with what is now called *agency theory*, or the *principal-agent model*. This model describes situations in which a "principal" delegates authority to an "agent": a CEO is an agent of shareholders, employees are agents of their leaders, and elected officials are agents of "We the People." Agency theory suggests that, because their incentives are imperfectly aligned, and because agents and principals do not have access to the same information, agents make decisions that are suboptimal from the point of view of the principals. These insights have resulted in significant findings about the optimal way of structuring contracts between principals and agents. They have also helped popularize the idea that the performance of executives should be evaluated (and rewarded) solely on the basis of the value that they create for shareholders.

The agency theory viewpoint is never far from our minds when we try to understand human behavior. We often take for granted the idea that individuals are selfish, cynical optimizers who seize every opportunity to pursue their personal interest at the expense of the institutions they are serving, who drown the common good in "the icy water of egotistical calculation," in Marx's memorable words. The paradox of this universally accepted explanation is that it is both generally true and, as we will see, very insufficient.

NO ANGELS

Many studies provide empirical support for the principal-agent model in the business world. Executives are not angels. There are clear connections between the strategic choices of corporate leaders and their personal interests. For instance, they seem motivated, both financially and emotionally, to increase the size of the companies they lead, even if this hurts shareholder value creation. This phenomenon, often called *empire building*, certainly contributes to the problem of overpaying for acquisitions—as when Quaker purchased Snapple.

Similar tensions often manifest within a company's management team. It is customary for a senior executive to be financially incentivized based on the results of her division or unit in the company, not on the company's overall results. Even when that is not the case and no direct financial incentives are in play, managers serve the interests of their division or department. In many companies, this is expected, even encouraged: defending the interests of one's unit or team is seen as a sign of conviction in one's plans, of personal commitment, and ultimately of leadership. This sort of corporate politics is not a pathology of organizations—it is a fact of life.

Corporate politics have an essential part in several of the mistakes that we have examined, especially when loss aversion comes into play. Recall the problem of risk-taking discussed in chapter 6. We saw that managers rarely choose to champion risky investments, and that this produces a level of risk aversion that is irrational in aggregate. One of the explanations for this behavior is that loss aversion for the individual does not focus on the same "loss" the company cares about avoiding. For the executive, the money the company may lose is secondary. What matters most is the loss of face she will suffer if the project fails. What impact will this failure have on her credibility, prestige, and career? The company will live to fight other battles, but the manager only has one reputation to lose.

Finally, principal-agent logic helps explain deviant behavior. At Wells Fargo, we saw that the sales targets set for employees were a key ingredient in the scandal. In other examples of large-scale transgressions, from stock-option backdating to anticompetitive collusion to the manipulation of engine emissions tests, financial incentives always play a large part.

THE LIMITS OF CYNICISM

Few readers will be surprised by these observations. The notion that managers can be tempted to place self-interest above their companies' interests seems so obvious that it has inspired universally accepted management practices. The alignment of individual financial incentives with the success of a company, for instance, is generally (and correctly) considered to be an essential prerequisite to building an effective organization.

Less obvious is the effect that adopting the principal-agent model has on the way leaders listen to the suggestions and opinions of others. Any executive knows she should expect colleagues to be self-interested to some degree. She knows she should ask herself at all times what the person sitting across from her is after. And she often prides herself on her ability not to be fooled by self-serving or self-promoting arguments. For experienced executives in large organizations, this precaution has become second nature.

This climate of mild cynicism creates a paradoxical sense of comfort: we generally assume that self-interest is a problem that is easy to manage, provided we know where each person's interest lies. Since executives generally understand their colleagues' motivations quite well (or at least think they do), they believe themselves completely capable of spotting their political maneuvering.

However, this generally accepted view of the manager as a

rational, even cynical, agent runs into some serious objections. Casual observation and careful empirical research alike have found ample evidence that individuals do not act out of self-interest alone. The facts do not support the assertion that people are acting as the archetypal *homo economicus*, or "Econ," as Richard Thaler calls this fictitious character, exclusively motivated by seeking personal gain.

A striking counterexample is provided by studies of the "ultimatum game." In this experimental setting, two participants (randomly assigned to one of two roles) must share a sum of money. The first one suggests a way to divide the money. The second can either accept and receive the amount of money allocated by the first or refuse. In the event of a refusal, neither participant gets anything.

An Econ proposer seeking to maximize personal gain should suggest taking the lion's share for himself. And an Econ respondent should accept any split offered, no matter how small his share: whatever he gets is better than the alternative, which is nothing. Yet this is not what happens. Generally, participants propose sharing the money in a relatively equitable way. When, on the contrary, they behave like selfish Econs and propose a very unequal division to their own advantage, most of their partners refuse. By doing this, they do not hesitate to deprive themselves of financial gain in order to "punish" the proposer who overplayed his hand. These results have been replicated many times over, notably in low-income countries, where the sums of money involved could represent three months' income for the participants.

The ultimatum game and, fortunately, many observations that we can make every day hold a reassuring message about human nature: our behavior is not always entirely driven by our immediate financial interest. Other considerations, such as fairness or the desire to preserve our reputation, influence our behavior. Obviously, these factors carry more weight in the context of an organization than they do in a game played by total strangers who will never see each other again. It's therefore too simple to assume that all managers and executives act in their own self-interest at all times and in all circumstances.

BOUNDED ETHICALITY AND SELF-SERVING BIAS

Does this mean we can disregard the weight of financial incentives? Not at all. Financial incentives are not our only source of motivation, but recent research suggests that they can influence us *much more than we realize*. Even if financial incentives do not determine all of our behavior, we cannot make ourselves immune to their influence. But this influence affects our decisions in quite different ways than we might generally imagine. When we observe that agents prioritize their personal interests, we usually suppose that they are doing it intentionally. We assume that they "respond" to incentives, and that this means they consciously calculate what behavior is best for them. Yet many researchers now hold a very different view. They believe that we are often *unable* to resist the influence of financial incentives, *even if* we sincerely intend to do so.

This is manifest with professionals who have a duty to place their clients' interest above their own, intend to do so, and sincerely believe they are succeeding. In reality, empirical evidence suggests that their interest colors their judgments. For example, lawyers have a duty to advise their clients in the best manner possible; but those who work on a contingency fee basis tend to recommend that their clients quickly settle, whereas those paid by the hour are more inclined to go to trial. Similarly, all physicians believe they are recommending the most appropriate treatment for their patients, but when surgeons' income depends on the number of operations they perform, they are more inclined to recommend surgery than medical treatment. And auditors arrive at different conclusions about the same financial statements depending on whether they're told the accounts belong to a client company or a company that is not a client—of course, the accounts are more often approved when they are presented as a client's.

Corporate executives are not immune to this form of bias. When taking part in strategic decision-making, a division head can be *genuinely* convinced (not *pretending* to believe) that her unit deserves significant resources. Whether or not financial incentives are in play, emotional attachments (to people, brands, places) can also affect her judgment.

This is not the behavior of an Econ consciously and selfishly maximizing personal gain. As a rule, nothing suggests that auditors are intentionally falsifying accounts to please their clients or that doctors intentionally mislead their patients. The problem, most of the time, is that these people are completely sincere. The phrase *bounded ethicality*, analogous to the *bounded rationality* of economics, describes, in the words of Max Bazerman and Don Moore, "the cognitive biases that lead honorable people to engage in unethical behavior without realizing that they are doing so." This is often called *self-serving bias*.

It's easy to dismiss this analysis as naive. How do we know these people are acting in good faith, and that their honest mistakes just so happen to coincide with their self-interest? How can we be sure they aren't just lying through their teeth?

The answer can be found by studying the way our biases work. Start with confirmation bias, discussed in chapter 1. It is easy to see how our first hypothesis would be one that favors our interests. Then, without realizing it, we will critically examine the data that contradicts this hypothesis but automatically accept the evidence that supports it. Since we are unaware of this distortion, we can remain convinced that we are examining the facts in a completely impartial manner.

Another bias that affects our ethical judgment concerns the difference between action and omission. Letting someone commit a reprehensible act seems less blameworthy to us than committing it ourselves, even if we benefit from it. One study illustrated this difference by asking people to evaluate the actions of a pharmaceutical company that takes advantage of its monopoly position to massively increase the price of a drug. Predictably, they wholeheartedly condemn the firm. However, if this company sells the patent to another player, knowing that the acquirer (in order to justify the purchase price) will make the drug even more expensive, they find the seller's actions tolerable.

The same mechanism helps us understand how a management team making a decision can let its leader make a bad decision, as we have seen in the cases of groupthink. They wouldn't have made that decision themselves, but contributing to it by omission is not ethically unacceptable. This helps explain why it is so rare to see a member of an executive team resign over strategic disagreements.

We could find many more examples of biases that consistently distort our interpretation of reality to our own advantage. As soon as there is any ambiguity about a judgment (and when a decision is difficult, there always is), we reason in a way that is selective enough to serve our interests and yet plausible enough to convince others (and ourselves) that we are not intentionally distorting the facts. Dan Ariely summarizes this behavior in a memorable sentence: "We cheat up to the level that allows us to retain our self-image as reasonably honest individuals."

The "sincere" nature of self-serving bias is further demonstrated by other experiments. In a 2010 study, neuroscience researchers asked paid participants to evaluate the quality of contemporary paintings. Some of the paintings were shown next to corporate logos. When the subjects were told that a corporation had sponsored the experiment and therefore made it possible for them to be compensated for participating in it, they expressed greater appreciation of the art shown next to that company's logo. The participants' judgment was biased, even though they would have no other interaction with the company in question, and despite the fact that the company was merely sponsoring the experimenters, not paying them directly.

What makes this experiment interesting is that the researchers did not just ask the participants to rate the quality of the art: the subjects were in an fMRI machine when they expressed their aesthetic opinions. The researchers were thus able to observe that the regions of the brain that encode preferences for art were indeed activated when the company-sponsored paintings were shown. In a manner analogous to the halo effect discussed in chapter 2, the positive impression made by the sponsoring company transferred to the paintings associated with it. It seems the subjects were not just being polite (or hypocritical) but *truly* enjoyed these paintings more.

WRONG DIAGNOSIS, WRONG REMEDIES

Why is it essential to understand that those who make decisions according to their own self-interest are doing so sincerely, and that unconscious, self-serving bias is quite distinct from conscious, self-serving calculation? For two essential reasons: misunderstanding self-serving bias leads us to misjudge the individuals who are subject to it. It also leads us to take ineffective measures to prevent its effects.

First, the way we judge the actions of individuals who are subject to a conflict of interest changes radically depending on whether we consider their decisions to be conscious or not. If we think that the lawyers, doctors, and auditors in the previous examples *are lying*, if we believe that they are consciously changing their decisions in order to maximize their income at the expense of their clients and patients, then we should find them blameworthy. And since we don't for a moment think ourselves capable of such corruption, we're convinced that we'd be able to resist this temptation if we were in their shoes.

An example of this kind of reasoning was expressed by the late Supreme Court justice Antonin Scalia. Scalia had to decide whether or not to take himself off a case involving then vice president Dick Cheney. The judge was on friendly enough terms with the vice president to have gone duck hunting on Cheney's property three weeks earlier. Scalia refused to remove himself and wrote a twenty-one-page memorandum justifying his decision. Like most of us, he believed himself able to set aside any friendships or self-interest when issuing his decisions. As he wrote, "If it is reasonable to think that a Supreme Court justice can be bought so cheap, the nation is in deeper trouble than I had imagined."

People who find themselves in a conflict of interest situation often voice the same indignant objection: "I can't be bought off so easily!" Many doctors are offended that people think they can be influenced by the token gifts pharmaceutical reps leave on their desks. Many researchers sincerely believe that their scientific results are not in any way influenced by the companies that have funded their research. As Bazerman and Moore put it, "Most members of these professions would agree that a conflict of interest exists.... These same professionals, however, assume that they themselves are immune from such conflicts of interest."

Understanding self-serving biases leads to a radically different analysis. If we cannot set our interests aside, no matter how hard we try, then it is inevitable that they will bias our judgments. We cannot be sure that Scalia (who joined the majority opinion by voting in favor of Cheney) would have issued a different decision if the case had concerned someone else, but we have every reason to suspect it is a possibility. Suggesting that he take himself off the case does not imply that he is easily bought but that his judgment might be altered. He is not presumed guilty of a voluntary offense: rather, he is a potential victim of involuntary error. He should be the first to want to remove himself from this situation.

Underestimating the power of self-interest bias has another consequence: it leads to an ineffective, even counterproductive, belief in the power of transparency to prevent conflicts of interest. Disclosure requirements have been imposed on many professions in various countries. For example, financial analysts must reveal the positions that they have in the stocks that they are covering. Physicians must state any links with the pharmaceutical industry. Politicians must disclose who donates to their campaigns. Researchers must list their sources of funding.

However, these transparency measures are a double-edged sword. They may dissuade a small number of malicious individuals from consciously lying in their own self-interest. Logically, however, they cannot change the behavior of people who are perfectly honest and sincerely convinced that they cannot be influenced.

Even worse, some studies suggest that disclosures, far from reducing conflicts of interest, make them worse. Apparently feeling "liberated" by the revelation of their conflict of interest, the individuals in question seem to pay less attention to the need to remain objective.

Like groupthink, self-serving bias is easily mistaken for moral weakness or an intentional transgression. Yet its harmfulness comes from the very fact that it is most often unconscious. Just as groupthink is not (at least not always) caused by the cowardice of someone who purposely conforms to the majority opinion, self-interest bias is not (at least not always) a calculated attempt to lie or cheat. This is why it is not enough to be aware of it in order to solve the problems it creates.

THE CONFLICT OF INTEREST TRAP
IN THIRTY SECONDS

- **"Agents" act in their own self-interest,** at the expense of those they are representing (*principal-agent model*).
  - ▶ *Directors acting on behalf of shareholders, elected officials acting on behalf of voters, and so on*
- **Political maneuvering** in companies is so obvious that people think they can easily discount the advice of self-serving individuals.
- **Beyond** these effects, which we assume to be conscious and intentional, we are also influenced by our self-interest **without realizing it.**
  - ▶ *Lawyers, doctors, and auditors are influenced by their compensation.*
- **Self-serving bias** produces **bounded ethicality,** which affects our ethical judgment.
  - ▶ *"The vast majority of unethical behaviors occur without the actors' conscious intention to behave unethically." (Bazerman and Moore)*
  - ▶ *"We cheat up to the level that allows us to retain our self-image as reasonably honest individuals." (Ariely)*
- It is thus essential to **avoid situations of conflict of interest,** even when one believes oneself to be immune to them.
  - ▶ *Justice Scalia was missing the point when he suggested that he could not be "bought so cheap."*
- **Disclosure requirements** do not make self-serving biases go away; sometimes they can even make them worse.

PART 2

DECIDING HOW TO DECIDE

10

HUMAN, ALL TOO HUMAN

Are Cognitive Biases the Root of All Evil?

We have met the enemy and he is us.

— Walt Kelly

Part 1 of this book listed nine "traps," mistakes that business lead-ers and organizations make repeatedly. I pointed out the role of cognitive biases in these mistakes. The bottom line is simple but troubling: the way we actually make decisions, including impor-tant business decisions, has little to do with the ideal, theoretical model of rational decision-making we all learned in school.

In part 2, I will outline an approach to decision-making that takes these biases into account. But first it will be helpful to review and recap the biases that we encountered in part 1 and organize them into a few easy-to-remember categories.

A PRACTICAL MAP OF BIASES

Categorizing biases is an entertaining exercise. At least, that's what we are tempted to conclude from the seemingly endless proliferation of classifications offered by experts. In *Decisive: How to Make Better Choices in Life and Work*, Chip and Dan Heath sort combinations of biases into groups they call the "four villains of decision making." Sydney Finkelstein, Jo Whitehead, and Andrew Campbell also identified four categories of biases (not the same four, of course). In their seminal 1974 article, Kahneman and Tversky cite twelve biases. Bazerman and Moore, in the authoritative textbook on management decision-making, have a different list of twelve. Others go for exhaustivity. The Swiss author Rolf Dobelli lists ninety-nine biases, including a large number of reasoning errors of all stripes. Wikipedia's list of cognitive biases contains approximately two hundred, collected in a hard-to-read but beautiful and much-circulated wheel-shaped visual. And that's just for starters.[*]

Of course, there is no single, "right" classification of biases— any typology is useful only to the extent that it meets its goals. The taxonomy of biases I suggest here is deliberately simplified to serve three purposes. First of all, it aims to be fairly easy to memorize, to help readers recognize biases in practice (something that is impossible with a very long list). To do so, it sorts biases into five families according to their effects rather than their purported psychological causes, which are largely invisible (and irrelevant) to the observer. Second, it is focused on the biases that affect business decisions, especially strategic ones. Many sources of error that are less relevant in an organizational context are intentionally left

---

[*] A distinct set of typologies categorize ways to leverage biases to affect behavior. The best-known are those developed by the British Behavioural Insights Team (or Nudge Unit), summarized by the acronyms MIND-SPACE and EAST.

out. Finally, it is designed to make the interactions between biases visible, an essential point that will be discussed further.

Page 153 shows the five families. The definition of each bias, with references to the chapters and page numbers where each has been discussed, can be found in appendix 1.

At the top of the diagram, we start with *pattern-recognition biases.* Confirmation bias is the main one here, but this group also includes the power of storytelling, experience bias, attribution error, and others.

All these biases work in a similar way: they use patterns we've previously experienced to shape our understanding of a complex reality. The pattern we think we recognize may be a hypothesis we confirm, the arc of an unfolding story, the personality of a key character, or something else. But the effect of recognizing a pattern is the same: it makes reality seem simpler, more coherent, and easier to deal with than it actually is.

Because pattern-recognition biases are the source of our assumptions and hypotheses, they underlie all our reasoning. To take but one example, the dominant bias in Procter & Gamble's disastrous offensive against Clorox was certainly a form of overconfidence. But it is easy to imagine that the P&G managers who proposed this plan had thought of, and perhaps used, analogies from successful past product launch campaigns. Through the lens of pattern recognition, the bleach market would have seemed similar enough to these past cases. This campaign's distinctive feature— the presence of a large, dominant, highly skilled competitor called Clorox—could easily be overlooked. Without these misleading analogies, perhaps P&G could have avoided the error.

The next two bias families—on either side of the diagram in figure 1—act as opposing forces. The first consists of *action-*

FIVE FAMILIES OF BIASES

PATTERN-RECOGNITION BIASES

- Confirmation bias, storytelling
- Experience bias
- Champion bias
- Attribution error
- Hindsight bias
- Halo effect
- Survivorship bias

INERTIA BIASES

- Anchoring
- Resource inertia
- Status quo bias
- Escalation of commitment, sunk-cost fallacy
- Loss aversion
- Irrational risk aversion
- Uncertainty aversion

ACTION-ORIENTED BIASES

- Overplacement
- Planning fallacy, unrealistic optimism
- Overprecision
- Competitor neglect

INTEREST BIASES

- Self-serving bias
- Present bias
- Omission bias

SOCIAL BIASES

- Groupthink
- Polarization
- Information cascades

oriented biases, which include the various forms of overconfidence. In general, action-oriented biases encourage us to do things we shouldn't do and take risks we shouldn't take. The opposite family contains *inertia biases:* these biases, on the contrary, dissuade us from acting when we should and lead us to spurn risks we should take. Anchoring, resource inertia, and status quo bias, among others, are inertia biases.

Despite this opposition, action biases and inertia biases sometimes coexist in a single syndrome. We saw this in chapter 6, with the paradox of "timid choices and bold forecasts." There are other examples. Companies like Blockbuster and Polaroid, which equivocated instead of responding to a deadly threat, were certainly giving in to inertia biases. But they also showed excessive optimism: their leaders were too easily convinced by plans to revitalize their traditional core businesses. And some pattern-recognition biases probably played a role, too. If you put yourself, for instance, in the shoes of John Antioco, the CEO of Blockbuster, it is very likely that, upon meeting Netflix, you called to mind many other small competitors you had easily defeated (or sensibly ignored). In these examples, it seems that combinations of biases are at work— which makes them all the more difficult to overcome.

The last two families, *social biases* and *interest biases,* appear at the bottom of figure 1. They, too, have a role in all large mistakes. When discussing the story of the Frenchmen who fell for the tale of the "oil-sniffing airplanes," for instance, we emphasized the importance of storytelling. But it is clear that the decision makers were powerfully motivated by the hope of discovering a new and highly profitable technology, and that the secrecy of their deliberations increased the risk of groupthink. The false beliefs that leaders adopt are likely to be beliefs they *want* to believe in; and when they act upon them, it's often because a group has collectively adopted them, too.

THREE COMMON MISCONCEPTIONS ABOUT COGNITIVE BIASES

Knowing about biases is essential, and having a shared language to talk about them is very valuable. In *Thinking, Fast and Slow*, Daniel Kahneman even makes this one of his main educational objectives: his goal is "to enrich the vocabulary that people use when they talk about the judgments and choices of others." Yet we must be careful to avoid reaching hasty conclusions. At least three common misconceptions set casual conversations about biases on the wrong track.

First misconception: seeing biases everywhere. Once you know about cognitive biases, it is tempting to see their influence everywhere (perhaps this is an effect of confirmation bias!). Yet not every mistake is caused by a bias. Some bad decisions simply reflect the incompetence or the sheer stupidity of those who make them. Many are the product of haste and carelessness. There are errors of reasoning that owe nothing to pattern recognition and errors in risk calculation that have little to do with overconfidence. Similarly, the choices that dishonest or corrupt individuals make are something quite different from well-meaning decisions influenced by self-serving biases: the existence of unconscious biases does not excuse or explain conscious wrongdoing. In short, the number of biases is large, but the number of ways things can go wrong is infinite.

Second misconception: attributing an undesirable result, in hindsight, to a bias. The clearest example of this blunder is the misidentification, after the fact, of overconfidence as the reason a bad decision was made. As Phil Rosenzweig eloquently points out in *Left Brain, Right Stuff,* those who comment on a failure often blame it on the leaders' overconfidence or hubris. But the same observers are just as quick to praise the visionary leadership of decision makers upon whom fate has smiled. Clearly, their analysis is colored by knowledge of the outcome: judgments about risky decisions are not nearly so sharp at the time these decisions are announced. Whenever we look for the biases that might have contributed to a decision that has turned out poorly, we are at risk of hindsight bias.

How, then, do we know we are not falling into this trap right now? When we discuss the story of Ron Johnson or the case of Snapple, we obviously know how the story ends. Is our reading of these stories the product of hindsight bias? Would we have given the same analysis of Procter & Gamble's reasoning if the launch of Vibrant had been a big success, or would we, on the contrary, be applauding the boldness and skill of its leaders? And when we note the inertia of Polaroid or Blockbuster in the face of disruptive change, would we judge them the same way if these companies were still thriving?

This objection has a simple answer. *These stories are not mere anecdotes; they are archetypes.* The cases that illustrated the nine traps in part 1 are not exceptional (except sometimes by their size): they are representative examples of frequent and easily recognized syndromes. They are exemplars of situations that frequently arise, and the choices leaders make in these situations go wrong in the same predictable ways.

The Snapple case, for instance, is not just a memorable story:

research has consistently shown that acquirers generally overestimate synergies and frequently overpay for acquisitions. The launch of Vibrant isn't just a story about Procter & Gamble: market entry plans that fail to fully anticipate the predictable reaction of competitors are the rule, not the exception. General Motors' infinite patience with its money-losing division Saturn is an outlier by its cost and duration, but hundreds of multinational corporations obstinately refuse to pull the plug on failing ventures.

This distinction between isolated anecdote and representative example is one we must make each time we suspect biases were at work in a past decision. Suppose, for example, that a new product did not meet its objectives and you are analyzing this failure. Was the launch team a victim of overconfidence in setting targets? Is this failure an isolated accident that has nothing to do with any kind of bias? Should we simply conclude that launching new products is a risky activity that inevitably entails a certain proportion of failures?

All these explanations are sensible; and unless an obvious mistake was made, we cannot tell which one is correct. To know whether biases—such as overconfidence—play a role in new product launches, we need a statistical approach, not an isolated story. By analyzing a sample of product launches, we may be able to discover, for instance, whether or not predictions are systematically overoptimistic. But without this kind of data, we should resist the urge to find a general explanation for a particular situation.

Third misconception: looking for "the" bias. Psychologists can identify a specific bias in the lab by controlling for all the other factors that may influence their subjects. In real life, however, it is rare to find a situation in which one bias is the sole cause of an error. However tempting it may be to look for a single "root cause," when we fall into one of the traps we discussed in part 1, it's usually the work of a combination of mutually reinforcing biases.

For instance, in the story of Ron Johnson at J. C. Penney, we pointed out the role of Johnson's past experience, which led him to reproduce many of the choices he had made at Apple. But other biases may have been at work. The board of directors—and, more broadly, all those who saw Ron Johnson's genius as the main reason for the Apple Stores' success—were probably led astray by attribution error. A strong optimism bias was also at work: Johnson (who invested $50 million of his own money in the business, a tangible sign of self-confidence) evidently under-estimated how long it would take to convince a younger and trendier customer base to shop at the new "jcp." By firing skeptics and surrounding himself with former Apple managers, he also created the conditions for powerful groupthink within his team. Finally, it's impossible not to see in this story an example of the escalation of commitment syndrome: despite immediate (and ongoing) disastrous results, neither the management team nor the board of directors reconsidered their radical transformation strategy or the speed of its implementation.

In the Snapple example, and in the broader problem of overpaid acquisitions it illustrates, we also see the combined influence of biases belonging to several of the five families. Pattern-recognition biases were evident in the misleading analogy with Gatorade. Action-oriented biases led to overestimating the synergies. It is plausible that some inertia biases contributed to Quaker's paying a very steep acquisition premium, if, as is often the case, negotiations were "anchored" on the initial asking price. Some members of Quaker's management or board of directors may have kept their doubts about the deal quiet: a form of groupthink. Finally, we should always suspect the presence of self-serving biases when executives expand their empire, or when the fees of the bankers advising them depend on the transaction price. Mergers and acquisitions are a minefield of biases!

To sum up, not all mistakes can be attributed to cognitive biases. When mistakes seem to be the result of biases, we should be careful not to draw conclusions until we have sufficient evidence, which a single case cannot provide. And we should make sure that we identify all the contributing biases, not just the most obvious one.

THE HUNT FOR BIASES

Once we know about cognitive biases and how to avoid identifying them erroneously, what can we do about them? Sure, as mentioned in the introduction to this book, it is tempting, and often quite profitable, to exploit the biases of others: that is the aim of behavioral marketing, behavioral finance, or—with different motives—of "nudges." But improving *our own* decisions by addressing *our own* biases is a very different matter. It is what the remainder of this book will cover.

THE MAP OF COGNITIVE BIASES
IN THIRTY SECONDS

- A practical way to categorize biases is to place them in **five families:**
- **Pattern-recognition biases** (confirmation bias and others) influence our initial hypotheses.
- **Action-oriented biases** (overconfidence and others) make us do things we shouldn't.
- **Inertia biases** (anchoring, status quo, and others) make us fail by inaction.
- **Social biases** allow organizations to let mistakes happen.
- **Interest biases** further color the judgments of individual decision makers.
- Nevertheless, **we should not see biases everywhere:** let's not forget incompetence, carelessness, dishonesty, and so on.
- In particular, it is **risky to "recognize" the effect of a bias in hindsight** once a negative outcome is known.
  - ▶ *The examples in this book are representative of recurring strategic errors, not isolated anecdotes.*
- **Biases reinforce each other:** serious mistakes almost always involve multiple biases.
  - ▶ *In Ron Johnson's failure and in bad acquisitions, we can assume that all five bias families are at work.*
- **Taking advantage** of other people's biases is one thing. Dealing with our own biases is another.

11

LOSE A BATTLE, WIN THE WAR

Can We Overcome Our Own Biases?

Why do you look at the speck in your brother's eye,
but fail to notice the beam in your own eye?

—Luke 6:41

Now that you know the traps decision makers fall into and understand the biases that make them do so, you might think yourself equipped to avoid them. Aren't these failures lessons that we can learn from? Once we know about a mistake, can't we simply make sure we don't repeat it? Problem solved!

This is precisely the promise that some authors make: self-discipline will protect you from your own biases. Some suggest that awareness of traps is sufficient to avoid them—forewarned is forearmed. Others promise to help us identify red flags that signal a risk of bias. Another writer explains his infallible method: "In situations where the possible consequences are large (i.e. important personal or business decisions), I try to be as reasonable and rational as possible when choosing. I take out my list of errors, and check them off one by one, just like a pilot does." Since his particular list contains almost one hundred mistakes to avoid, this practice must delay decision-making quite a bit.

In truth, we cannot just decide to shed our biases like so many extra pounds. Attempts to self-correct biases, in fact, run into three distinct problems.

CAN YOU REALLY BECOME AWARE OF YOUR BIASES?

The first problem, to use the biblical parable, is that we can easily see the speck of other people's biases, but we don't see the beam of our own. We simply aren't aware of them.

This is the key difference between a bias and a simple mistake. We all know what a mistake is; we are usually able to recognize when we've made a mistake and avoid making the same one twice. But we are almost never aware of bias in ourselves: on the contrary, we feel unchallenged, comfortable, confident in our reasoning. For instance, when we give in to confirmation bias, we're not aware that we're favoring data that justifies our hypothesis instead of looking for evidence that would contradict it. Our entire mind is mobilized to find evidence that will, in fact, confirm our preexisting viewpoints. How can we possibly learn to overcome an obstacle if we are never aware that it is in our way?

Overconfidence (an easy bias to measure) provides a striking illustration of this problem. Remember the experiment in which about 90 percent of people interviewed thought they were among the top 50 percent of drivers? If you ever have the chance, try this experiment yourself in front of an audience—any group of more than a dozen adults will do. When the audience members raise their hands, everyone can see that the group is collectively overestimating itself: the percentage of people who think they are above the median is well over 50 percent. Wait a moment to let the embarrassed laughter dissipate, and then ask this simple question: "Who in this room *has changed their mind* about *their own* driving abilities during the last few minutes? Do any of you now think you're a less good driver than you thought when entering this room?" Almost no one will say yes! Everyone can see the collective mistake, but no one draws any individual conclusions. Sure, someone must be overestimating themselves, but it's not me, it's them!

If this kind of statistical feedback is not sufficient to eliminate bias, what about stronger, more personal, loud and clear feedback? One study considered groups of drivers who not only had poor driving records but also had been hospitalized after car accidents caused, in most cases, by their own negligence. The researchers found that members of this group were just as overconfident as the members of a control group of drivers with good driving records. Most of the drivers whose poor driving skills landed them in the hospital, some of whom were still hospitalized at the time they were interviewed, believed they drove better than average, too!

As these examples show, reminders to "pay attention to our biases" cannot be expected to produce real results. Even when we're intellectually aware of the existence of biases in general, we underestimate their effect on us in particular. This is called the *bias blind spot*. As Kahneman observes, "We can be blind to the obvious, and we are also blind to our blindness."

The difficulty of catching biases in the act also explains the limited success of interventions that aim to train people to debias their individual judgment. An old joke says that the rude man who steps on your feet to walk out of the theater in the middle of a bad movie is probably an economist who has learned to recognize the sunk cost bias. But what this economist has more likely learned to recognize is a mistake he's previously made by enduring bad movies until the end, not necessarily the underlying bias. There is no guarantee that the same economist will recognize sunk costs in other situations. It is unlikely, for instance, that he will be faster than average to pull the plug on a failing PhD or to leave an unhappy marriage.

This example reflects the general conclusion that emerges from research on debiasing: given sufficient training, people can recognize and thwart their own biases in a specific domain. But, with few exceptions, this training does not improve their performance on other problems and in other contexts, because, unless prompted to do so, they do not recognize the need to apply their learnings.

There is thus a fundamental difference between "normal" mistakes and cognitive biases. After all, would Daniel Kahneman have won the Nobel Prize in economics if he had simply rediscovered, two thousand years after Seneca, that "to err is human"?

CORRECT A BIAS, BUT WHICH ONE?

In the preceding chapter, we touched briefly on the second reason biases are hard to combat: in real life, unlike in laboratory experiments, there's never just one bias. Mistakes usually occur when several biases are present, reinforcing, or sometimes counteracting, each other. Even if we manage to correct one of these biases, there's no guarantee that our decisions would end up improving.

For instance, suppose that you have learned from experience that you are very susceptible to overconfidence. Could you come up with a simple way to routinely remind yourself to pay special attention to this peril? What a practical way it would be to teach yourself some much-needed humility!

Some, in fact, have tried this before. One of them was Bill Bernbach, the legendary ad man credited with the 1959 "Think Small" campaign for the Volkswagen Beetle. It's said that he always kept a laminated card in his jacket pocket that read: "Maybe he's right." Bernbach didn't know what a bias was, but he was keenly aware that he could, like anyone, be wrong. Since he was regarded as a genius in his field and was therefore in a position to confidently trample over any disagreements, he became aware of the dangers of overconfidence.

But could he still escape all cognitive biases? By paying more attention to his colleagues' opinions, was he at risk of tolerating a form of groupthink? When he chose to take out his "Maybe he's right" card in response to one comment but not another, wasn't he giving in to champion bias, listening to some of his colleagues more than others? Interestingly, the wording of his reminder suggests that his humility didn't go so far as to imagine he could be usefully contradicted by a woman...

Hopefully, Bernbach sometimes managed to catch himself redhanded in the act of overconfidence. But he could not identify, let alone control, all the other biases that interfered with his judgment. A more accurate self-admonition might have been, "Maybe I'm wrong." Unfortunately, such a reminder isn't very helpful. "Maybe I'm wrong, but how?"

WHAT WOULD BE THE COST OF CORRECTING YOUR BIASES?

The third problem is perhaps even more important: even if we could repress our own biases, even if we could become entirely rational, cold, calculating decision makers, it would be a bad idea! As we saw when discussing intuition in chapter 3, our biases are a by-product of *heuristics*, intuitive shortcuts we use as a powerful, fast, and effective method to make most of our daily decisions. And for the vast majority of our decisions, our heuristics give excellent results.

Consider pattern-recognition biases. When we recognize patterns based on our experience, we use a decision-making heuristic. Evidently it is not *always* wrong to use our past experience, rely on analogies, and cultivate our instincts! Similarly, action-oriented biases are the flip side of a productive heuristic: being optimistic is generally advantageous. Social biases arise as a result of a heuristic that suggests that the judgment of others is generally sound—because in many situations it is. The same is true when we defend our interests (at the risk of self-serving bias) or when we prioritize stability over sudden changes of direction (at the risk of inertia biases).

With all that we hear about the damage biases do, it's easy to forget that we have them for a reason: our heuristics can lead us astray, but they also render us indispensable services. Kahneman and Tversky made it clear in the very first paragraph of their seminal 1974 article introducing "Heuristics and Biases": "*In general,* these heuristics are quite useful, but *sometimes* they lead to severe and systematic errors." (Italics mine.) Depriving oneself of tools that are *in general* essential in order to avoid *sometimes* making mistakes would be a very bad deal.

INDIVIDUAL BIASES, ORGANIZATIONAL DECISIONS

To summarize, becoming aware of our biases is extremely difficult; knowing in advance which biases to neutralize is impossible; and even if it were possible to become a bias-free decision maker, this would do us more harm than good. The bottom line: we can't will our own biases away. Self-help is not the sort of help you need against biases.

This combination of challenges has led many experts to be quite pessimistic about the possibility of debiasing. Asked about the possibility of individuals debiasing themselves, Daniel Kahneman once replied: "I'm really not optimistic. Most decision makers will trust their own intuitions because they think they see the situation clearly." Dan Ariely, who has written bestselling books on irrational decision-making, resists the temptation to promise his readers "recipes" for avoiding biases and acknowledges: "Despite the fact that I understand and can analyze some of my decision biases, I still experience them. They never completely cease to influence me (this is something to keep in mind as you attempt to become a better decision maker)." Moreover, if knowledge of our biases was sufficient to improve decision-making, we should have seen a noticeable improvement in the quality of all kinds of decisions by now, given that nearly half a century has passed since Kahneman and Tversky's first publications. Such improvement is, to say the least, not obvious.

But wait…if there is no way for us to overcome our biases, and if biases cause mistakes, why aren't these mistakes even more frequent? Logically, if biases sometimes, but not always, cause mistakes, there must be *other* factors at work. What are these factors?

167

As we shall see, the answers to these questions will put us on the path to reliably making better decisions. This is because it introduces an essential distinction we have not emphasized so far, a distinction between two levels of analysis: individual and organizational.

The *biases* we have discussed here, for the most part, affect the *individual.* Overconfidence, loss aversion, the halo effect, self-serving bias, and others all affect the judgment and decisions of individuals. Even groupthink only concerns small groups, like management teams. Yet the *strategic errors* we have analyzed are not made by individuals alone. When we note the high frequency of overpaid acquisitions, of project overruns, or of escalating investments into failing subsidiaries, we're observing the error patterns of *organizations.*

Confusing these two levels of analysis is frequent in casual conversation: observers routinely attribute the errors of organizations to the individuals who lead them. It is nonetheless a dangerous oversimplification. The traits, strengths, and weaknesses of individuals do not simply scale up to determine the behaviors of organizations. We can all see, for instance, that an organization's ability to make enlightened choices cannot be predicted from the average IQ of its leaders; or that a company may hire many enterprising and creative individuals and nevertheless fail to bring successful innovations to market.

This should make us think twice before we attribute the mistakes of companies or governments to the biases of individuals. We know that individuals commit systematic errors of judgment, but in order to explain the mistakes of organizations, we need to look at the *mechanisms* through which individual choices are translated into an organization's decisions.

Conversely, in order to prevent mistakes at the organizational level, we will have to seek organization-level decision-making mechanisms that counteract individuals' biases instead of tolerating or amplifying them. Most research on debiasing has found, as we've discussed, that debiasing the decision maker is very difficult. But methods that change the *environment* of the decision maker, instead of her way of reasoning, often give good results.

The bottom line: obsessing over our own biases and how to reduce them is a waste of time. *The way to improve decisions in an organization is to improve the decision-making practices of the organization.*

This apparent tautology has a crucial consequence: if a decision must be the organization's decision, not just its leader's, then this leader cannot decide alone. The art of decision-making must have a collective dimension. A smart leader facing a strategic choice will rely on her team, ask experts, consult the board of directors, and speak to advisors. She knows that she cannot correct her own biases, but she trusts others to see them quite clearly and help her avoid mistakes. Even if she is the one making the final call, she will never be alone in the decision-making process. By conceding defeat in the individual battle against her own biases, she improves her chances of winning the collective war against bad decisions.

But input from multiple individuals, though necessary, is not sufficient. If groups always made good decisions, none of the mistakes described earlier in this book would have happened. In terms of decision-making, teams are capable of both the best and the worst.

KENNEDY VS. KENNEDY

A historical example provides a striking illustration of the two extremes of collective decision-making. Chapter 8 described how President Kennedy's team made a disastrous decision regarding the Bay of Pigs invasion. Eighteen months later, Kennedy would nevertheless succeed in handling the Cuban missile crisis with such clearheadedness that it remains a case study in negotiation and international relations courses today. The difference between these two sets of decisions does not lie in the makeup of the team—it was essentially the same. It lies in the method that Kennedy implemented in the second case.

Following the futile Bay of Pigs offensive, Cuba had strengthened its ties with the Soviet Union. The Americans suspected that the Soviets had set up nuclear ballistic missiles in Cuba, and on October 14, 1962, they confirmed that this was true. The missiles put all cities on the Eastern Seaboard within easy reach of a nuclear strike. This represented an unacceptable threat for the United States.

JFK quickly set up a fourteen-person committee he called ExComm to manage the situation. This committee would look for ways to resolve the crisis. ExComm also assisted Kennedy in managing his communications with the American people, their allies, and his Soviet counterpart, Nikita Khrushchev.

At the beginning of the Bay of Pigs crisis, JFK faced a binary choice proposed by the military: to do nothing or to invade Cuba (the plan many of his advisors favored). In the Cuban missile crisis, Kennedy took a different approach suggested by his brother Robert: as his character memorably puts it in the movie based on his memoir, *Thirteen Days*, "We've got a bunch of smart guys.

We lock 'em in a room and kick 'em in the ass until they come up with some solutions." ExComm identified several intermediate options between inaction and invasion, including the idea of a naval blockade, which would prove decisive.

The members of ExComm then worked as a team to evaluate these different options. According to historians of the crisis, in the first days following the discovery of the missiles, ExComm was leaning toward "hard" options. It then gradually moved away from these ideas and adopted the idea of the blockade, first introduced by Defense Secretary Robert McNamara. Despite the overt opposition of some members, the president gradually became convinced of the merits of this option.

Discussions were heated and sometimes took an unexpected turn. When the option of an air strike seemed to predominate, Undersecretary of State George Ball undermined it by making a counterintuitive analogy: he compared the planned strike on Cuba to the surprise attack on Pearl Harbor that the United States had suffered twenty years earlier. By doing this, he forced his colleagues to consider its consequences from the point of view of the adversary and of international public opinion.

Most of the members of ExComm, starting with the very influential Robert Kennedy, changed their views at one point or another during the crisis, not only because new facts appeared (for instance, through secret contacts with Soviet diplomats), but because their judgment of the various options' chances of success and of consequences evolved. Two of JFK's advisors were explicitly tasked with acting as "intellectual watchdogs" (another name for the well-known devil's advocate) to uncover the weaknesses of the plans under consideration. The ongoing and often passionate debates about each plan were key to finding a solution to the crisis.

The management of the Cuban missile crisis is considered a classic example of successful teamwork. This team behaved in a radically different way than the team that decided on the Bay of Pigs invasion—even though it was made up of many of the same people. It avoided making a rushed decision. It forced itself to reject a binary choice and to generate and consider several alternatives. It encouraged the expression of diverse and contradictory viewpoints on these options and their possible combinations. It accepted that its members could change their minds. It searched for information to evaluate the reactions each option would elicit and the consequences it would produce.

In a word, ExComm adopted a working *process* that was conducive to effective decision-making. JFK understood that it was not enough to simply surround himself with a team of brilliant individuals. This team had to follow the right method, to use the right process.

Luckily, the decisions corporate executives make do not involve nuclear strikes. But when the time comes to sit around a table and make a strategic decision, they would benefit from asking the same questions Kennedy answered in 1962: *What team* should they put in place to inform the decision? *What process* should they establish in order to get the best out of this team? By focusing first on team and process, they will ensure a better decision.

As we will see in the next chapter, this is exactly what we do when the stakes are high and failure is not an option.

THE IMPOSSIBILITY OF OVERCOMING YOUR OWN BIASES IN THIRTY SECONDS

- Trying to **debias yourself** generally doesn't work, for several reasons:
- Biases are **not ordinary mistakes: being aware that they exist is not enough** to correct them.
  - ▶ *No one becomes less confident after participating in a test that shows collective overconfidence.*
- Bias blind spot: *"We can be blind to the obvious, and we are also blind to our blindness." (Kahneman)*
- In any situation, there are multiple potential biases: It's not easy to decide **which bias to combat.**
- **Heuristics,** of which biases are the flip side, are essential to us.
- Unlike individuals, **organizations can improve their decisions by changing their decision-making practices.**
  - ▶ *"Changing the environment"* instead of *"changing the decision maker."*
- **Two conditions** exist to do this: **collaboration,** so some individuals can correct the biases of others; and **process,** so the group does not devolve into groupthink.
  - ▶ *The decision-making process was the difference between the successful management of the Cuban missile crisis and the disastrous decision in favor of the Bay of Pigs invasion.*

WHEN FAILURE IS NOT AN OPTION

Collaboration Plus Process

Failure is not an option.
—Attributed to Gene Kranz, flight director, in
the movie *Apollo 13*

One rainy afternoon you are wandering through the slick streets of a small city you have never visited before. Your business meeting was just canceled at the last minute. Bad luck: you have to bide your time in this town until your flight. The rain is coming down harder now. Hugging your briefcase, you seek shelter under an archway and notice that groups of people are coming in. As it happens, this is the courthouse, and a trial is about to start. With time on your hands, you may as well sit in on the proceedings. At least this way you will have a story to tell your colleagues when you return.

You take a seat in the courtroom as the trial begins. The case concerns an alleged burglar who shot the homeowner when confronted. The victim died soon after the paramedics arrived. A gloomy story in a gloomy town…but at least you've found an interesting way to pass your time, sheltered from the rain that continues to beat against the windows of the courthouse.

That's when things take a surprising turn. Instead of the usual proceedings of a trial, seen in countless TV crime shows, the prosecutor walks over to a projector, opens his laptop, and begins presenting a deck of slides. Deftly using PowerPoint, he starts with the timeline of events on the night of the crime, challenging the defendant's alibi: he had ample opportunity to reach the crime scene between the time when he was last seen by a witness and the time when the murder was committed. The prosecutor calmly proceeds with his demonstration, holding the room's attention as he clicks through exhibit upon exhibit: photos of the crime scene, the weapon, the forensic findings, the fingerprints left by the defendant, even a Google Maps plot of the murderer's escape route. As he reaches the end of his argument, the prosecutor displays a one-page summary with clear, concise bullet points recapitulating his previous slides. He then gives his closing statement: the defendant should be found guilty and sentenced to life in prison with a minimum of twenty years.

Sitting in the back of the courtroom, you have completely forgotten your setbacks this morning and are absorbed in this solemn moment. You are more than a little impressed by the prosecutor's presentation style: the justice system is much more professional than you thought! Naturally, you now expect the defense attorney to use the same techniques to try to show to the jury that the defendant is not guilty, or at least to establish reasonable doubt.

But nothing of the sort happens! First, you just noticed that no jury is present in the room. This case is tried before a judge. This is strange enough already.... Then, instead of giving the floor to the defense, the judge starts a conversation with the prosecutor, challenging some of the points he has made: could he go back over the third slide and explain how one piece of evidence fits into his story? The prosecutor goes back and explains. Could the prosecutor confirm that the crime weapon was properly identified by ballistics experts? Yes, it was, the prosecutor replies confidently. After a few more questions and answers, the judge thanks the prosecutor for his clarifications. Finally, without further ado, he declares the defendant guilty and puts him behind bars for the next two decades.

THE COURTROOM AND THE BOARDROOM

You wake up from this nightmare with a start, seated in a plane soaring above the rain clouds, already far from this strange little town. Stretching, you think how odd this dream was. Clearly, no trial would ever look remotely like this! Even some of the world's worst dictators, when they want to send their political opponents to a labor camp, maintain a facade of proper procedure in order to create the illusion of due process. The appearance of a fair trial has such a grip on our collective imagination that even terrorist groups often stage morbid mock trials before executing their hostages.

So why aren't we shocked by the fact that the scene in this imaginary, nightmarish courtroom looks very much like what we see in boardrooms when reviewing an investment proposal, a restructuring plan, or a planned product launch?

A CEO, surrounded by a management team, is hearing the "case." She must make the final decision. A manager who has studied the project, is in favor of it, and makes no mystery about that defends the proposal. As this "prosecutor" makes his case, the rest of the audience may ask questions or voice opinions, but they are not required to. If they do speak up, their interventions do not have to follow any specific rules of procedure. After the presentation, the CEO plays two roles at once: she must act as the attorney for the opposite side, who challenges the presenter's facts and recommendations, and also as the judge who, once convinced, makes the final decision.

Of course, you might object that managerial decisions are very different from legal rulings. They must be fast, unlike the notoriously slow justice system. The stakes are not necessarily as high. Plus, executives are assumed to be competent and correctly incentivized, and we trust them to make decisions.

But these differences hardly justify such an astonishing discrepancy in method. Just like the people in whose name justice is rendered have a right to demand the best possible judicial decisions, the stakeholders of a corporation expect quality business decisions. Speed is irrelevant: there can be varying degrees of urgency in companies, as in courtrooms; and when justice is slow, it's not because of the time it takes to hear both sides of an argument. The importance of the stakes is not a meaningful difference, either: we do not drop all expectations of due process when the infraction is a minor one; and some corporate decisions are quite consequential. Finally, our confidence in the competence of the decision makers is just as irrelevant: requiring judges to observe procedural rules does not imply that we doubt their wisdom or their impartiality.

To understand the roots of the difference in approach between corporate choices and judicial decisions, we must understand how they came about. Legend has it that Louis IX, king of France (later canonized as Saint Louis), rendered justice to his subjects while sitting under an oak tree. His decision-making system looked quite a bit like our imaginary trial: although thirteenth-century petitioners did not resort to PowerPoint, they had a chance to make their case, and the wise, omniscient king, after he questioned them, issued his ruling. If modern justice systems no longer look like this, it is because the obvious limitations of this medieval decision-making model became unacceptable to the people. Any observer could see that judges, even if they were kings or lords, were subject to their emotions and biases, could be personally connected to one of the parties, could be influenced by a deceptive presentation of the facts, and so on. Regardless of personal qualities, a judge is a human being, and many factors can lead him to make an unjust decision. This risk can never be completely eliminated, but democratic judicial systems evolved to reduce it. The procedural requirements generally known as "due process of law" act as safeguards against arbitrariness and human error.

Corporate decision-making has not evolved in the same way, except for certain specific processes (for instance, the development of rules that prevent conflicts of interest). Unlike citizens who scrutinize the justice system, shareholders and directors of companies have apparently not perceived the importance of accurate decision-making. That is, in essence, why CEOs still make decisions in much the same way Saint Louis did under his oak tree.

This observation isn't meant to question the skill, and certainly not the integrity, of these executives. (No one questioned the good judgment of Saint Louis, either!) And of course some individuals are better than others at keeping their biases at bay. Some leaders may be clear-sighted enough to resist many pattern-recognition biases. Others will be humble and cautious enough not to fall prey to action biases. Some will have the courage to overcome inertia bias within their organizations; others will be independent-minded enough to liberate themselves from groupthink. One hopes that some will even have enough integrity to be impervious to self-serving bias.

But this is quite a list of virtues to expect from business leaders. Sure, biases do not lead *all* decision makers astray *all* the time. Conversely, we cannot expect that *all* our leaders embody *all* these virtues and overcome *all* their biases in *all* their decisions. In boardrooms just as in courtrooms, it's not enough for a decision maker to be virtuous. The individual must also be able to collaborate with others; decisions can't be made alone. And wisdom must arise from process, not from individual virtues. *Collaboration* and *process* are the principles on which sound decisions are based.

WHEN FAILURE IS NOT AN OPTION

It is striking to note that collaboration and process can be found in many situations in which the cost of error is unacceptable. When, like the Apollo 13 astronauts, we know that "failure is not an option," we count, of course, on talented individuals—but we also rely on teamwork and on carefully designed methods.

French astronaut Jean-François Clervoy, a veteran of three missions on the *Atlantis* and *Discovery* space shuttles, knows what "failure is not an option" means. Space travel is a high-risk activity: "Based on historical data," he says, "an astronaut knows that the chances he won't come back are somewhere between one in two hundred and one in one hundred." Fourteen astronauts on American vessels and four Russian cosmonauts have lost their lives since space exploration began.

However, none of these accidents happened while astronauts or cosmonauts orbited Earth. Only one accident, which cost three Russian cosmonauts their lives in 1971, occurred outside the atmosphere, during the pre-reentry phase. All the others took place during takeoff or reentry into the atmosphere, for reasons that had nothing to do with the astronauts' behavior.

This is not to say that all other missions were uneventful. Astronauts have managed to face and survive countless serious crises, including the Apollo 13 incident. They have been in spaceships struck by lightning. They have faced module separation failures. They have dealt with toxic gas leaks, fires on board, collisions in space, and engine malfunctions. How did these serious accidents in an incredibly hostile environment not cause any loss of life?

First of all, because the equipment is engineered to minimize risks. As Jean-François Clervoy observes, "From the time the equipment is designed, all possible failures that are either too likely or too consequential are identified and addressed." Second, because the astronauts' training prepares them to make the right decisions in the most challenging and unpredictable situations: "Seventy percent of our training time is spent in high-fidelity flight simulators, practicing how to handle all possible situations, with instructors who imagine increasingly complex combinations of equipment failures in order to trick us."

But, above all, space explorers depend on a rigorously standardized process. As Clervoy explains, "For each type of emergency situation—fire, air leak, exposure to toxic products—and for less serious incidents, there is a checklist that we follow meticulously. In the space shuttle, this documentation, which was available in paper form, was a massive set of books. There's no room for improvisation."

Obviously, astronauts are an elite group, selected from thousands of candidates. Through extensive training in extreme conditions, they acquire "perfect knowledge of the vessel, leaving no room for the unknown," Clervoy says. Yet when an incident occurs, they will first and foremost rely on a predetermined process. What a lesson in humility for those of us who believe we can trust our instincts.

That's the process. What about collaboration? As Jean-François Clervoy explains, even if all astronauts are thoroughly trained, each one must share his or her doubts and be able to speak with complete trust. Each astronaut must admit any mistakes or hesitations. The "cowboy culture" seen in *The Right Stuff*, where errors were shameful and had to be hidden away, is long gone. Instead, astronauts are encouraged to discuss any doubts and report any mishap. They are thanked for doing so and debriefed so that lessons can be drawn for training the next crew or refining the checklists. If astronauts make sound, lifesaving decisions, they owe it to process, not improvisation, and to collaboration, not individual genius.

Airline pilots have had their share of "avoidable" disasters, too. One of these changed the history of civil aviation. In 1978, the crew of United Airlines flight 173 discovered a malfunction with its landing gear while preparing to land in Portland, Oregon. The captain began to circle above the airport and search for the cause of the problem in order to solve it. Thirty minutes later, the plane crashed just a few miles from the airport, killing eight passengers and two crew members.

Incredibly, the plane had just run out of fuel. The captain was so completely and single-mindedly focused on the landing gear problem that he failed to check the fuel gauge. Cockpit voice recordings showed that he ignored repeated warnings from his copilot and flight engineer about the fuel level. It also revealed that the crew members had not expressed these warnings to their superior in the clear, assertive, and urgent manner the situation demanded. This is the defining characteristic of this type of human error: it happens when the most senior person, not a subordinate, is at the controls. Sure of himself, surrounded by a crew that is too deferential and fails to challenge him, the captain confidently pilots his plane straight into disaster.

The crash of United flight 173 did at least have the benefit of raising awareness of this problem. It led to the development of *cockpit resource management,* or *crew resource management* (CRM), in the late 1970s. Developed by the National Transportation Safety Board and NASA, this set of techniques is designed to improve communication among crew members and to give them the tools to handle unexpected problems together. How does CRM reduce the incidence of human error? Quite simply, by relying on collaboration and process. Subsequently, CRM techniques have been adapted and adopted by professions as varied as firefighters, air controllers, and some medical teams.

Yet CRM is only one of the processes that civil aviation depends upon. The most basic component is the checklist. To realize how completely we have internalized the value of checklists in this setting, imagine yourself comfortably seated in a plane about to take off and hearing the following announcement from the cockpit: "Ladies and gentlemen, this is your captain speaking. Welcome on board. We are running late and I really want to get you to your destination on time. So I've decided not to waste time going over the pre-takeoff checklist. Don't worry, I know this plane like the back of my hand. Fasten your seat belts!" Chances are you would not be reassured.

This thought experiment illustrates an important point: when we *benefit* from the quality of decisions, we all see the value of collaboration and process, and of the tools that embody these principles. It is only when we picture ourselves as the *decision maker* that we fail to see this value and don't like a systematic discipline forced upon us.

Atul Gawande makes this point forcefully in his remarkable book *The Checklist Manifesto*. Gawande headed the development of a universal surgical safety checklist for the World Health Organization. Checklists serve the same purpose in the high-risk environment of an operating room as they do in an aircraft: they impose process and force a degree of collaboration. The surgical safety checklist asks medical teams, for instance, to verify the patient's identity, to confirm that they are performing the right procedure, and to make sure that all members of the medical team have introduced themselves by name and role. These simple checks have a significant effect: they reduce complications by one-third and postoperative mortality by half. As Gawande points out, if a medication could guarantee such results, it would instantly become a blockbuster drug.

Nevertheless, introducing the checklist is not easy. Even after testing it and verifying its positive effects, about 20 percent of surgeons refuse to adopt it, claiming that it's not worth the time it takes. As Gawande explains, experienced surgeons can some-times see themselves as above the need to slavishly follow a list of standardized steps. So Gawande asked the same surgeons a different question: *if you were the patient* and you were about to have an operation, would you like the checklist used? The answer: 93 percent of surgeons would insist upon it. Clearly, when you are the patient, failure is not an option.

"TOTAL QUALITY" IN DECISION-MAKING

Justice, space travel, civil aviation, surgery: in all of these arenas, collaboration and process demonstrably improve decisions. But what about in "ordinary" companies and in universities and government offices?

Fortunately, they too use elements of "collaboration plus process." The most widespread example is the total quality approach in manufacturing, which aims to systematically reduce waste while improving the quality of finished products. It includes methods such as Toyota's "Five Whys": by asking "why" five times instead of just once, you aim to go beyond superficial explanations and get at the root causes of a problem. Collaboration is also a core element of most quality management approaches, which rely on the active involvement of workers and managers to discover problems and find solutions.

Consider other examples of this. For instance, there is nothing revolutionary about the idea of building a working team that collaborates to solve a problem, or about giving that team a formalized process to work with. But, curiously, the propensity of organizations to use collaboration and process is inversely proportional to the importance of the decision at hand. Most organizations have much more formalized methods for making daily decisions than for making strategic ones. Almost all companies have a procedure for buying office supplies, but very few have a formalized process for buying a company and merging with it!

In other words, most companies have rigorous processes to ensure a high degree of quality in their manufactured products, but few apply the same rigorous standards to their decision-making. Any organization, regardless of whatever else it makes, is a factory that makes decisions, but this virtual factory is not held to the same quality standards as the real one.

In theory, corporate governance has a role in ensuring decision quality. When a board of directors or supervisory board is required to approve certain types of decisions (for example, investments above a certain amount), this is a form of process; and since the board is a collegial body, there is, in theory, some collaboration. Yet even if boards operate in an effective and collaborative way (and that is a big "if"), good governance is not enough. To return to the factory analogy, governance is quality control: it checks that the "product," the decision submitted to the board of directors, meets certain standards. But quality control doesn't make good products. A good manufacturing process does. Similarly, effective governance can encourage leaders to establish a good "manufacturing process" for decisions, but on its own it is not sufficient to improve the quality of decision-making.

Indeed, in situations in which failure is not an option, the presence of a supervisory authority is not the main reason for the presence of high-quality decision-making systems. Judges' respect for the due process of law is not based on the fear that they will be voted out if they fail to observe it. And the reason NASA astronauts use their checklist has nothing to do with the fact that mission control is watching from Houston. In both cases, the decision makers are trying to make the best decisions possible, and they are sincerely convinced that collaboration and process are the best way.

This leads to an important question. When it comes to strategic decisions, are we as convinced of the value of "collaboration plus process"? How do we know that they produce better results than any other possible approach? That is the question we explore in the next chapter.

COLLABORATION PLUS PROCESS
IN THIRTY SECONDS

- We consider **due process** essential because we know that a judge's individual merit is not sufficient for avoiding bad decisions. However, **organizations generally do not hold themselves to the same standards:** Do they care less about the accuracy of their choices than citizens care about justice?

- In general, organizations enforce "collaboration plus process" whenever **failure is not an option...**

  ▶ *Astronauts are trained to apply the rules, not follow their instinct.*

  ▶ *Airline pilots are encouraged to rely on the crew and on procedures.*

  ▶ *Surgeons can reduce the incidence of complications by using checklists.*

- ...or for **lower-level decision-making...**

  ▶ *Formalized procedures for buying office supplies, not for buying companies*

- ...but usually **not for strategic decisions.**

  ▶ *Good governance is not enough.*

  ▶ *Why don't we demand "total quality" in the "decision factory"?*

A GOOD DECISION IS A DECISION MADE THE RIGHT WAY

Is Paul the Psychic Octopus a Good Decision Maker?

'Tis not in mortals to command success,
But we'll do more, Sempronius; we'll deserve it.

—Joseph Addison, *Cato*

During the 2010 FIFA World Cup in South Africa, soccer fans and sportswriters paid a lot of attention to a specimen of *Octopus vulgaris* living a tranquil life in Oberhausen, Germany. This octopus, which went by the name of Paul, seemed to demonstrate an extraordinary gift for prophecy: he predicted the winner in each game Germany played.

To facilitate this ritual, before each game, Paul's owner placed identical amounts of food on either side of the aquarium in boxes decorated with the respective flags of the competing countries. Paul the Psychic Octopus "chose" where to feed. In this manner, Paul repeatedly selected the future winner: he correctly signaled that Germany would beat Australia, Ghana, England, and Argentina. But don't mistake Paul for an undiscerning supporter of the

Mannschaft, prone to patriotic wishful thinking: he did not hesitate to announce that his team would lose to Serbia at the group stage, then to Spain in the semifinal. Paul was right again in predicting that the Germans would beat Uruguay in the third-place playoffs. As a bonus, Paul foretold that Spain would beat the Netherlands in the final, sealing his worldwide reputation as an infallible prognosticator. All told, he correctly predicted the results of eight out of eight games.

Obviously, most experts and commentators did not predict as well as Paul the Octopus. This raises the question of whether, if you are a bookie or the head of an online betting company, you should invest in raising a stable of clairvoyant octopi. At least one man thought so: Oleg Zhuravsky, a Russian online betting entrepreneur, offered to buy Paul for the exorbitant sum of 100,000 euros. When Paul's owner refused, the businessman tripled his offer but was rejected again.

LUCK AND SKILL

Zhuravsky's objective must have been a PR stunt: no one in their right mind could possibly believe that Paul the Octopus was a skilled forecaster. To put Paul's feat in perspective, consider the possibility that it is merely a matter of chance. The probability that a random process will choose the winner eight times in a row, like the probability of tossing heads or tails eight times in a row, is 0.4 percent: unlikely, but certainly not impossible.[*] Given the

---

[*] Ties are excluded from this calculation, which is a slight simplification concerning the three group stage games.

global popularity of the World Cup, we can assume that thousands of animals were "trained" to predict game results. A quick online search shows pictures of cows, hamsters, turtles, even elephants attempting the same feat. If we haven't heard of them, this is a simple case of survivorship bias. If there was a chicken in China or a goose in Slovenia who selected the *losing* team eight times in a row, we never heard about it—even though that result would be statistically just as improbable as Paul's. In any case, what made Paul such a brilliant "decision maker" could be one thing only: chance.

Outside of casinos, chance is usually not the only factor that determines the results of human decisions. Skill does matter. But how much, exactly? The most extensively studied example is surely the performance of investment managers, which is measured, analyzed, and compared year after year. Despite the required warning that "past performance is not indicative of future results," investors scrutinize past results carefully before choosing which funds to invest in. Whatever we may or may not believe about efficient markets, when a fund manager beats the fund's benchmark indices several years in a row, it's hard to resist the conclusion that this person has superior skill. And if this success persists over a very long period of time, it seems clear that we're dealing with an exceptional manager.

This was just the reputation that Bill Miller, the manager of Legg Mason's flagship fund, had acquired in the early 2000s. Miller managed to beat the S&P 500 index not for one, three, or five years but for fifteen years running. So impressive was this streak that Miller was named "The Greatest Money Manager of the 1990s" by *Money* magazine and "Fund Manager of the Decade" repeatedly by Morningstar Inc. An informational letter published by a rival bank observed with respect that "for forty years, no other fund had beaten the market for twelve years in a row" (and certainly not, therefore, for fifteen).

The enthusiasm is understandable: the probability that such a streak could be the product of chance alone seems astronomically small. At least at first sight. If we look more closely, however, the same reasoning applies to Miller's performance as to that of Paul the Octopus. The probability that *one particular manager*—Miller—would regularly beat the market *during those specific years*—from 1991 to 2005—is indeed infinitesimal. But that's not the right question! There are thousands of managers, and dozens of fifteen-year periods, during which this result could have been observed. Assuming that markets are completely efficient and that the work of managers is just a big game of chance, what is the probability that we would observe this result at least *one* time, for *one* manager, over *one* fifteen-year period? Approximately 75 percent, as calculated by physicist Leonard Mlodinow in his book *The Drunkard's Walk: How Randomness Rules Our Lives*. This puts the exceptional nature of the event, and Miller's achievement, into perspective.

"Sure," you might reply, "but still—Bill Miller did it, and no one else! Isn't it a bit petty to deny Miller the glory he deserves?" If that's what you think, there's one more element to consider. During the fifteen years that Miller's "winning streak" lasted, there were *over thirty periods of twelve consecutive months* when he *underperformed* the market. In other words, if his performance had been measured over twelve-month periods running from February through January, or from September through August, instead of calendar years, his exceptional performance would disappear. Miller himself good-naturedly admitted this: "That's an accident of the calendar.... We've been lucky. Well, maybe it's not

100 percent luck. Maybe 95 percent luck." For that, at least, he deserves a lot of credit: it's a rare survivor who doesn't forget what he owes to survivorship bias.

Paul the Psychic Octopus and Bill Miller have an incredibly important lesson to teach us. When we evaluate a decision maker, especially a senior executive, we want to judge her on her results. It is natural to assume that a good decision maker is one who makes good decisions, and that good decisions are those that produce good results. Yet this is a dangerous assumption: when we evaluate decisions by their outcomes, we often underestimate the role of chance.

But that's not all. In addition to the inevitable intervention of chance, many decisions entail some level of risk. When we evaluate decisions in hindsight, we should not forget to take that level of risk into account. Recall the example of the risky investment from chapter 6: a high-risk, high-return bet can be a perfectly rational choice and nevertheless lead to a loss. Conversely, imagine an executive who gambles the company's assets at a roulette table and happens to win; or, for a more realistic example, a trader in a bank who engages in unauthorized trades well beyond his limits and ends up producing profits. Neither should be congratulated for making a good decision, as the level of risk they had their company assume was unjustifiably large.

And there is one more complication. The results we observe do not just depend on the initial decision. A sound decision can be poorly implemented and a mediocre one rescued by flawless execution. It is often said that in business the quality of implementation matters more than the decisions themselves; and although this is an overstatement (just think of some of the strategic decisions described in part 1), it has a core of truth.

In sum, when we consider the outcome of a decision, what we see is not a pure result of the quality of the initial decision. It is also the result of good or bad luck, an appropriate or inappropriate level of risk-taking, and good or bad execution. Except for extreme cases of success or failure (like some of those related in this book), it is therefore risky to attribute good or bad results solely to a good or bad initial decision. Jacob Bernoulli, one of the founders of probability theory, made the point succinctly in 1681: "One must not decide about the value of human actions from their outcomes."

The problem, of course, is that we *do* decide about the value of human actions from their outcomes...and we will never stop! It's even one of the most solidly established managerial axioms: "It's the results that count!" Or, even more clearly: "Better lucky than smart!" As we've seen, hindsight bias leads us to hold a decision maker responsible for a failure, even when it was impossible to predict. Conversely, attribution error makes us give the decision maker credit for success, even if luck played a big role. In many circumstances, there's a lot to be said for the simplicity of focusing on results, and for the accountability it creates. But the price we pay for this simplicity is steep. When we judge decisions (and those who make them) by their results alone, we are making the same mistake as the Russian business-man who offered 300,000 euros to "hire" Paul the Octopus as a forecaster.

This observation raises many practical questions. How are we supposed to evaluate decisions if not on the basis of their results? And specifically, how can we know if relying on collaboration and process will truly improve our performance?

After all, there are plenty of counterexamples. There are

tyrannical leaders who don't give a fig about what their collaborators think. There are dyed-in-the-wool intuitive thinkers who break out in hives at the very word *process*. And quite often they succeed! The image we have of Steve Jobs—rightly or wrongly—is that of a charismatic leader who cared little about collaboration and not at all about process, and whose success was nevertheless unquestionable. Or consider how Masayoshi Son, the founder of SoftBank, describes his decision to invest $20 million in Alibaba in 1999: "He [Jack Ma, Alibaba's founder] had no business plan...but his eyes were very strong. Strong eyes, strong shining eyes. I could tell." This, to say the least, is not anyone's idea of a collaborative decision, much less one that follows a process. Yet it turned out to be perhaps the most successful investment decision anyone ever made: twenty years later, SoftBank's share in Alibaba was worth roughly $130 *billion*.

The flip side, of course, is that the same individuals have made mistakes, too. Steve Jobs's spectacular failures are part and parcel of his legend. And Masayoshi Son apparently relied on the same gut-feeling approach to make much more questionable decisions than the Alibaba one. These include a much-derided $300 million bet on Wag, the "Uber for dog-walking." More consequentially, Son made a $10 billion investment in the parent company of WeWork, whose cofounder, Adam Neumann, certainly had strong shining eyes, too (Son compared him to Jack Ma). Neumann, however, had to resign when his eccentric behavior and controversial accounting practices led the company to cancel its initial public offering; and SoftBank had to invest an additional $8 billion to bail out WeWork and stave off immediate bankruptcy.

Such striking (and contradictory) stories provide great material for after-dinner conversations between businesspeople: "Sure, relying on gut feeling does not work every time! But sometimes it does..." The heart of the matter, of course, is that in an uncertain world, no approach can possibly guarantee success. The question we should try to address is a more nuanced one: how much of a difference, if any, does one decision-making approach make, relative to another approach? Specifically, what is the effect of "collaboration plus process" on the quality of decisions?

ONE THOUSAND AND ONE INVESTMENT DECISIONS

We cannot hope to answer this question by discussing isolated examples. Just as there are examples of successful gut-based decisions, and counterexamples in which they fail miserably, we can produce many anecdotes to support—or dispute—the claim that collaboration and process produce good results. Examples cannot lead us to a conclusion, especially when risk-taking, execution, and chance greatly affect the results.

We can, however, approach the problem as a statistical one. To do so, we must consider a large sample of decisions and compare those in which "collaboration plus process" was used with those in which it was not. The outcomes of these decisions will all be affected by chance factors, of course, but there is no reason to expect that chance will favor those who decided in one way rather than the other. Accordingly, we can expect chance factors to cancel each other out and the decision-making method's effect on the outcome, if it exists, to become visible.

This is the idea behind a 2010 study covering 1,048 decisions in all industries. The decisions in question were all investment choices (because the return on an investment is an indisputable measure of its success) and included mostly strategic investments (mergers and acquisitions, new product launches, and so on). In order to determine the impact of collaboration and process on decision quality, for each one of these decisions, the respondent answered a series of questions about how the decision was made.

Half of the questions concerned the analytical tools used: for example, did you construct a detailed financial model? Did you perform sensitivity analyses of the main parameters of this model? These questions tested the thoroughness of the number-crunching and fact-finding—in short, whether the decision makers did their homework. This is the "what" of the investment decision.

The other questions were not about the "what" but about the "how," and specifically about collaboration and process: Was the decision team composed of people chosen for their skills, not just for their rank? Did you explicitly discuss the uncertainties surrounding the decision? Did you have a decision-making meeting during which someone suggested *not* making this investment?

The conclusion: "How" factors—the quality of collaboration and process—explain 53 percent of the variance in return on investment. "What" factors—the quality of analysis—explain only 8 percent of the results. The remaining 39 percent is explained by variables related to the sector or the company, which are not specific to the investment in question and over which the decision maker has little or no control.

This result is so surprising that it bears repeating. If we leave aside the factors in an investment decision that we cannot control, "collaboration plus process" counts more than analysis—*six times* more. The way we make the decision—the "how"—is six times more important than the contents, the "what"!

ANALYZE LESS, DISCUSS MORE!

To get a sense of how counterintuitive these results are, think back to your most recent investment decision—or reflect on the next one you'll make. If your company works like most large organizations, you will rely on an array of calculations: sales forecasts, cost projections, cash flow forecasts, expected return on investment and payback time, and so forth. You can count on teams of professionals to conduct and review these analyses, applying rigorous standardized methods. Experts in your finance department probably have debates about these methods: Should we change the hurdle rate we use to evaluate investments? Should we introduce multiple scenarios with "optimistic" and "pessimistic" cases? In the end, if this research is given the attention it deserves, your company spends a massive amount of time on it.

Now, how much time you do really spend *discussing* these analyses and the hypotheses underlying them? Moreover, have you given any real thought to the decision-making process during which this discussion takes place? For instance, in what meeting should the discussion occur? Who should participate? At which stage of project development should the meeting happen? In many organizations, these questions are never asked. Instead, a decision maker or decision-making committee meets periodically, with an investment review as one of its agenda items. It receives a set of analyses supporting the proposed investment, which it knows have been done carefully and according to procedure. It reviews them (possibly after a presentation by the investment's chief advocate) and decides to approve or reject the proposal.

In other words, we spend most of our efforts on the "what," the content of the analysis. We invest very little in the "how," even though it is decisive. When the time comes to decide, we are so focused on the rational, quantifiable, objective aspects of the project that we simply do not realize the impact of collaboration and process.

To understand why this impact is so large, it is useful to look at the specific aspects of the "how" that make a difference. What are the practices of our 1,048 decision makers that are most closely associated with investment success? Those that enlist collaboration and process to fight the biases that are typical of investment decisions. Four questions in particular separate the best decisions from the worst ones.

First of all, *did you have an explicit discussion about the risks and uncertainties* associated with the investment proposal? It's clear that if such a discussion does not happen, the risk of overconfidence is high. Yet it often does not take place, because when the mood around the investment is positive, no one wants to preach doom and gloom and spoil the party.

Next, *in the discussion of the proposal, were points of view that contradicted those of senior leaders aired?* It's easy to see why this practice can combat groupthink. If meeting participants tend to align, consciously or unconsciously, with the boss, it's unlikely that contradictory views will be openly voiced.

Third, *did you deliberately seek out information that would contradict the investment thesis*, instead of focusing only on data that supports it? As you will recall, this is a direct countermeasure against confirmation bias, which naturally leads us to acquiesce to proposals.

Finally, *were the criteria for approval predefined and transparent for all those taking part in the discussion?* This practice helps shield the decision-making group against storytelling bias. We have seen how easy it can be to justify any decision by building a good story from cherry-picked data. Without clear, predefined criteria, the risk is that your reasoning and the choice of data that supports it will be dictated by the conclusion you want to reach: "Sure, this investment doesn't meet any of our financial criteria, but we should do it for 'strategic' reasons, such as..." Or, on the contrary, if it meets all your investment hurdles but you don't like it, "It looks good on paper, but I don't think it'll work, because..."

Part 3 of this book will discuss techniques you can use to organize and stimulate discussions such as those held by investment committees. But the key takeaway from this study of investment decisions is a simple one: if you have an hour to spare before you need to make a big decision, don't spend it doing more analysis, looking for additional information, or running the financial model one more time. Instead, invest this time in quality discussion. Analyze less, discuss more!

PROCESS VS. FACTS?

You may wonder why, according to this study, analysis seems to have such a small impact on the quality of decision-making. Does this mean that discussion, all by itself, leads to good decisions? Can we just have a friendly talk over a couple of beers and spare ourselves the number-crunching? Of course not. The reality is more nuanced.

In truth, almost all of us are capable of producing good financial analysis on proposed investment decisions. Most people (and most companies) run through the same analytical rituals and use the same formulas and software. The technical quality of financial analysis is no longer a source of differentiation between good and bad decisions: it's a prerequisite.

Admittedly, the quality of the information and data underlying such analysis can sometimes make a big difference. But in the case of investment decisions, this is relatively rare: the data that supports the financial model (sales targets, cost forecasts, estimated timetables, and so on) is often gathered in the same standardized way, by the very people who are proposing the investment. Except when an inquisitive boss or an especially persistent analyst takes it upon herself to challenge the project champion, a routine investment analysis is generally not based on very original data.

In other words, analysis that makes a difference does not happen naturally. What makes it more likely that it will be produced? Good process! For instance, to go back to one of the four elements most closely associated with quality decisions: deliberately seeking out information that contradicts the investment idea is not a "standard" practice, but it is certainly the mark of a good decision-making process.

Above all, even the best research and the most insightful analysis will be useless if they are not discussed. This problem jumps out at us when we look at postmortems. I once worked with an investment fund that had the good sense, after a particularly disappointing investment, to reexamine its decision process. The fund's leaders wanted to understand how the due diligence team and then the investment committee decided to acquire a company that—in hindsight—had serious issues. When they dug up and looked over the successive versions of the discussion documents submitted to the investment committee, they noticed something strange. In the very first presentation, three questions were listed as potential deal breakers: the low skills of some key executives, weakening demand for one of the product lines, and concerns about the solidity of one patent. In the second presentation, two of these problems had disappeared, with the third just mentioned in passing. In the final presentation before the investment decision, the three deal breakers had simply vanished. No explanations were given to justify how these issues were addressed, and apparently no questions were asked. Naturally, with each new presentation, the overall tone became more optimistic as the deal came closer to its conclusion.

Interestingly, the fund's forensic analysis did not stop there. It also looked at the reports made by the team handling the company after the acquisition. What were the most urgent issues to deal with as the ink on the acquisition contract dried? The same three that had been raised, months earlier, in the first due diligence report. One of them would turn out to be the main reason for the bitterly disappointing outcome of the acquisition. The issues hadn't gone away; they had just been swept under the rug, under the pressure of groupthink and collective overconfidence—the "deal fever" well known to anyone who has been involved in mergers and ac-quisitions. In this case, as in many, the facts had been dug out. All the necessary analysis had been done, and done right. But a flawed decision-making process had rendered it completely useless.

As this example shows, it does not make much sense to pit facts and figures against good process. If statistical analysis shows that process makes more of a difference than calculations, that's not because analysis is pointless: it's because it is almost always there, but it takes a good process to exploit it.

The practical implication is that, if you're trying to improve the quality of your decisions, the place to start is the decision-making process. After all, a good team following a good decision-making process should be able to realize when important information is missing, and to make sure the required analysis is quickly carried out. Good decision meetings will get the missing spreadsheets produced. But the reverse is not true: no one has ever seen a spreadsheet call a meeting.

FROM PROCESS TO DECISION ARCHITECTURE

So, process is key to making good decisions. But—and this is an understatement—the word *process* often evokes mixed feelings. Many leaders have an allergic reaction to the term. To some, letting a *process* take care of decisions is the opposite of exercising business judgment, which they see as the very essence of their role. Others instantly associate it with bureaucracy and red tape, producing procedure upon procedure and reams of paperwork littered with boxes to check off. When associated with the idea of collaboration, the mention of *process* raises another specter: the danger of "analysis paralysis" and endless discussions that result in a wishy-washy consensus—if they produce any decision at all. "Management by committee," it is often said, is a recipe for the dilution of responsibility and the lack of any strategic vision or managerial courage.

These concerns are entirely understandable, and anyone who has lived inside public or private bureaucracies will sympathize with those who voice them. But they misunderstand what is meant here by *collaboration* and *process*. Yes, *collaboration* means that more than one person is required. But, as we have seen in the examples of the Cuban missile crisis, of encouraging dissent in aircraft cockpits, or in the analogy with a judicial trial, this sort of collaboration is the exact opposite of seeking consensus: it's about debate, about ensuring that diverse, conflicting viewpoints are expressed and heard. Neither does this imply that the final decision is in any way "democratic" or made by majority vote: whether in the cabinet, in the cockpit, or in the operating theater, it is very clear who is in charge.

What about *process*? It is true that many procedures and processes in organizations consist in mandating predefined tasks and analyses that must be performed before a decision can be made. Over time, this often becomes a mindless box-ticking routine. As we saw in the example of the investment fund, routines like this are useless if the end product is not noticed and discussed. That is what good processes are about: making sure that decision meetings are effectively organized and led, under the leadership of open-minded executives who are able to take a step back from the situation and apply their critical judgment.

Nothing about this looks like a Rube Goldberg machine! And if the words *collaboration* and *process* don't work for you, why not use different ones? Some prefer to talk about *best practices* in decision-making (despite the risks associated with the very idea of *best practices*, which we discussed in chapter 2). Some managers characterize these ways of deciding as their management style or personal *system* for decision-making. Companies that have made them systematic describe them variously as their *governance principles, rituals,* or *playbook*.

In part 3 of this book, I'll use the term *decision architecture*. In *Nudge*, Richard Thaler and Cass Sunstein emphasize the crucial role of *choice architects*, who, deliberately or not, design the way in which choices are presented to consumers or citizens. In the same vein, an executive who designs the decision-making procedures of her company is a *decision architect*. If this decision-making architecture relies on collaboration and process to combat biases, those who "live in" this architecture—the architect herself, first of all—will be likely to reach the best possible decision more often.

The choice of the term *architecture* also has useful associations. First of all, architecture is not a science but an art. Viewing yourself as a decision architect should remind you that the art of decision-making cannot be reduced to purely quantitative analysis.

Second, you don't call on an architect to build a toolshed. Similarly, it's worth thinking about decision architecture when the importance of the decision justifies it—that is, for choices that determine a company's future. These can be choices that are made only once, such as a diversification or a merger. Or they can be repetitive decisions that, as a whole, define the strategy of a company—for example, research and development decisions in a pharmaceutical company or investment decisions in a mining company. But there is no point in overthinking decision architecture for minor choices. That may be precisely what too many companies do when they entangle their employees in a web of procedures, but that is not decision architecture: it is bureaucracy.

Finally, the idea of architecture suggests plans that are drawn up before the work begins. It makes sense to define the architecture of the decision, to choose *how* you will decide, before the decision-making process begins. Respecting this sequence is not always feasible—for example, in crisis situations—but it is generally desirable.

The remainder of this book discusses decision architecture. It aims to help you think about your own decisions and how to make them—to help you, in other words, decide how you will decide. It is organized around three themes, or three pillars of good decision-making architecture. The first pillar is *dialogue*, an authentic exchange of viewpoints among people who sincerely want to listen to each other and not just convince each other—a prerequisite for effective collaboration. Next comes *divergence*, which provides relevant, fact-based, and original content for this dialogue so that it doesn't end up a mere conflict of preconceived ideas. Finally, decision-making *dynamics* in the organization must promote dialogue and divergence—which many organizations tend to suppress.

Of course, these general principles are not enough. The decision architect needs practical tools to turn them into reality. Some call them rituals, *countermeasures* against biases, or *bias busters*. Here, I'll simply call them *decision-making techniques*. Each technique acts as an antidote to some of our biases. As we shall see, the majority are organizational techniques, not individual ones: biases are individual, but the remedies that we apply will most often be collective.

In part 3, you will find forty different examples of these techniques (summarized in appendix 2). Chapter 14 outlines fourteen practical techniques for creating a decision architecture that fosters real *dialogue*; chapter 15 proposes fourteen techniques to stimulate *divergence*; and chapter 16 suggests twelve techniques to foster productive *dynamics* at every stage of the decision-making process. All these techniques come from the observation of decision processes and conversations with executives in companies of all sizes (from start-ups to multinationals), in financial investment firms, in professional service firms, and in the public sector.

As you will see, most of the examples used to illustrate these techniques are anonymous. This choice protects the confidentiality of conversations in which senior corporate leaders shared their methods, their mistakes, and the lessons they learned from them. Just as importantly, it is a way to avoid the trap of imitating "best practices." When you read about a tool applied by a particular company, the reputation of that company colors your judgment of the tool in question. Not knowing where the idea comes from leaves you free to judge it on its merits, and to ask yourself whether you might apply it to your own situation.

This list of techniques is of course not exhaustive. Its goal is to inspire you as you think about your own decision architecture. Each organization will need its own techniques, and each leader should feel free to adapt those that are proposed here or to invent new ones. After all, good architects follow common principles, but no two of them will ever design exactly the same building.

DECISIONS MADE THE RIGHT WAY
IN THIRTY SECONDS

- **Success does not mean a decision was good:** chance, risk, and execution also come into play.
  - ▶ *Paul the Psychic Octopus beat all the experts... by sheer luck.*
  - ▶ *A trader who exceeds his risk limits and wins is not a good trader.*
  - ▶ *Bad execution can make a good decision look bad.*
- **Survivorship bias** often makes us forget this.
  - ▶ *Bill Miller beat the market for fifteen years... thanks to a fluke of the calendar.*
  - ▶ *"One must not decide about the value of human actions from their outcomes." (Bernoulli)*
- We **can judge a decision-making method** if it has been applied to a large number of situations; and data suggests that **collaboration and process make a difference.**
  - ▶ *Study of 1,048 investment decisions: process has six times more impact than analysis.*
  - ▶ *This is not because analysis doesn't matter but because it must be used: good meetings get spreadsheets done, but spreadsheets don't call meetings.*
- A key task of a leader is, therefore, to be a **decision architect who "decides how to decide,"** introducing collaboration and process in the organization's decision practices.

PART 3

THE DECISION ARCHITECT

14

DIALOGUE

Confronting Viewpoints

I take it we are all in complete agreement on the decision here. Then, I propose we postpone further discussion of this matter until the next meeting to give ourselves time to develop disagreement, and perhaps gain some understanding of what the decision is all about.

—Alfred P. Sloan

You are in Mountain View, California, the heart of Silicon Valley, in the early 2000s. A new day is starting at Google. You might think the "Googlers" would be parking their cars in the parking lot and getting settled at their desks, ready to conquer the world. Not yet. In fact, the parking lot is the site of a furious game of roller hockey. And the players are not holding back: hockey sticks smack each other, shouts are heard, and several players collapse, either because they're exhausted or because someone has shoved them to the ground. The most aggressive players are cheered by a small crowd. When Larry Page and Sergey Brin, the founders of Google, are on the court, "the gloves are off with them—it's full contact," says one of their colleagues. When the game is over, the sweaty employees head into the office—except for those who have to stop at the infirmary first.

A strange way to start the day, you might think. Google's leadership must want to channel the employees' aggression through sports. But inside the office, even though the roller skates and hockey sticks are put away, the "game" is just as intense. In meetings, Googlers shout at each other left and right and don't handle their colleagues' feelings with kid gloves. It's not unusual to hear an employee call an idea "stupid" or a coworker "naive"—name-calling of all kinds is commonplace.

This management style is certainly not a "best practice" to be emulated. And the Google of today is certainly less brutal than it was in those days. But however extreme, the example holds a lesson: it takes some conflict, some discomfort, to reach good decisions. Yet many companies, because they fear discomfort, avoid conflict.

The question, therefore, is how can we stimulate the right amount of conflict without creating more discomfort than is strictly necessary, and certainly without using hockey sticks? That's the first pillar of good decision-making: tension between opposing ideas that does not degenerate into a clash between people. This can only be achieved by orchestrating an authentic dialogue around the decision at hand.

YOU CAN'T IMPROVISE DIALOGUE

Picture an "ordinary" decision-making meeting you may have recently attended, such as an executive committee review of an investment proposal. A manager presents a project, backed up by a barrage of PowerPoint slides. Several attendees support the proposal: as is customary in many companies, the project champion "pre-sold" the idea to key participants in order to enlist their support, or at least to secure their neutrality. The executive in charge asks attendees to give opinions, seeking to achieve a quick consensus. Each person soon gets a sense of how the boss feels about the proposal and is careful not to voice unproductive concerns: everyone understands it's too late to air doubts at this point. As expected, the proposal is approved. The triumphant presenter returns to his anxious team and is asked how the meeting went. "Brilliantly," he says. "There was no discussion at all!"

In many organizations, a meeting that "goes well" is one *where there is no debate.* The discomfort caused by conflicting ideas is so great that people suppress it by avoiding any real discussion. If any disagreements are expected, a wise presenter will resolve them one-on-one with key stakeholders before the meeting. The meeting itself ends up being a perfunctory affair, rubber-stamping a decision already made. It's easy to see how this behavior paves the way for multiple biases: groupthink, of course, as a majority is already in favor of the project; confirmation bias, when the audience follows the presenter's story; overconfidence, when no one challenges an overly optimistic plan; interest biases, when members of a committee implicitly (or sometimes explicitly) trade support for each other's projects. The decision-making meeting is a cauldron where all these biases bubble up to the surface.

Here's an interesting paradox: not all meetings are like this. For instance, have you ever participated in a creativity seminar? Usually, before anything else, participants are reminded of the rules of brainstorming: no criticism or self-censorship, no "bad ideas," you should build on other people's suggestions before sorting through the ideas, and so on. Whether these methods are effective or not (and much evidence suggests they are not), no one minds being told what rules to follow: creativity seems too mysterious an activity to be left to a "normal" meeting. What a contrast with the typical decision-making meeting, which follows no specific rules. When it comes to decision-making, we think we can play it by ear, without any specific tools or techniques.

The explanation for this paradox lies, once again, in the invisibility of biases. If we gather to generate creative ideas and we don't produce any, we immediately experience our own failure. So we're glad to embrace meeting techniques that help us avoid this outcome. But when we get together to make a decision, we are not aware of the biases that derail us. That's why we're satisfied to run decision meetings without a formal procedure.

But you can't improvise dialogue. It's not easy to tolerate, much less encourage, the expression of different points of view. It's not easy to make the tension between ideas explicit without creating conflict between the people who are expressing them. It's not easy for managers who have firm viewpoints, and who want to advocate them passionately, to engage in a dialogue, to speak openly, and to listen actively to each other. But there are routines you can use to stimulate real dialogue.

SETTING THE STAGE FOR DIALOGUE

Technique #1: Ensure Sufficient Cognitive Diversity

The first prerequisite for a successful dialogue is almost a tautology: it's to bring together a sufficient diversity of viewpoints.

What is usually meant by *diversity*—that is, diverse *backgrounds*—naturally contributes to this. But bringing together people of different genders, ages, nationalities, or ethnic origins is not enough. When people have long worked in the same organization or on the same team, they will share the same training, experience, successes, and failures. They will likely form the same hypotheses, believe the same stories, and generally be subject to the same biases. Some studies of problem-solving in groups suggest that effectiveness is associated with *cognitive diversity*—a variety of preferences in terms of handling information—but not necessarily with demographic diversity. Diverse skills and perspectives matter more than diverse identities.

An example of cognitive diversity is provided by a bank chairperson who picked the members of the bank's board of directors to include specific profiles: risk management specialists, legal experts, macroeconomists, and experts in the main countries and sectors in which the bank invests. Obviously, these backgrounds allow the board members to make valuable substantive contributions on their respective areas of expertise. Less obviously, they are also valuable for the diversity of perspectives and mindsets the directors bring to the meeting. Each director considers a decision through the prism of his or her own experience and individual inclinations, viewing the issue at hand a bit differently than the others, even without specific subject matter expertise. This diversity of perspectives was sorely lacking, it seems, on certain bank boards before the 2008 financial crisis.

Technique #2: Make Time

A second condition for dialogue—which, like the first, is both obvious in principle and often ignored in practice—is to give yourself enough time. Engaging in dialogue takes longer than obtaining superficial agreement.

The bank chairperson mentioned above generally asks board members to devote twenty-five days per year to this board. Each meeting lasts two full days. Of course, this particular case does not suggest a general rule. But the chair insists that it is a key to the effectiveness of the board: if people who have very different backgrounds and areas of expertise are to collaborate effectively and engage in real, thoughtful dialogue, they must spend time together. Diversity and the need for time go hand in hand: the greater the similarity between the way the people present think, the faster they will agree with each other—even if they're all wrong together! The more diverse they are, however, the more time it will take for them to listen to each other's viewpoint, and for some to change their minds.

Technique #3: Put Dialogue on the Agenda

The third prerequisite for dialogue concerns meeting agendas. Probably in reaction to the very real problem posed by the proliferation of useless, time-consuming, soul-draining meetings, many executives now believe that *any* meeting must lead to decisions, duly recorded in meeting minutes as *decisions made*, *next steps*, and *action items*. The flip side of this view is that any meeting that ends without a decision is a failure. By extension, no item should be put on the agenda if the meeting cannot definitively settle it.

This view is well intentioned but misguided. There is a time to discuss and a time to decide. An essential prerequisite for dialogue is to know when we are doing one and when we are doing the other.

Sometimes this can happen in the same meeting, with the discussion naturally followed by a decision. Sometimes it can't. A simple way to materialize this distinction is to mark some topics on the agenda as *for decision today* and others as *for discussion only*. These designations will lead to very different kinds of conversations.

Whether a topic is for discussion or for decision depends on how far along its development is. This is a judgment call, and it is the prerogative of the leader to make it. Any effective leader senses the distinction between subjects that are "decision ready" and those that aren't yet. If she makes that distinction explicit, her team will know when it's no use to press her to make a decision yet. They will also know when debate is over and the time to make a decision has come.

THE GROUND RULES OF DIALOGUE

Once we have brought together a diverse enough group for a long enough time and with a well-defined agenda, is dialogue guaranteed to happen? Not yet. We need some ground rules.

Just to be perfectly clear, this list is not like the "rules for good meetings" taped up on the walls of many conference rooms. Advice such as "Always start on time" and "Clean up the room before you leave" is excellent, but quite distinct from the ground rules you need to prevent counterproductive meeting behaviors: the behaviors that foster groupthink, discourage the expression of different ideas, or generally speaking hinder dialogue. Setting ground rules for dialogue means accepting a paradox: to encourage free expression, we need certain prohibitions.

Technique #4: Limit the Use of PowerPoint

If you're looking for impediments to dialogue, for those things that freeze discussion and put participants to sleep, PowerPoint slides are a good place to start. The all-powerful PowerPoint presentation has its own special way of smothering discussion, by turning a meeting into a one-way street dominated by a single point of view. Even Marine Corps General Jim Mattis, when he was U.S. Joint Forces Commander, lamented that "PowerPoint makes us stupid."

PowerPoint is helpful for presenting facts and arguments, and even for establishing the foundations of a productive discussion. But in practice it is often used to hide the weakness of an argument, to distract the audience with visual tricks, and to hold the floor and limit the time available for debate.

PowerPoint is ubiquitous, and that is why few executives dare to ban it altogether. But those who do so are pleased with the results. "Those presentations were preventing us from having a discussion," says the head of a family company, visibly happy with the change in the tone of the meetings. Many years ago, Scott McNealy, who had banned the use of PowerPoint at Sun Microsystems, was so happy about the results that he did not hesitate to make a surprisingly strong claim: "I would argue that every company in the world, if it would just ban PowerPoint, would see their earnings skyrocket."

If only it were so easy! But alternatives to "death by PowerPoint" are gaining ground. Amazon, for instance, does not use presentations but requires "narratively structured six-page memos" that all participants read at the beginning of the meeting in total silence.

This is not just a choice of software, or a preference for using paper vertically rather than horizontally: as Amazon CEO Jeff Bezos puts it, "If someone builds a list of bullet points in Word, that would be just as bad as PowerPoint." The value of the memo is that it forces the writer to clarify the issues, make assumptions explicit, and articulate a coherent argument, rather than "gloss over ideas" and "ignore" their "interconnectedness," says Bezos. Readers can discover this reasoning at their own pace, using their critical judgment. But why read the memo in the meeting rather than send it in advance, as is standard practice in most organizations? Because, says Bezos, "just like high school kids, executives will bluff their way through the meeting as if they've read the memo." (How shocking! Of course, *you* have never done this.) Reading the memo together, study hall–style, may look odd, but it guarantees that when the debate starts, "everyone has actually read the memo, they're not just pretending."

The same principle can be applied to boards of directors, who usually use "board books," thick compilations of PowerPoint presentations that are circulated before meetings. Netflix has replaced these board books with memos, to which board members can electronically add questions and comments. The memos are about thirty pages long and contain links to supporting data. The goal is the same as it is at Amazon: time can be devoted to a real discussion instead of its being taken up by presentations and clarification questions.

Why is this practice not widespread? Why does PowerPoint retain a chokehold on our meeting rooms, despite its severe, long-acknowledged downsides? Why don't we just all write memos instead? Quite simply, because it's very hard! The difference between a slide deck and a good memo is not just a format choice;

216

it is a considerable commitment of time, effort, and skill. Netflix's memos to the board are reviewed by ninety senior executives. And it's worth quoting Jeff Bezos at length again on good memos: "The great memos are written and re-written, shared with colleagues who are asked to improve the work, set aside for a couple of days, and then edited again with a fresh mind. They simply can't be done in a day or two....A great memo probably should take a week or more." This is why banning PowerPoint altogether is probably too radical for most organizations; putting limits on its use is a more realistic goal.

Technique #5: Ban Misleading Analogies

Another useful ground rule is to ban certain kinds of arguments from the meeting. Turning to censorship may seem a paradoxical way to stimulate dialogue. But, as in a courtroom where rules of procedure prohibit using inadmissible evidence or arguments that would unfairly sway the jury, some fallacious arguments must be banned.

This is especially the case with some analogies, which, as soon as they are made, lure us into the storytelling trap. The CEO of one venture capital firm says that when his investment committee reviews a possible investment, references to similar companies are prohibited: presenting a candidate as "the next WhatsApp" or "the Uber of its industry" biases the discussion irremediably. Even if you later identify differences with the comparison company, that company's success anchors your evaluation. The power of the analogy wins out over any kind of rational argument.

Technique #6: Discourage Hasty Conclusions

The same venture capitalist also suggests a technique to avoid hasty group decisions. When he and his colleagues meet the founders of start-ups in which they are considering investing, no one is allowed to respond immediately to the pitch. After the entrepreneur's presentation, the investment committee members go their separate ways and do not debrief the meeting until the next day. This cooling-off period goes against all the principles of productive meetings (including, again, the misguided belief that "every meeting must end with decisions"). But when people are asked to decide immediately, says the investor, "it becomes a debating match based on first impressions." The strongest reactions, which aren't necessarily the best-advised, may have the most weight and sway the group. Banning quick decision-making leads to better decisions.

Technique #7: Encourage Nuanced Viewpoints
by Asking for "Balance Sheets"

Another renowned venture capitalist, Kleiner Perkins's Randy Komisar, takes this idea one step further. He dissuades members of the investment committee from expressing firm opinions by stating right away that they are for or against an investment idea. Instead, Komisar asks participants for a "balance sheet" of points for and against the investment: "Tell me what is good about this opportunity; tell me what is bad about it. Do not tell me your judgment yet. I don't want to know." Conventional wisdom dictates that everyone should have an opinion and make it clear. Instead, Komisar asks his colleagues to flip-flop!

The idea, of course, is to prevent positions from becoming entrenched, to give people the opportunity to change their minds after they've heard the views of others. It is also, as Komisar puts it, to "emphasize...that each participant is smart and knowledgeable, that it was a difficult decision, and that there is ample room for the other judgment."

This is a key insight that few organizations are able to put in practice. When handling difficult, complicated decisions, we have to accept that they are difficult and complicated. A culture in which leaders are expected to appear totally confident in their judgment sends them down the slippery slope of overconfidence and pushes the group into groupthink. The much better alternative is to recognize uncertainty and encourage its expression.

This requires welcoming the expression of balanced, complex, nuanced viewpoints. Nuance must be regarded as a sign not of indecisiveness or incompetence but of lucidity. Yes, the role of leaders is to decide; and sometimes this requires taking a complex problem and making it simple. The time to choose will come. But it is dangerous to force too much simplification, too much confidence, and too much unanimity too soon. Remember the famous principle often attributed to Einstein: "Everything should be made as simple as possible, but not simpler."

STIMULATING DIALOGUE

Once the meeting has started and the ground rules have been laid, you still have to stimulate dialogue. There are a lot of ways to do so; which ones you choose will depend on your own management style and company culture. The following examples only illustrate the range of possibilities.

Technique #8: Appoint a Devil's Advocate

This tried-and-true strategy still has supporters today. An executive interviewed for this book said that he uses it without fail: "When everyone tells me an idea is good, a little warning light goes off in my head. So I choose someone to play devil's advocate and tell me why the proposal on the table is actually a bad idea." And how does he choose someone to carry this out? Based on character, he says. "I make sure to choose a troublemaker, someone whose personality fits the part."

This is not so easy. Your management team may not include many people who, by temperament, enjoy arguing the opposite of what they really think (and perhaps this is not a bad thing!). Furthermore, the devil's advocate runs a big risk: if she puts her heart into the task and uses her rhetorical skills against her own allies, they are likely to hold it against her. Kennedy was well aware of this when he asked two advisors, not just one, to take on this thankless role during the Cuban missile crisis.

For these reasons and several others, the technique is hard to implement: there is a high risk that the defense will be halfhearted or worse. Research bears this out and suggests that contrived dissent is less effective than *authentic* dissent, the expression of genuine dissenting beliefs.

But cultivating authentic dissent presents other challenges. It may conflate the content of the dissent and the personality of the person voicing it. Ideally, choosing between two alternatives shouldn't mean choosing between two people. This is why the following techniques, which can be seen as alternatives to the devil's advocate, are often preferable.

Technique #9: Use Mandatory Alternatives

One powerful yet little-used technique is to require anyone who wants to propose one project to bring not one but two. The chief financial officer of a large industrial company has adopted this rule: he will not listen to an investment proposal unless the person who is presenting it offers an alternative at the same time.

This technique stimulates debate by creating additional options, allowing the decision maker to escape a binary choice "for or against" a single proposal. As an added benefit, it helps combat the problem of inertia in resource allocation, discussed in chapter 5. After all, the financial director may approve both proposals from a single division and reject all those from another. If each unit had brought only one investment proposal, he would have been more tempted to approve them both.

Technique #10: Run the Vanishing Options Test

Another way to generate alternatives is by using the *vanishing options test*, described by Chip Heath and Dan Heath in *Decisive*. It means asking yourself what you would do if, for some reason, the options on the table became impossible. This forces participants in the decision to generate additional, sometimes unexpected, ideas.

It's easy to see how one might think that having more options makes a decision more difficult—which explains why many leaders try to simplify things by narrowing down the range of options. Yet the opposite is true. The simple fact of having multiple options improves the quality of decisions. The Heath brothers make this guideline the first item in their method for improving decision-making. They cite a study showing that only 29 percent of business decisions are choices among several options, whereas 71 percent are "yes or no" decisions on a single proposal. But the failure rate is much lower for the multiple-option decisions (32 percent vs. 52 percent).

Technique #11: Tell Alternative Stories

Sometimes, generating more options is impractical. Indeed, the more important, unusual, or unique the decision is, the more difficult it may be to generate credible alternatives. Also, even before any options can be considered, decision makers must share an understanding of the situation and the problem or opportunity these options are meant to address. In such cases, the variety they need is not a variety of options: it is a variety of ways of looking at the situation, or at the one option under consideration.

One routine that can help achieve this goal involves generating multiple stories or scenarios that feature identical facts but lead to different conclusions.

Recall, for instance, the example in chapter 1 in which a sales director, based on a call from one of his salespeople, concluded that a price war was starting. An alternative story based on the same facts might have been: "This sales rep has run into some isolated difficulties with one or two important clients, and that's why he's feeling down right now. His difficulties have less to do with the price positioning of our products and are more about the way he is presenting them, because price is not, and should not be, our main selling point. We don't need to lower our prices—we need to strengthen the training and motivation of our salespeople."

This alternative story is not necessarily true, but neither was the first one. The benefit of generating it is that it pushes the sales director to seek different pieces of evidence, supporting a broader range of possible conclusions than the simple "we should lower our prices." For example, to confirm or disprove the second story, he would need an objective assessment of the company's competitive positioning, including but not limited to the prices of its products. The sales director may not ask for such an analysis if he remains focused on the first story. The alternative story broadens his viewpoint.

At a private equity firm where a version of this technique is used, people presenting an investment proposal are expected to use the same facts supporting their "positive" story to construct an alternative story according to which the fund should reject the investment. It's not an easy exercise: those who are asked to practice it may find it uncomfortable at first; and those who see it used for the first time sometimes find it artificial. But, as with the "balance sheet" technique mentioned above, alternative stories make participants aware of the uncertainty inherent in the decision. Recognizing that an investment choice is a subject about which reasonable people can disagree creates a climate that is favorable to dialogue.

Most of all, having the same person present alternative stories defuses and depersonalizes any possible disagreements. Unlike a devil's advocate, who inevitably appears to attack the person behind the story she is critiquing, the person who is presenting two stories gives others the option to agree with some of the arguments supporting each story. Dialogue becomes easier.

Incidentally, this technique shows how you can take advantage of one bias—the power of storytelling—to fight another—confirmation bias. Generating alternative and equally believable stories is a way to fight fire with fire.

Technique #12: Run a "Premortem"

Another effective technique for stimulating real dialogue in a management team and, especially, fighting the deadly combination of overconfidence and groupthink is the premortem. Invented by Gary Klein, the expert on "intuitive" decisions who made an appearance in chapter 3, the premortem is a method for identifying flaws in a plan that would otherwise go unnoticed. It takes place before the final decision, at a stage when certain objections or concerns may have been identified but not expressed. The technique involves collectively imagining a future in which the project has failed, and conducting a postmortem—hence the coinage, suggesting an advance autopsy.

The specifics of how premortems are conducted can vary slightly, but the core principle is simple. The meeting organizer announces: "We are in the year X, and this project has been an unmitigated disaster. Why did it turn out to be so catastrophic?" The participants then write down a series of possible reasons. They then take turns sharing them with the group. Everyone must contribute.

How does a premortem differ from what almost all teams do— have a discussion of the risks and uncertainties facing the project? In two small but very important ways. First, remember what hindsight bias teaches us: we are much more talented when explaining what has happened (in the past) than when imagining what may happen (in the future). The premortem astutely takes advantage of this bias: it asks us to travel in time to the future so we can look back, and it asks us to explain what "has happened" in this imagined past. In a clever oxymoron, Klein calls this *prospective hindsight*. Second, asking people to write down their reasons, and setting a norm—that everyone must contribute—helps dissenters and doubters overcome their tendency to silence themselves, which is the root of groupthink.

When done right, premortems are often very helpful. If all the participants are worried for the same reasons, perhaps these concerns have not been sufficiently explored. Even if the concerns raised are simply part of the uncertainty inherent in any risky project, it is useful to identify them as key focal points to monitor during implementation. But the most valuable outcome of a premortem is the identification of flaws that have not been discussed. As Smithburg, the CEO of Quaker, acknowledged a few years after the failed acquisition of Snapple: "There was so much excitement about bringing in a new brand, a brand with legs. We should have had a couple of people arguing the 'no' side of the evaluation." A premortem would have given them the license—indeed, the obligation—to do just that.

Technique #13: Assemble an Ad Hoc Committee

If asking your executive committee to imagine the worst isn't radical enough, here's another idea: replace the committee altogether. The norm in most organizations is that the top team—whether formally called the executive committee or something else—decides on everything. But the best way to avoid groupthink and other political games may be to vary the makeup of the group for different decisions.

A business leader interviewed for this book described a technique he calls the "Six Amigos" for reviewing investment proposals.

"We bring together six people chosen from different parts of the company. They don't know about the project and they learn about it at the same time we do. We tell them to ask the right questions and challenge the idea using whatever skills they've developed in their jobs."

And it works! When they're given this unexpected role, the employees play along. They will be much less prone to play political games, to engage in the "you scratch my back, I'll scratch yours" approach that sometimes develops in a standing committee. It's sensible for members of the top team to worry that the person whose project they criticize today will criticize theirs tomorrow. But the Six Amigos do not have this concern. Their focus is on the chance they have been given to demonstrate their analytical skills and business judgment when they present to the CEO. Giving high-potential junior executives an opportunity for exposure is indeed an added benefit of the technique. But its main use is as a way to stimulate dialogue—by changing the participants.

Technique #14: Lock the Memo in the CEO's Drawer

It is difficult to implement these techniques at all in certain situations. Dialogue may be limited to a very small group because the decision must be kept secret—for instance, if a large acquisition is being explored. But the smaller the group, the more biases come into play. In such cases, dialogue needs to be orchestrated between the ultimate decision maker . . . and himself. But himself at a different point in time.

One of the challenges raised by acquisitions is that excitement—"deal fever," as some have called it—takes hold of decision makers and their teams, as Smithburg's remark about bringing in people

226

to argue "the 'no' side of the evaluation" suggests. The fund whose reports at successive stages of the acquisition process made problems vanish one by one without resolving them is an example of this. When teams are working day and night, and when negotiation requires rapid response times, it can be hard to keep a cool head.

The "memo in the drawer" technique consists of the team and the CEO sitting down a few weeks before the planned date of the transaction to write a memo listing deal breakers that absolutely must be resolved. The CEO will then put the memo away in her drawer until the day of the decision.

When that day arrives, the CEO can have a dialogue about the decision with someone who has all the required expertise and her complete trust: herself. Or, more precisely, her self of a few weeks earlier, when she was less subject to the emotions and biases of the moment. Was this question properly answered? If not, was it unimportant? After all, she is the very person who put it on this list just a short time ago. . . . This "conversation," of course, is not the same as true dialogue. But at a crucial time, it can help the CEO achieve the necessary distance from the pressures of the moment.

THREE FALSE CONCERNS ABOUT DIALOGUE

Three frequent objections arise when the topic of dialogue in decision-making is brought up. These concerns must be addressed here, because all these techniques for stimulating dialogue are useless if you don't really believe in its value.

The first concern is the fear that dialogue will degenerate into endless discussion, postponing the decision and wasting precious time, or even preventing the decision from being made at all. This is the danger of "analysis paralysis," briefly mentioned above; and it is true that some organizations suffer from this disease. A leader who deals with this culture might be tempted to shorten or even eliminate discussion in order to take action. (One consumer products multinational even made it, for a while, one of its informal mottoes: "Action, No Debate.") This, however, is generally a mistake: to improve the speed of decision-making, it is not necessary (and certainly not sufficient) to sacrifice its quality. A core feature of all the dialogue tools featured in this book is that they're often very quick. A typical round in a premortem session, for instance, takes no more than two minutes.

Eric Schmidt, the former CEO of Google, calls this "discord plus deadline": organizing discord, confrontation, and dialogue but also establishing in advance the time when you will stop discussing, make a decision, and begin implementing it. "Who enforces the deadline?" Schmidt asks rhetorically: "Me. That's my job. Or whoever's running the meeting." As Schmidt observes, "If you just have discord, well, then you have a university."

The second concern is that dialogue around a strategic decision will end up reaching an agreement by compromise—a mediocre, soft consensus. But this is a simple misunderstanding: dialogue does not imply democracy. When the dialogue is over, the decision maker is the one who decides. She does so after listening to the discussion, but without any obligation to adopt the point of view of the majority.

Admittedly, this is not easy. One of the executives quoted above notes that orchestrating dialogue "is not comfortable at all, a lot less comfortable than gently bringing people around to an agreement." This is why leading a team through dialogue requires true managerial courage: the courage to be ready to call the deadline and make the final decision, but also the courage to go against the opinion expressed by part of your team. If wishy-washy compromises happen, it is not because of dialogue. It is because of wishy-washy decision makers.

The third concern is a consequence of this need for a clear final decision. If there has been real dialogue, people will have expressed conflicting viewpoints. Once the final decision is made, people who were in the minority must still participate in implementing the decision. Will they balk at having to execute a strategy that they argued against? Isn't it better to avoid the overt expression of diverse points of view, so no one is placed in that awkward situation?

Experience and research both suggest that in fact the opposite is true. A real dialogue in which everyone gets a fair hearing inspires those who participate in it. Authors W. Chan Kim and Renée Mauborgne call this "fair process": if people have had a chance to express their point of view and be heard, once the final decision is made, the motivation of all contributors is increased, not reduced. Provided, of course, that some important conditions are met: the rules of the game must be clear, dialogue must be respectful, and listening must be sincere. A sham consultation that creates the appearance of agreement is a motivation killer. Nothing makes managers more cynical than bosses who pretend to listen to them but in fact only expect them to endorse the decisions they already made.

Orchestrating dialogue is not easy, especially when organizations are not used to it. But dialogue is a prerequisite for fighting most of our biases. Dialogue combats pattern-recognition biases by suggesting different stories. It thwarts action-oriented biases because it gives a voice to those who are skeptical. It can also prevent inertia biases, because when we compare conflicting viewpoints, we must challenge the status quo. Finally, when done right, dialogue prevents groupthink. For all these reasons, dialogue is the first pillar of a sound decision architecture.

DIALOGUE IN THIRTY SECONDS

- In too many companies, a successful meeting is one in which there is no discussion. But **dialogue is essential to fight biases** (groupthink and others).
- **Set the stage for dialogue:** dialogue does not "just happen."
    - ▶ *Cognitive diversity and sufficient time.*
    - ▶ *Explicit agenda: "For decision" or "for discussion"?*
- **Establish ground rules for dialogue.** Some prohibitions are good for debate—for example:
    - ▶ *Limit PowerPoint.*
    - ▶ *Ban misleading analogies, hasty conclusions, advocacy of strong viewpoints.*
- **Stimulate dialogue:** Use techniques that change the nature of the debate by broadening options and interpretations.
    - ▶ *To broaden options, use devil's advocate, mandatory alternatives, vanishing options, alternative stories.*
    - ▶ *The premortem: "It's five years later and the project has failed. Why?"*
    - ▶ *Ad hoc team—for example, a "Six Amigos" construct.*
    - ▶ *Memo in the drawer: What should stop us when we decide six weeks from now?*
- **Don't be afraid of disagreement:** it's up to the leader to decide.
    - ▶ *Dialogue is not an absence of decision: "Discord plus deadline" (Eric Schmidt).*
    - ▶ *Dialogue doesn't demotivate those who didn't win—but fake consensus does.*

15

DIVERGENCE

Seeing Things from a Different Angle

In God we trust. All others, bring data.

—Anonymous

When the subprime mortgage crisis hit in 2007–2008, it took most of the big banks by surprise. All their models, all their analyses, and all the scores from the ratings agencies suggested that the loans that brought about the crash weren't risky. The banks and other investors lost huge sums, triggering an unprecedented financial crisis.

Except, of course, for those who saw the crisis coming. One of them was Michael Burry (later played by Christian Bale in the movie *The Big Short*). Early on, the problem jumped out at him: if there was a downturn in the housing market, the borrowers, who were fundamentally insolvent, would default on their loans, and the bubble would burst. As he later wrote, "Nobody in Washington showed any interest in hearing exactly how I arrived at my conclusions that the housing bubble would burst when it did and that it could cripple the big financial institutions." When his prediction came true in 2007, Burry's fund raked in some $750 million. Taking positions that go against the general opinion, being what investors call a contrarian, can sometimes be very profitable.

But who is Michael Burry? Is he a prominent strategist in a big bank? Or a trader in a Wall Street brokerage firm? Not at all. A medical doctor by training, Michael Burry stopped practicing medicine to devote himself full-time to his hobby, the stock market. He started a small investment fund with his savings and some money borrowed from family and friends. To investment professionals, Burry is an outsider. In fact, he's an outsider in other ways, too: antisocial and suffering, by his own assessment, from Asperger's syndrome, he met his wife through a personal ad in which he described himself as follows: "I'm single and have one eye and a lot of debt." It's easy to see why Burry doesn't work for Goldman Sachs.

SEEKING OUT DIFFERENT VIEWPOINTS

Contrarian, "divergent" ideas like Burry's are priceless. But ideas don't emerge in a vacuum. Within many banks, some employees voiced similar concerns about the subprime mortgage bubble, but no one listened. Was it because these individuals weren't as persistent as Burry? Or because their environment dissuaded them from pushing ahead with their ideas? In the end, these are the same thing. Companies rarely welcome people with divergent ideas, tolerate rebellious thoughts, or integrate their results into their strategic decisions.

Obviously, this is problematic. We saw in the previous chapter that dialogue is essential for good decisions, but if this dialogue takes place between people who all have the same ideas, it's a waste of time. How can we make sure that when we discuss situations and opportunities, the people present have different ways of looking at them? How can we overcome groupthink and confirmation bias, which naturally incline us toward unanimity? How can we make ourselves see things from a different angle?

For divergent ideas to flourish, we must welcome those who have them. This means cultivating diversity, bringing in challengers, and tolerating sometimes disturbing differences.

Technique #15: Cultivate Informal Advisors

Many political leaders who want to make sure they are not cut off from civil society have a network of informal, unofficial advisors who can provide them with "offbeat" ideas. In the same spirit, many business leaders make sure that they do not cut themselves off from reality by cultivating an informal network of gadflies, mavericks, and troublemakers. This fulfills the same function: bringing them divergent viewpoints.

Because informality is the essence of the role, these counselors go by a variety of names: *maverick* isn't exactly a job description. Some are called special advisors to the CEO or in-house consultants. Many play this role in addition to their official position in the organization (usually a staff role, such as director of transformation, head of innovation, or coordinator of special projects). But the real value they add lies in their ability to offer divergent viewpoints.

Besides the ability to "think different," it's important to have the CEO's ear. As such, not all of these mavericks are eccentrics. One executive, who has turned around several struggling companies, brings a small cadre of advisors with him in all his adventures. He trusts this core group of faithful followers not only for their brainpower and creativity but also for their absolute loyalty. "The risk for me," he says, "is to think I'm all-powerful and not listen to anybody. Since I come into companies where I don't know anyone and everybody thinks the same way, I need to bring independent people with me. Only they will tell me when I'm wrong."

Additionally, many business leaders ensure access to divergent viewpoints by maintaining informal networks of contacts inside their organization. They establish or maintain connections with people in the company hierarchy to whom they would not normally be exposed, and use them as an unfiltered sounding board on important decisions. One executive who spent twenty years working the way to the top of his company took great care to maintain a friendly network of those who were his peers at each step of his career. These men and women know they can still speak to him frankly now, despite the fact that he is the CEO.

Technique #16: Get Unfiltered Expert Opinion

In-house divergence only goes so far: often, if you want different viewpoints, you need to seek them outside the organization. The most obvious way to do this is to look for outside experts. The challenge here is that outside expertise often provides more convergence, not divergence.

Consider the example of an acquisition that involves a complex tax issue. The tax attorney who is consulted will naturally study the issue in detail, highlight the risks that the acquiring company runs, and calculate the potential costs if these risks materialize. Her mission is to draw attention to the risks, not to judge whether or not these risks are justified. Plus, she needs to protect her reputation by making sure that no one can blame her for anything that may happen later. The people she interacts with are the tax experts inside the legal or finance department: they, too, share a risk-averse perspective. When, after many detours, this expert opinion finally ends up on the CEO's desk, it is nothing more than one supporting point in an overall recommendation.

One of the CEOs interviewed for this book has an interesting way to proceed in this kind of situation. His approach is to eliminate the hierarchical levels between the expert and himself and to have her talk to him in person. This way, he can sound out her opinion on a deeper level. In essence, he tells her: "I read your report, and I understand that you're supposed to warn me about the risk. But my job is to decide whether this risk is worth taking. Just between us, off the record, I'd like to know: if it was your money, would you take this risk?"

Not all experts are willing to answer the question, of course. But those who try must adopt a different viewpoint—and often a divergent one. They abandon the viewpoint of an expert listing all the dangers and take on that of a leader taking calculated risks. In addition, an expert's true opinion is often revealed to be slightly different from what it had appeared to be in writing. Not surprisingly, it is not always as perfectly aligned as it seemed to be with the viewpoint of the insiders interacting with the expert.

Technique #17: Keep Your Consultants in the Dark

In addition to experts who address focused, technical issues, outside consultants can bring a different viewpoint on an entire project. They can thus be an invaluable source of divergent insights. (Admittedly, as someone who was a strategy consultant for many years, perhaps I do not escape my own biases in making this observation.)

Like insiders and experts, however, consultants can sometimes contribute to convergence and groupthink instead of divergence. To mitigate this risk, it helps to select independent consultants whose compensation structure does not affect their judgment: if people are paid to make a transaction happen or to implement an information system, you can hardly expect them to deliver unbiased advice about whether the deal is justified or what technology to choose.

In addition to this seemingly obvious (yet often ignored) principle, another idea can help you make the most of your consultants: keep them in the dark. Or, more precisely, formulate the questions you ask them in such a way that you don't influence their recommendations.

One CEO's approach to acquisitions illustrates this counterintuitive principle. In general, companies bring in consultants to perform due diligence on a specific acquisition target—to check, for instance, that the company they are considering acquiring is in good shape strategically and will be easy to combine with the acquirer. This CEO, however, is aware that his own belief in the project will influence his advisors, however hard they may try to remain independent. So instead of asking the consultants to analyze the company he has in mind, he asks them for a broad perspective on the industry and a general view of strategic options for his company. This unconventional approach, of course, takes longer and costs more. It makes the consultants quite uncomfortable: instead of answering a closed question, they have to consider a wide range of possibilities. But the CEO will know that, if their recommendation supports his hypothesis, it is as free of bias as possible. And when, on the contrary, the consultants give different advice, this divergent opinion is of great value to their client.

Technique #18: Appoint Outside Challengers

Another source of divergent views also has its proponents: outside challengers. A large pharmaceutical company has made this an integral part of its strategic planning process. When considering the two or three most important issues of the year, the company asks an "outside challenger" to perform a critical analysis of a division's plan on the issue in question and to present it to the management team.

The value of the method depends heavily on the expertise of the challengers, and whether the company has been able to tap them from a variety of places. Physicians who are regarded as key opinion leaders can provide perspective on the evolution of their specialty or some therapeutic area. A retired executive of the company can advise on a sensitive organizational change. The head of a start-up in which the company has invested can bring a fresh view from the technological frontiers of the industry. Challengers are compensated for their work, as a board member would be, but they generally don't accept the assignment for the money (and in fact often redirect it to a charity of their choice). They do it for the intellectual challenge on a topic of interest to them, and for the chance to present their conclusions to the top team of a global industry leader.

As a result of the challenge process, the strategic plan of the division under review is usually amended on some points to integrate the challenger's suggestions. On other points, the management team and the challenger simply agree to disagree: this gives the top team a chance to hear two different viewpoints on the same issue.

Technique #19: Organize a Red Team or a War Game

An even more radical approach to creating divergence is to mandate it. Instead of seeking out a second opinion and finding out whether it diverges from the first, you can direct a team to intentionally prepare an opposite assessment. If you call the team submitting the first proposal a "blue team," this means that a "red team" is tasked with defending the opposite point of view.

The red team, in essence, is a devil's advocate on steroids: rather than relying on the critical thinking skills and rhetorical talent of one individual, it has access to independent fact-finding and analysis. The benefit of this method is that the final decision maker can come up with her own opinion after hearing two equally well-researched viewpoints. She is in the situation of a judge who has heard both the defense attorney and the prosecutor, each one conducting the best research and constructing the best argument they can muster.

This duplication is not free. Assigning two teams to every routine assessment would not be economically sensible. Moreover, orchestrating confrontation between the "blue" and "red" teams inevitably gives rise to tensions. For these reasons, the red team approach can only be justified for high-stakes decisions. It's not surprising that it originated in the military and in intelligence agencies, where a misinterpretation of evidence can have tragic consequences.

A variation on the same technique, in which the role of the red team is to anticipate the reaction of the adversary, is called *war gaming*. Some companies use war games to anticipate the reactions of their competitors—and thus overcome the trap of competitor neglect discussed in chapter 4 and illustrated by Procter & Gamble's ill-fated offensive against Clorox.

Another use of red teams is to offset the effects of interest biases. Warren Buffett recommends a variation of this method for studying acquisition proposals, especially if a stock swap is involved (making the evaluation more complex). According to the Oracle of Omaha, "When directors are hearing from an advisor [that is, an investment bank], it appears to me that there is only one way to get a rational and balanced discussion. Directors should hire a second advisor to make the case *against* the proposed acquisition, with its fee contingent on the deal *not* going through."

Buffett sums up his point in his typical style: "Don't ask the barber whether you need a haircut." What he advises is more interesting: if you want to know whether you need a haircut, ask two barbers—and tell them what answer you want!

Technique #20: Tap the Wisdom of the Crowd

Last but not least, there is a way to seek out different viewpoints that too few companies use: consulting their people. Back in 1907, statistician Francis Galton demonstrated the paradoxical phenomenon of the "wisdom of crowds." He found that the average estimate of a group was more accurate than that of the vast majority of individuals within that group: when individuals do not share a particular bias, and their mistakes are therefore not correlated, they cancel each other out. The vox populi can therefore be remarkably lucid.

A simple average of estimates from a relevant "crowd" usually provides a good estimate. Many techniques offer further refinements of this idea, by selecting the "right" crowd or combining forecasts in more sophisticated ways. One technique is to set up a *prediction market.* Instead of making simple estimates, participants in a prediction market trade contracts that depend on the value of future events. Suppose, for instance, that you are wondering whether a competitor will start building new production capacity. Your prediction market could enable trades in a contract that pays one dollar if the competitor announces a capacity addition by a certain date, and zero if the competitor does not. At any time, the equilibrium price in the market will reflect the aggregated belief in the probability of that future event. When the contract trades at 70 cents, for instance, this means that traders in the market collectively believe there is a 70 percent chance the competitor will move. As new information becomes available, traders will take it into consideration: if your competitor announces disappointing quarterly results, participants who think this makes capacity additions less likely will sell the contract, driving its price down. The new equilibrium price will thus reflect a new aggregate probability, weighted by the amounts the traders are betting.

Some companies use wisdom-of-crowds approaches to obtain reliable forecasts when getting ready to launch a product. Unsurprisingly, salespeople are in the best position to produce sales forecasts, and the aggregation of their estimates can be a very reliable indicator.

The main downside of wisdom-of-crowds approaches—and the main reason they are not used more broadly, despite being widely known and highly effective—is the transparency they create. A forecast created by aggregating the individual forecasts of salespeople, and visible to all of them, is likely to become a self-fulfilling prophecy. This is good news if the forecast is optimistic, as it will certainly boost morale. It is also probably a good thing if the forecast is frankly pessimistic: after all, if your salespeople overwhelmingly think the new product is a dud, you should know—and perhaps reconsider the launch. But what if the forecast is merely tepid? Once a half-convinced salesperson realizes that he's not alone in doubting the new product's appeal, won't he be further demotivated? If you fear this might doom a launch that still had a decent chance of moderate success, it may be a risk you don't want to take.

Leveraging the wisdom of the crowds is less risky when the aim is not yet to make a decision but to generate and evaluate ideas. This is the case, for instance, in the early stages of a strategic plan, a corporate transformation, or an effort to stimulate innovation. Tapping the brains of thousands of employees used to be impractical, but technology is getting more effective every year at processing massive numbers of qualitative contributions. This has the potential to become the primary way of collecting divergent opinions on the ground.

USING BIASES AGAINST BIASES

Among other ways of bringing out divergent points of view, three methods stand out as particularly effective when it comes to counteracting some of the most resistant biases. Their common feature is that they fight fire with fire, turning the power of a bias against itself.

Technique #21: Fight Anchoring with Re-anchoring

We saw in chapter 5 how hard it is to defeat resource inertia, which arises in large part from anchoring on past numbers, and discourages companies from reallocating resources as dramatically as they should. The power of anchoring comes from the fact that it happens unconsciously, so we can hardly resist its pull. To fight the pull of an anchor, we need a different anchor, one that will pull us in the opposite direction. This is *re-anchoring*.

Large companies that have adopted re-anchoring methods as part of their budgeting process use multiple variations of the technique, but the principle is always the same. Re-anchoring requires, first, a simplified model of what budget allocation would look like if it was done "mechanically." The model is typically based on a small number of criteria used to evaluate the strategic appeal of each unit: market size, growth, profitability, and so forth. But one input it does *not* consider is the amount of resources allocated to the unit in the past. Using these relevant (if not sufficient) inputs, the model proposes a "clean-sheet" allocation of resources—that is, one that ignores the previous years' figures.

Obviously, this simplified model cannot be used to determine the real resource allocation. But it changes the terms of the discussion. If last year's marketing budget was $100, the discussion of next year's budget would ordinarily revolve around this figure— between $90 and $110, perhaps. But, look, the model suggests a budget of $43! Of course, no one proposes actually using this figure. Perhaps there are excellent reasons for keeping the budget at $100, or even for increasing it. But what are these reasons? We now have to ask ourselves this question, which otherwise wouldn't have been raised. Now that the debate is "anchored" by two numbers instead of just one, it has a very different tone.

In principle, the allocations proposed by the model should not *all* be radically different from historical numbers. Assuming that historical numbers were relatively consistent with the overall strategy, that this strategy is reflected in the criteria used by the model, and that the model is correctly calibrated, the model and the history should produce broadly consistent numbers in most cases. There's not much point in spending hours discussing the numbers: the discussion is likely to produce small changes only. It's better to spend more time on the units for which previous budgets and model estimates diverge radically. Focusing management time on those units whose budgets are in real need of in-depth examination is a secondary benefit of re-anchoring.

Technique #22: Fight Confirmation Bias with Multiple Analogies

Just as anchoring can be fought with re-anchoring, confirmation bias, which leads us to embrace misleading analogies without realizing it, can be tamed by *multiple analogies*. This practice involves seeking out analogies that provide an alternative, or counterweight, to the first comparison that pops into our minds, which is usually based on personal experience or highly memorable situations.

Coming up with multiple analogies is not as difficult as it seems. For instance, during the Iraq war, Kalev Sepp, a strategic analyst with the American army command, soon realized that an analogy with the Vietnam War served as the main mental model for all the officers stationed there. Vietnam is an interesting analogy, thought Sepp, but aren't there any others that might be just as relevant? Are there other examples of counterinsurgency situations from which U.S. forces could draw lessons about what works and what doesn't? In a few days, he drew up a list of two dozen analogies, each at least as relevant as Vietnam. Using multiple analogies opens the mind and forces us to resist the pull of the dominant analogy that first pops into our heads.

Technique #23: Fight the Status Quo by Changing the Default

Just as anchoring blocks the reallocation of resources, status quo bias blocks companies from questioning their choices—leading them, for instance, to hold on to businesses they should sell. Here again, it's possible to fight fire with fire. To do this, challenging the status quo must become the default choice instead of being the one that requires special effort. You can create a routine to challenge the routine.

A large diversified corporation has adopted this principle: it systematically submits all its business units to a regular portfolio review (annually or every two years). The review asks a simple question: if we didn't own this company, would we buy it today? This is quite different from the traditional strategy review, in which corporate executives review the business unit's performance, challenge its management, and try to identify growth potential. Such reviews operate on the unstated premise that the unit rightly belongs in the corporation's portfolio. The portfolio review shifts the burden of proof to the unit: it must propose plans that create enough value to justify its continued presence in the corporation. If it cannot, the question of disposal is immediately raised.

Another company applies this principle in its HR processes. Its CEO describes talent reviews as "rehiring" senior managers and executives every year. The core question the reviews aim to answer is: if this person did not work for us, given the performance we observe and the growth potential we estimate, would we hire her today?

Of course, these examples are special cases. Not all companies can, or should, follow the purely financial logic that inspires the diversified group to conduct portfolio reviews. Even fewer would accept the radical HR philosophy that the second example illustrates. But the same principle applies wherever the status quo must be challenged: routines must be in place to make challenge the default option.

GETTING THE FACTS RIGHT

Divergence is indispensable, but a time comes to choose, to converge again. Once you've heard multiple perspectives, encouraged outside challenge, and generally achieved divergence, how are you supposed to decide which viewpoint is right?

The choice, of course, must be grounded in facts. As Senator Daniel Patrick Moynihan famously said, "Everyone is entitled to his own opinion, but not to his own facts." How to find the right facts and interpret them correctly is a vast subject that goes well beyond the scope of this book, but five relatively simple routines can help. All of them help fight biases and are generally underused by decision makers.

Technique #24: Use a Standardized Framework

The first routine is based on the same principle as the checklist: establish a framework that lists the criteria to consider whenever a decision must be made. Codifying standardized decision-making frameworks and sticking to them is an effective way to bring discussions back to the relevant fundamentals after all the necessary divergence has taken place.

This idea often seems shocking at first glance, especially if the decision under consideration is an important one. We tend to think that our decisions are unique and can't be reduced to a framework or checklist of predetermined criteria. Atul Gawande insightfully observed that making and following checklists "somehow feels beneath us....It runs counter to deeply held beliefs about how the truly great among us...handle situations of high stakes and complexity."

But using frameworks does not mean turning a complex decision into a check-the-box routine. It simply recognizes that many decisions, although they may seem unique to those making them, belong to known categories, and that each category can be associated with a decision-making framework. It should be easy for a pharmaceutical company to define the hurdles an R&D project must meet to proceed from one development phase to another. A venture capital fund knows the key questions that any investment proposal must address.

When they are written down and shared, such decision-making frameworks become the basis for discussion and decision. Of course, a leader can always decide to set the framework aside: some decisions really are exceptional. But even in those cases, the mere existence of the framework offers a benefit by forcing a discussion about why, exactly, a certain decision is like no other.

Rather than formalizing their frameworks as checklists, many companies embed them into mandated presentation formats that cover the criteria associated with each type of repetitive decision.

For instance, one CEO has refined, down to the smallest detail, standardized investment proposal templates. This is his way of limiting one kind of risk—the risk that the person proposing the project has cherry-picked arguments supporting his storytelling while ignoring or downplaying less appealing aspects of his proposal.

Some worry that the definition of frameworks, the formalization of decision rules, and the imposition of templates have negative effects. They fear that implementing these tools will sterilize discussion, eliminate the possibility of original arguments, and ultimately abolish risk-taking. This is a valid concern: in some companies, frameworks and checklists are indeed used as substitutes for managerial decision-making, not as aids to it. Some bureaucratic organizations view them as a way to smother debate and make any kind of managerial courage unnecessary. If your company's practice is to use decision meetings merely to rubber-stamp proposals, fine-tuning the frameworks is not going to change that.

But the effect of a well-defined framework is just the opposite when it is used in combination with other techniques described here, in a company that values real dialogue and the expression of divergent ideas. As the CEO mentioned above (and many others) discovered, a common framework does not hinder dialogue: it enables it. Adhering to the template prevents project leaders from presenting facts selectively to minimize risks or otherwise distort reality. It also means that the basic data can be absorbed more quickly in the decision meeting, which frees up time for debate. Participants are then free to take the necessary step back, express their points of view, and engage in genuine dialogue about them— a dialogue that will be fruitful precisely because they all agree on the same set of facts. In the end, the CEO does make risky decisions, but he makes them because the level of risk the project entails is justified, not because it has been hidden from him.

Technique #25: Define the Decision-Making Criteria in Advance

Predefined frameworks and templates can only be used for re-petitive decisions. Unique, once-in-a-lifetime choices, such as a major restructuring or a huge merger, do not lend themselves to a predefined checklist. Yet they can benefit from applying the same logic. In these decisions as in repetitive ones, the danger that must be avoided is the storytelling trap, grounded in an excessive reliance on intuition and in confirmation bias. As we've seen, the power of a good story may lead the decision maker to give undue weight to certain considerations and to neglect others. But a remedy exists, even if it's not easy to put into effect: you can explicitly define the criteria for making the decision *far in advance* of the final decision.

The deputy CEO of a family-owned company saw the power of this approach in a decision his chairman made. The deputy was about to ink the deal on an important overseas acquisition after protracted negotiations between the management teams of the two companies. To everyone's surprise, the chairman vetoed the agreement at the last minute. From the beginning, he had drawn up a list of decision-making criteria, including the following: "Am I confident that our team and the management of the target company will be able to work hand in hand to make the deal a success?" The chairman had purposely refrained from telling his deputy that he would make up his mind on this decisive issue by observing the interactions between the two management teams during the negotiation phase. You can imagine the deputy CEO's surprise and frustration at the chairman's eleventh-hour decision, and at the justification he offered, which he seemed to have pulled out of his hat. Yet in hindsight, as he reflected on the tense inter- actions he had had with the target company's management, the deputy CEO acknowledged that the chairman's decision was wise, and that integrating the two companies would have been much more difficult than anticipated. Only by referring to his predefined criteria was the chairman able to keep the necessary distance from the dynamics of the negotiation.

Technique #26: "Stress-Test" Your Assumptions

Regardless of the framework and criteria you use, your decision probably relies on some quantitative analysis. The quality and depth of this analysis are, of course, critical. Most companies use the same analytical tools, but their level of sophistication in using them varies greatly. The best ones spend time exploring and "stress-testing" the assumptions that underpin their calculations, and not just when the proposals are prepared but in the decision- making committee itself.

For instance, a common practice when considering investment proposals is to develop multiple scenarios, including a "worst-case" scenario. This makes sense, of course, as a way to stress-test a plan. But it can also backfire by providing an illusory sense of comfort. That happens when—as is too often the case—the "worst case" is not the worst case at all but a slight downgrade of the base case. Stress-testing the assumptions behind your plans should not just mean tweaking the most obvious variables. It should include a thor- ough challenge of assumptions the base case takes for granted.

One CEO tells of buying a troubled company in a rapidly declining market in hopes of salvaging some of its assets. Knowing it was a risky gamble, he had developed a series of scenarios, all of them rather pessimistic. His worst-case scenario anticipated a 40 percent drop in the target company's revenues in the year following the acquisition: conservative enough, you might think. Yet the factor that turned out to be decisive was one he had not included in his model: how much time it would take to get a green light for the transaction from the antitrust authorities. This turned out to take much longer than the CEO had—implicitly—expected. Given that revenue was falling just as quickly as the worst-case scenario anticipated, a six-month delay meant another 20 percent drop in revenues. The deal ended up producing heavy losses.

Technique #27: Take the Outside View by Finding a Reference Class

We saw in chapter 4 the danger of the planning fallacy, and more broadly the tendency to produce exaggeratedly optimistic forecasts. The principle that can combat this bias is the *outside view*, described by Daniel Kahneman in *Thinking, Fast and Slow*. Its practical application to a forecasting problem is known as *reference class forecasting*.

To illustrate it, let's first consider how a project's time frame and budget are typically planned. If you are in charge, you will plan for all the project's phases and costs, add them up, and, of course, include an additional safety margin. This is the *inside view*: it starts with your project and what you know about it. If, for instance, you are in charge of organizing the Paris 2024 Olympic Games, you will be confident that you have budgets under control: as the French minister for sports explained in 2016, "There is no reason why the costs should balloon."

Now, consider what an outside view would tell you. Taking an outside view means regarding this project as one among many similar cases. The set of comparable projects, called the *reference class*, provides statistical information about the time frame and budget that similar projects required. In the example of the Paris 2024 Olympics, the most natural reference class is, of course, previous Olympic Games. Bent Flyvbjerg and his colleague Allison Stewart at Oxford University compiled data about Olympic Games from 1960 to 2012 and found that *all* went over budget. The average percentage overrun was, in nominal terms, 324 percent (or "only" 179 percent when adjusted for inflation). Knowing this, if you had to place a bet on whether the Paris 2024 Olympics will remain within their initial budget, what would you say?

The disparities between the inside and outside views are not always so striking, but the outside view generally turns out to be more reliable than the inside view. Paradoxically, the estimate is better when the specific characteristics of the focal project are ignored. Less information results in better accuracy, because confirmation bias and excessive optimism are kept at bay. In the UK, the Treasury and Department of Transport have included reference class forecasting in the required forecasting methodology used for all large infrastructure projects.

Technique #28: Update Your Beliefs as New Data Becomes Available

John Maynard Keynes was frequently criticized for changing his opinion. In one such instance, he is said to have replied: "When the facts change, I change my mind. What do you do, sir?"

This sums up a fundamental problem: in the decision-making process, we all discover new facts along the way. We have to take them into consideration, of course—but to what degree? When is new information important enough to make us reconsider our position? No one wants to flip-flop with every new piece of data, but it's not good to be stubborn as a mule, either.

Fortunately, there is a tool to guide our judgment in this area: Bayes's theorem of conditional probability. Provided we agree to express our judgment quantitatively—that is, as a probability— Bayes's theorem tells us exactly how much we should revise that probability in light of new facts. Without presenting it here in its algebraic form, we can illustrate its application to the simple example we introduced in chapter 8: an investment committee that tries to avoid the traps of groupthink and information cascades while making a decision about a prospective investment.

Suppose that you sit on this committee, and after careful consideration of the investment opportunity being discussed, you have concluded that it is not attractive. However, the first one of your committee colleagues who speaks up has arrived at the opposite conclusion: she supports the investment. Should you change your mind?

Intuition suggests that the answer depends on two factors. First of all, what is the strength of your original conviction, the *prior probability* that you are right? If you were 99 percent sure that it was a bad investment, you will be less likely to change your mind than if you were only 60 percent sure. Second, what is your colleague's credibility? Naturally, the quality of her judgment (as estimated by you) also influences your propensity to change your mind. If you think her judgment is generally unreliable, you will stick to your guns; but if you consider her practically infallible, you will be much more likely to change your mind and join her.*

Bayes's theorem lets the decision maker quantify these intuitions by calculating a *posterior probability*. Posterior probability is the adjusted level of confidence you will have in your answer after taking new information into consideration and weighing it appropriately. In our example, let's suppose that your original degree of confidence in your judgment was quite high: you think there is only a 33 percent chance that the investment will turn out to be profitable. But let's also suppose that you have a lot of respect for your colleague: in your estimation, her judgment is correct 80 percent of the time. Bayes's theorem suggests that you should radically change your opinion: if you run the numbers, you will find that the posterior probability that the investment is attractive is 67 percent. In other words, on the basis of the new information you are taking into account, your estimate of the probability that the investment is a good one has gone up from one in three to two in three. If this level of confidence is sufficient for you to invest, you should change your mind.

The value of quantifying your guesses and using Bayes's theorem is that you can find out how different these numbers would need to be for you to change your mind. In this example, if you

---

* More specifically, you need to consider the likelihood that she will be mistaken in one direction or the other. For example, if you consider your colleague to be very cautious, you might then expect that it would be highly unusual for her to recommend a bad investment—but not unusual for her to miss out on a good one. In other words, you must estimate the frequency of her "false positives" and "false negatives," respectively. In this example, we make the simplifying assumption that her reliability is the same in both directions.

believe your colleague is correct "only" 70 percent of the time, the posterior probability that the investment is attractive will only be around 50 percent. This is more than your initial level of 33 percent, but perhaps still not enough for you to support the investment. The strength of your initial belief also counts a lot: for example, if your prior probability estimate that the deal is good was 20 percent (instead of 33 percent), your colleague's opinion, assuming it is 80 percent reliable, would still only take you to a 50 percent posterior probability. These are the two key parameters when updating your beliefs: the value that you should give to new information depends partly on your confidence in your prior judgment, and partly on the diagnostic value of the new information.

Needless to say, expressing beliefs as probabilities is useful, but it remains a simplification. In a case such as this one, it would be good to quantify beliefs, but it would be even better to use some of the dialogue techniques described in the previous chapter to get to the bottom of your disagreement! Your colleague's viewpoint may seem a lot more persuasive to you, for instance, if it is based on facts you had neglected rather than merely on a different interpretation of the same data.

Nevertheless, learning to update your beliefs by using Bayes's theorem can be very valuable in situations of great uncertainty. Nate Silver, in *The Signal and the Noise*, describes in detail many practical applications of the theorem (and provides a valuable how-to guide for those who want to use the formula). Additional evidence comes from Philip Tetlock, the psychologist whose work on political expertise was mentioned in chapter 3. Tetlock and his colleagues have been conducting a multiyear project to improve the accuracy of the political and military forecasts produced by

American intelligence agencies. In particular, they have identified "superforecasters," amateurs whose forecasts are more reliable than those of professional analysts. One of several distinguishing characteristics of superforecasters is their willingness to update their beliefs in response to new information—and their ability to do so in Bayesian fashion, avoiding both overreaction and under-reaction.

CULTIVATING HUMILITY

A final ingredient is essential for both tolerating divergent views and preventing them from taking us too far: a healthy dose of humility in the face of tough decisions. Practicing humility is easier said than done, of course. But instead of thinking of humility as a permanent trait of virtuous individuals, we can try to cultivate it.

An amusing example of this principle comes from Bessemer Venture Partners, one of the oldest American venture capital firms. Its website features an "anti-portfolio" listing all the deals that the company could have made but passed on. There are some great investments on this list. Apple? A Bessemer executive thought it was "outrageously expensive." eBay? "Stamps? Coins? Comic books? You've *got* to be kidding....No-brainer pass." PayPal, Intel, and Google are also on the list. This exercise—which has since been copied by other funds—may look like public self-flagellation, but it serves as a reminder that investment decisions are complex and difficult.

In addition, it's a reminder that the direction of error matters. In many fields, it is much more important to avoid errors of commission than errors of omission: for an airline pilot or a bridge engineer, "better safe than sorry" is an excellent rule of thumb. But venture capital is the opposite: nothing is worse than being overly cautious. As another venture capitalist interviewed for this book observes, "When you invest one dollar and you're wrong, you lose one dollar. But when you pass on an investment whose value is multiplied by one hundred, you lose ninety-nine times more." This is why Bessemer's list emphasizes the false negatives but not the false positives, the investments it did make and that turned out poorly. The "anti-portfolio" does not just cultivate abstract humility but focuses everyone on the sort of humility that matters. It's up to you to know which sort of humility matters most in your own field, and to find the right technique to cultivate it.

To make good decisions, it's not enough to eliminate our mistakes—we also need to have good ideas, and to choose wisely between them. This is what makes divergence an indispensable component of a sound decision architecture.

DIVERGENCE IN THIRTY SECONDS

- **Divergence** means **seeing the facts from a different angle** to limit biases, especially pattern-recognition biases.
- Certain **contrarian personalities** do this naturally...but rarely survive for very long inside large organizations.
  - ▶ *Michael Burry saw the subprime crisis coming, while most people in big banks did not.*
- **Divergent, challenging viewpoints** can come from multiple sources:
  - ▶ *From the outside: informal networks, experts, consultants, and challengers—if used the right way.*
  - ▶ *From the inside: "red teams" or war games when confrontation is acceptable; crowd wisdom when collective opinion is relevant.*
- We can also generate divergent ideas by using **one bias to fight another.**
  - ▶ *Re-anchoring vs. anchoring—budget discussions.*
  - ▶ *Multiple analogies vs. confirmation bias—Iraq is not comparable just to Vietnam.*
  - ▶ *Changed defaults vs. status quo bias—systematic portfolio reviews.*
- Deciding between divergent ideas requires **high-quality, fact-based analysis:**
  - ▶ *Standardized frameworks for repetitive decisions; predefined decision criteria for unique ones.*
  - ▶ *Stress-test assumptions; take the outside view with a relevant "reference class," and update your beliefs as new data becomes available.*
- In all cases, it is good to **cultivate humility** when dealing with divergent viewpoints.
  - ▶ *Bessemer Venture Partners' "anti-portfolio" of great investments they passed up.*

16

DYNAMICS

Changing Your Decision-Making Processes and Culture

If at first you don't succeed, try, try again. Then quit.
There's no point in being a damn fool about it.
—attributed to W. C. Fields

It is quite likely that you found at least some of the ideas listed above about creating dialogue and divergence ill-suited to your own professional environment. Perhaps, as you read some of these suggestions, you thought, *This would never work in our culture.* Or: *It looks like an interesting idea, but I don't know where this would fit in our existing decision processes.* Indeed, dialogue and divergence will remain pipe dreams if the processes and culture of your organization block them.

You cannot improve your decision-making if you do not take into account your decision processes, the hierarchies, committees, and calendars that answer the practical question: *Who* decides *what when?* For instance, your company certainly has processes for coming up with marketing plans, drawing up budgets, and approving investments. If these processes bring divergent viewpoints back onto the "straight and narrow" of a single way of thinking, and if they crush dialogue instead of stimulating it, the quality of your decision-making will suffer.

Similarly, an organization's culture (also called its *core values, guiding principles,* or *shared beliefs*) is critical, because—among other things—it answers the question: *What matters* when we make decisions? It is a truism that corporate culture can get in the way of sound decision-making. For example, we saw how difficult Polaroid's culture made it for the company to perceive the urgency of technological change.

This is why decision architecture relies on a third pillar, without which the first two will soon collapse: the *dynamics* of decision-making, which concerns an organization's decision processes and decision culture.

There is, of course, no silver bullet that will magically change an organization's culture, and this is true of an organization's decision-making culture, too. But big corporations and government organizations can draw inspiration from the decision-making methods and styles of small companies and entrepreneurs, for whom agility in decision-making is a condition of survival.

INFORMALITY AND FORMALISM

To any observer of the way large organizations make decisions, one thing is striking: decision meetings are often formal, solemn affairs. Stiffness, tension, and even fear are often the dominant emotions. Naturally, this atmosphere is not conducive to establishing open dialogue—even less so to the expression of divergent opinions. Why does it have to be this way?

Technique #29: Cultivate a Friendly Atmosphere

Sometimes a solution is so simple it seems obvious. Many smaller organizations and some large ones value good personal relations between members of the management team. One serial entrepreneur goes as far as making it a rule: "In all my companies, I've always brought in friends, including very close ones. People often say I'm crazy. But it's priceless to know that I can count on them not playing politics, because we've known each other for years."

This may be extreme, and if you are in a leadership position, hiring your friends has obvious downsides, too. But on a management team or a board of directors, it is often wise to foster an environment of friendly discussion. As one board chairman relates: "I try to create the atmosphere of a bunch of friends talking together. It might sound strange to say it that way, but it's very important to create this feeling. There can't be any freedom of speech in a group where people hate each other." Even small details can contribute to this. The executive who put together the group of "Six Amigos," described in the previous chapter, points out that "even the fact that we call it 'Six Amigos' instead of 'the committee for X' contributes to creating an informal atmosphere." However you decide to pursue this goal, the underlying reason is the same: it's hard to make dialogue happen unless the participants feel comfortable together.

The suggestion of an informal, even casual atmosphere may seem at odds with the precise ground rules for dialogue that we discussed earlier. But there is no real contradiction. On the contrary, it is the informality that makes the regulations bearable. It's much easier to ban "storytelling arguments" or to enforce "alternative stories" if you feel confident, relaxed, and surrounded by friendly faces. Conversely, imagine that an authoritarian boss, in a tense atmosphere, forbids you from using certain comparisons, or orders you to defend a point of view that is the opposite of the one you just expressed. Would you be able to play along in good faith? A friendly and informal atmosphere is not the enemy of organized dialogue: it is an enabler of it.

Technique #30: Foster a "Speak Up" Culture

Another problem that bedevils large companies more than small ones is that people do not speak up. This is not limited to the self-silencing behavior in meetings that we have discussed with regard to groupthink: in many organizations, people are reluctant to freely express not only their disagreements, doubts, and concerns but also their ideas and suggestions. Of course, executives always say that they want to encourage their employees to speak up. But speaking up is harder than it looks.

The head of a large European company says his technique for encouraging a culture of speaking up is "rewarding and promoting people who have the guts to disagree. Not only do you have people who speak up, but the others can see that political operators have no future." Another business leader took the helm at a company where he found the culture too deferential. He didn't hesitate to hire the services of a professional coach for some of his executives. He told them, "I want you to work with your coach on learning to tell me to my face, 'You made a mistake.' Politely, of course, but clearly and quickly."

These two leaders share the same conviction, which a third executive expresses in his own way: "I hope I'm right more often than not. But I can make mistakes, and I do. It's essential for my teams to tell me so." Speaking up is key. Making it happen takes effort.

Technique #31: Align the Incentives with the Common Interest

Of course, it would be naive to expect a friendly atmosphere and some encouragement from the top to produce divergent viewpoints if incentive systems go against these objectives. As one of the executives quoted above explains: "It's the mother of all solutions. If you haven't established a compensation system where people work in the interest of the group, they will just optimize their personal bonus." Cass Sunstein and Reid Hastie, in their book *Wiser*, also count "rewarding group success" as one of the key ways to make groups more effective. How to design motivation systems that balance individual and collective rewards is beyond the scope of this book, but the issue cannot be ignored.

Taken together, these suggestions make up a simple and rather appealing picture: a "group of friends" who aren't afraid to speak openly to each other, especially since their interests are perfectly aligned. Who wouldn't prefer this environment to the uptight, tense atmosphere of many management committees?

RISK-TAKING AND CAUTION

We saw in chapter 6 that large companies often do not take enough risks, and that their leaders often urge their executives to "be more entrepreneurial." While the model of entrepreneurship is inspiring, the lesson taken from it should be qualified. Ask entrepreneurs how they think about risk, and they will state the obvious: precisely because they are running their own business, they take as few risks as possible, and always calculate them carefully. Clichés notwithstanding, much research suggests that entrepreneurs are not gamblers: they do not have an irrational or unhealthy appetite for risk.

What distinguishes entrepreneurs from managers of large businesses is not so much the amount of risk they take as their agility in managing it. This agility is manifest in at least five techniques that large companies can take inspiration from.

Technique #32: Find Ways to Learn for Free

The first idea is summed up by the founder and CEO of a midsize luxury goods company: "When we take a gamble on something new, we want to see if it works, but we don't want to spend money on it."

One of his strategic choices illustrates this principle. Most of his competitors, especially those owned by large luxury conglomerates, operated their own stores in addition to relying on third-party retailers. The CEO was considering adopting the same business model. But this raised many questions: Would he be able to develop the right store concept, and how much revenue would it generate? What was the maximum rent he could afford? What sorts of locations would be best? How would his current retailers respond? These questions could be analyzed on paper, and he knew how his competitors answered them, but he couldn't resolve them for his own brand until he explored the terrain.

In other words, before taking this risk, he needed to learn a new skill: managing retail points of sale. The conventional way of learning would be to open a few pilot stores to refine the strategy before deploying it on a large scale. But as a majority shareholder playing with his own money, he wanted to learn without paying for this sort of pilot. It would be too big a risk for him to commit to renting, setting up, and managing stores for several years (given the length of commercial leases) without knowing how much revenue to expect.

The CEO decided to look for partners who would be willing to share the risk with him. In one country, a landlord eager to attract a luxury brand agreed to a variable rent indexed on sales. In another country, one retailer agreed to open a shop for the brand in his own space, knowing that if it failed, he could easily reconvert it. Through these different formulas, the entrepreneur improved his new model without ever risking more than he could afford. He accepted the fact that the process would take longer than it would for a large company, but his approach also had its advantages. For instance, it would give him the opportunity to make adjustments during the process as he learned from his experiments.

Technique #33: Conduct Experiments and Allow Them to Fail

What about the approach of large companies, which, in a similar situation, open pilot stores? Isn't that a way to test and learn, too?

It is... or, rather, it should be. In truth, the interchangeability of the terms *test* and *pilot* often reveals a confusion of objectives. A test serves to refine a plan and help you decide whether to launch it or not. A pilot is intended to measure and demonstrate a plan's effectiveness so that you can rally the organization before rolling it out. This is not at all the same thing.

Let's take the example of a retail chain that is preparing to launch a new store concept to breathe life into the organization. The plan must, of course, be tried out in a few pilot stores. How does it work? First, the retailer carefully chooses the store locations, which receive additional funds and are showered with top management's full attention as they implement the new concept. Next, their results—sales, profits, customer satisfaction—are compared with those of a group of other stores (usually not defined in advance), which, during this time, have been almost totally neglected. Naturally, the results are conclusive: the new concept works! Management can now roll it out on a large scale.

Ask anyone involved in the project, and they will tell you: the company wasn't trying to test the new concept so much as it was trying to demonstrate its success. This was not about deciding but about beginning to implement a decision that's already been made. No wonder, then, that once the pilot is declared a success, the results of the rollout to the full store network are so often disappointing. It's impossible to tell if the pilot stores' success is the result of the new concept or of the special attention they received during the pilot phase. This is the "Hawthorne Effect," the business equivalent of the placebo effect: nearly a century ago, organizational psychologists discovered that almost any change they made to the environment of a factory had a temporary positive effect, simply because the workers were aware they were being observed.

It's easy to see the decision-making dynamics that lead large corporations to repeat this mistake. Naturally, the team that developed the new concept on paper wants it to succeed. Senior management is convinced it will—otherwise, they would not bother to test it. They task another team with managing the pilot in the field: this team, too, is keen to see it succeed—it doesn't want to get blamed for an experiment that "fails." Meanwhile, top management has already told its board, its shareholders, and the financial analysts how confident it is that the new store concept will revive the retail chain. It has no Plan B in case it flops. When everyone wants a test to succeed, they'll make sure it does.

Contrast this fake "test" with a true experiment. Online retailers and other digital service providers routinely use "A/B testing" to evaluate the effect of a planned change, such as a modification to their website design. To do this, they compare the results of two customer groups, A and B, who either experienced these changes or did not. These two groups are defined in advance, randomly selected, and no other actions are taken that could affect the evaluation. This is the equivalent of a randomized controlled trial in science. In the same spirit, nudge units such as the UK's Behavioural Insights Team rigorously test multiple proposals in order to quantify their impact on the behaviors they aim to modify.

If a controlled trial is impractical, another way to conduct real experiments is to adopt a mindset of continuous experimentation. For example, the retail company mentioned above could develop several different concepts and test them at the same time, allocating the same resources to each test. It wouldn't have its results as quickly, and these results would not be as easy to interpret, but at least it would create a healthy rivalry instead of a paralyzing fear of failure. Alternatively, instead of testing an overall concept, the company could test each element of a new concept and measure its effects separately. It could even develop its new concepts on an ongoing and continuous basis by integrating the lessons of previous tests.

Whatever approach is chosen, the key principle to bear in mind is simple: it's not a real experiment if it's only allowed to succeed.

A real experiment is one in which failure *is* an option, because you can learn as much from failure as from success. Entrepreneurs intuitively know this: they break down large decisions into smaller ones so they can conduct true experiments and take calculated risks. Managers, whose objective is to convince their organization to move forward, tend to forget it. They must reengineer their decision-making processes to include real experiments.

Technique #34: Do Postmortems of Successes, Too

Learning from experiments is great, but learning from real-life experience is important, too. Most companies have—at least on paper—a routine for debriefing failures and drawing lessons from them. Conducting such postmortems in the right way, so that they don't become a finger-pointing exercise or a witch hunt, is sometimes difficult. But in principle, everyone recognizes the importance of learning from failures.

A much less frequent habit is to learn from successes by debriefing them just as systematically and as rigorously. French navy commandos, like many units of the American armed forces, practice systematic mission debriefs. To facilitate candid conversations, one principle features prominently on the wall of their debriefing rooms: "nameless, rankless." As one officer notes, a key purpose of these debriefs is "to answer a question that would otherwise never be asked: Where were we lucky?" If the mission succeeded merely because of good luck, there may be a lot to learn from it—perhaps more than from some failures. And this matters: next time, luck may not be on your side.

Many businesses would do well to take this page from the military playbook: by the time they discover that their success was largely a function of good luck rather than superior talent or strategic advantage, it is often too late.

Technique #35: Increase Your Commitments Gradually

Low-cost learning, ongoing experiments...couldn't this be a way of limiting the stakes, of refusing to commit, of thinking small and playing small? Shouldn't a big company use the strategic advantage of its size and take bold risks that others can't?

Of course. But it should still do so with agility. A fourth way of being agile consists in making gradual commitments instead of big gambles. This is the way of venture capitalists, who sometimes back the same company from seed stage to unicorn valuations, increasing their financial commitment at each stage based on past achievements and future plans.

Here again, the dynamics of large organizations make this kind of approach unusual. Faced with an investment decision, the expected answer in a big company is a straight yes or no. It is rare to hear something like: "Tell me what intermediary objectives you can reach with 10 percent of this amount, and then let's see if you've done it in a month's time." Yet this would be an excellent way of making decision-making more agile.

Companies that establish this kind of gradual commitment process have to overcome obstacles related to both their processes and their culture. First, they have to engineer exceptions to the annual budget process, create a nest egg that they can gradually apply to financing these projects over the course of the fiscal year, or dedicate a separate unit to take care of these projects in the manner of an internal venture-capitalist. Second, they have to find time to do progress reviews at each stage, even though these discussions may seem small-scale in comparison to the large investments they usually review.

But the main difficulty is a cultural one. It is hard for those proposing projects at the company to accept that they will be constantly challenged. (In the same way, start-up founders must perpetually tout their company as they seek their next round of financing.) As a general rule, the firm's employees do not have the same tolerance for risk and financial expectations as entrepreneurs. As we have seen when discussing how difficult it is for corporations to divest unsuccessful businesses, it's also hard for senior executives to learn to "pull the plug" on a project if, at one stage or another of its development, it hasn't reached its objectives.

Technique #36: Recognize the Right to Fail,
Not the Right to Make Mistakes

The final condition for agility is the most important one: it's to create a real right to fail.

To be clear, the right to fail does not mean the right to make a mistake. One CEO recounts his employees' surprise when he promoted the manager of a unit that had suffered heavy losses. "It was my decision to buy this company, he accepted the challenge, and he acquitted himself as honorably as possible. The market collapsed; it was not his fault. He had nothing to be ashamed of—on the contrary."

As this example shows, the right *to fail* is a simple issue of fairness and logic: as we have seen, when we undertake risky activities, there will be failures without mistakes. The right *to make a mistake* is something very different. You may wish to forgive someone who made a bad decision and choose to give him or her a second chance . . . but maybe not a third.

The fact remains that many managers are paralyzed by the fear of failure. The retail company's "pilot" was biased because the managers in charge were afraid of being associated with a fiasco. When large corporations are reluctant to take on a portfolio of small risks, it is because the person in charge of each project dreads the prospect of having to report a failure. Loss aversion is at work. But it is quite difficult to conduct a true experiment if you don't accept the possibility of failure. You can't be agile if you're petrified.

Some executives are well aware of this problem, and know the signals they send personally are essential for fighting the fear of failure. As one CEO says, "Speeches about 'I want you to take risks' are useless. When people take risks and it backfires—that's when you send the real messages. When a manager tries something sensible and that doesn't work, that's when you walk the talk. If you go out of your way to make him feel valued, everyone will remember it."

The same CEO adds: "If we want people to believe they have a right to fail, we have to show them our own failures." During annual seminars with his managers, this executive doesn't hesitate to openly share the decisions he has made that have not produced the expected results. Basically, he is willing to reveal that he is a mere mortal, someone who endures failures. A simple idea, right? But not one you see applied every day.

VISION AND FLEXIBILITY

The CEO of a family-owned business describes his strategy in this way: "In a diversified family company like mine, many strategy decisions are opportunistic. Trying to have a predefined strategy would be very dangerous. I don't want to lose my ability to move or prevent myself from seizing opportunities in the name of a so-called strategic vision."

This refusal to formalize a strategy may seem paradoxical: if there is one thing that everyone believes a CEO should do, it's defining the company's strategy. However, many shrewd CEOs of large corporations share this view and strive to maintain flexibility in their strategic outlook.

Technique #37: Strategize Like a Texas Sharpshooter

You may have heard the joke about the Texas "sharpshooter" who shoots randomly at the barn door, then walks over to it and paints a target circle around the densest cluster of bullet holes. A sure way to score!

This story is generally used to describe a reasoning fallacy: it is an error to define the target after the results are known. But it also illustrates the value of flexibility. The CEO of a publicly traded corporation puts it this way: "When people tell me, 'Your strategy is so astute!,' I tell them: 'I hate to disappoint you, but I don't have a strategy. I just make good decisions that create value for shareholders, and they end up making a coherent whole.'"

What pitfall is he trying to avoid? "The most serious errors I've seen," he explains, "were committed by executives who had a grand design in mind, and who bought and sold whatever they needed at any price so they could have their dream as quickly as possible." In other words, these leaders start off by telling their shareholders and their management a compelling story of value creation. They lock themselves into their own storytelling, and it quickly leads them to make bad decisions.

By contrast, this executive tells the story only afterward, once it has become reality. Like the Texas sharpshooter, he draws the target after he shoots. But, of course, he doesn't shoot just anywhere. While his strategy is flexible, his company's mission of creating value for shareholders is not. Strategic flexibility is only possible because the goals and the long-term vision are crystal clear.

Technique #38: Change Your Mind, Proudly

The flexibility that these leaders show in their strategy is also visible in their everyday behavior. They're able to change their minds and are proud of it. Not because they are dictators subjecting their team to their every whim, of course. But because they set an example of flexibility.

The bank president quoted previously says: "I've gotten the members of my board accustomed to seeing me change my mind. Not arbitrarily, but on the basis of the discussion and the facts." Or, as another executive puts it: "I can say one thing in the morning, receive new input during the day, and change my mind that night."

Obviously, as this same executive is careful to add, "this is only possible with people at a certain level." When you are speaking in front of thousands of employees, you have to deliver a clear message that doesn't change every day. But that's when the time for decision-making has passed and the time for execution has arrived. When you are still in the decision-making phase, stimulating dialogue and bringing out divergent viewpoints, only a leader who is able to change her mind can encourage her colleagues to do the same.

She can even congratulate them on this flexibility. As venture capitalist Randy Komisar enthusiastically proclaims: "I think comfort with uncertainty and ambiguity is an important trait in a leader. . . . I love a leader who changes his or her opinion based upon the strength of the arguments around the table. It's great to see a leader concede that the decision's a hard one and may have to be retested."

Not getting locked into your own story, maintaining the necessary flexibility to change the narrative or tell different stories: this is a good way of fighting confirmation bias. It's also a discipline that few of us are accustomed to. Hence the importance of a leader's setting a good example by changing her mind, proudly.

TEAMWORK AND SOLITUDE

Throughout these examples, we have seen that the team is essential. But the final decision belongs to the leader alone. She needs to orchestrate dialogue, but ultimately she must accept responsibility. She has to appeal to others to fight against her individual biases, but when the time comes, she has to make a decision without knowing if biases are leading her astray.

How and when can we make this final decision? Of course, there's no single, miraculous answer to this question. But, once again, a few examples offer helpful paths to take.

Technique #39: Share the Power

One unusual but powerful way of operating is to share power. When two people (or more) share the responsibility for making important decisions, the risk of one individual's biases dominating is reduced.

One executive explains his situation: "We are two cofounders, and we complement each other extremely well, with complete trust. The fact that there are two of us deciding is the best defense against going off on an ego trip." It's also a defense against political games: "No one tries to guess our opinion in order to conform to it, because everyone knows that at the beginning of an important discussion, we never agree!" Another demonstration of the power of this approach can be found where governance dictates power-sharing—for instance, in the partnerships of professional service firms.

Technique #40: Build an Inner Circle

Power-sharing is difficult, and in most organizations may not be a realistic option. In a traditional company, one possible way to benefit from "several heads in one" is for the leader to establish a small decision-making committee, a kind of "inner circle." Many people have adopted this practice informally. Some have made it official.

One of the leaders previously quoted established a "strategic committee" alongside his regular executive committee. Surprisingly, he included only members with staff positions, and not the line management of various units. This choice violates one of the most universally acknowledged principles of strategic decision-making: make sure the people who will implement the decisions are involved in making them.

Why this unusual choice? Because when it comes to making corporate strategy decisions, this leader wants to be able to rely on people who are "neutral" about the decision and who share the same incentives. Having division heads involved in decisions that affect the fate of their units means bringing in self-interest bias, accentuating inertia in resource allocation, and opening the door to excessive optimism. Of course, these managers have been closely involved in researching the decision before the strategic committee gets involved. But when it's time to decide, the key factor should not be which division head is the most persuasive about obtaining resources or who thumps on the table the hardest.

SLEEP ON IT

In spite of everything, at the end of the day, when the meetings are over, when you have gone over the research and examined it from every angle, the decision is still yours to make. An age-old piece of advice applies here: sleep on it. This is the one thing that all the business leaders I interviewed have in common: they make their decisions in the morning.

This is true of leaders of large corporations and of small business owners. Only after a night of sleep (even if it's short) do they feel they have a clear understanding of what they need to do. One executive says that he wakes up at 5:00 a.m. to decide on any outstanding issues. Another states that "sleeping on" an important decision always provides a clear sense of what to do the next morning. Letting a night go by is a simple way to attain some distance and to avoid deciding while in the grip of emotions.

Decision-making dynamics are deeply rooted in organizations, and none of the techniques that affect them will instantly change a company. But many will amend its decision-making processes, and others will subtly modify its culture. Decision dynamics, in combination with techniques that foster dialogue and encourage divergence, have the potential to transform an organization's decision-making.

DYNAMICS IN THIRTY SECONDS

- Dialogue and divergence cannot thrive without **agile decision-making dynamics** (the organization's **processes** and **culture**). In this respect, large organizations can often **learn from smaller ones.**
- **Cultivate informality:** personal relations; a culture of speaking up; appropriate incentives.
- **Take risks with agility:**
  - ▶ *Learn for free: a luxury brand has its partners shoulder the risk.*
  - ▶ *Carry out real experiments that can fail, not "pilots" that are fake tests.*
  - ▶ *Debrief both failures and successes.*
  - ▶ *Make gradual commitments, like investors in rounds of start-up fundraising.*
  - ▶ *Recognize the right to fail (which is something other than the right to make mistakes).*
- **Combine vision and flexibility:** only tell the story once it is complete (like the Texas sharpshooter); don't hesitate to change your mind for good reasons.
- **Finally, decide: in a partnership; with a small committee; or alone, after sleeping on it.**

CONCLUSION

You're About to Make Excellent Decisions

> Progress is impossible without change; and those who cannot change their minds cannot change anything.
> —George Bernard Shaw

You know the decision-making traps you want to avoid. You understand the five families of cognitive biases that underpin them. You realize that even the best possible decisions can never guarantee success in an uncertain world, but you believe in the importance of collaboration and process to make better decisions. And you are intrigued by a few techniques that could help you orchestrate dialogue, encourage divergence, and promote agile decision dynamics. Well done! You're now ready to build your own decision architecture.

The prize is large. If every organization, whatever else it makes, is a decision factory, and if strategic decisions are those that shape the future of the organization, then improving the quality of strategic decisions should make a very large difference. Superior decision-making can become a source of competitive advantage, perhaps even *the only real source* of competitive advantage. What better way could there be to outsmart your competitors than to reliably make better decisions than them?

BETTER PEOPLE MAKE BETTER DECISIONS... AND VICE VERSA

You might object that this reasoning ignores an important driver of decision quality: the people who make them. And of course, even with the best decision architecture, mediocre managers won't make brilliant decisions! So, if you want to raise the quality of your organization's decisions, perhaps you will be tempted to conclude that hiring and promoting the best people is a shorter route to achieving that goal than designing a decision architecture.

This would be shortsighted. Organizations that have a better decision architecture do not just produce better decisions and better results. They also produce better people.

If this sounds counterintuitive, start at the beginning—when recruiters compete to attract the best talent. Ask graduates of the top business or engineering schools, and they will tell you: they want to work in companies that give them a say in decisions.

Millennials would often rather join a start-up than a Fortune 500 corporation, and many HR executives interpret this as a tectonic shift in the values and preferences of this new generation. There isn't much we can do to attract the best talent, they say, if these kids don't want to have anything to do with big business.

In reality, one of the key reasons young managers join smaller companies is the belief that their contribution will make more of a difference there. But some very large companies have managed, despite their size, to remain highly attractive to the best graduates.

In large part, they owe this advantage to a decision culture that places a premium on open dialogue, real divergence, and agile decision-making. Amazon's Leadership Principles dictate that its people "seek diverse perspectives and work to disconfirm their beliefs," "are obligated to respectfully challenge decisions when they disagree," and "do not compromise for the sake of social cohesion." McKinsey consultants are expected to "uphold the obligation to dissent." At Google, core values include "we challenge each other's ideas openly" and "we value diversity in people and ideas."

Despite their size, these companies make a clear promise to their new hires: *Here, your voice will be heard. You will not call the shots on your first day, of course. But if you're right, your ideas will make a difference. You will not be a nameless cog in a bureaucratic machine.* This had better be true: in the age of Glassdoor and social networks, propaganda is short-lived. But when companies deliver on their promise, candidates get the message. Organizations with a healthy decision architecture are a magnet for talent.

What happens, then, once these managers have been hired? As we saw in chapter 14, people are more engaged when their opinion counts. When they participate in real dialogue and know their opinion is heard, they are more committed to the final decisions, even when things do not go their way. When divergent thoughts can become new products, new strategies, and new methods, people work harder to come up with innovative ideas. When decision processes are agile and make room for ongoing course correction, people take more calculated risks and are more attentive to measures of success. A sound decision architecture is a reliable way to produce the elusive commodity, anxiously monitored by HR departments everywhere, known as "employee engagement."

Finally, how do organizations decide who gets promoted and who gets the boot? Not always in the best possible way. We have all seen executives who got promoted on the basis of results that owed more to chance than to talent. (And think of Paul the Psychic Octopus.) Conversely, we all know talented, hardworking individuals who languish in middle management because they never got the big break they deserved. And business news keeps bringing us fresh examples of CEOs who, like Ron Johnson, develop a reputation for genius and infallibility, and who take bigger and bigger bets—until they suddenly crash and burn.

This hit-and-miss pattern is a direct consequence of a business culture in which "it's the result that counts." Where outcomes are the only way of assessing whether or not a decision was sound, where luck is mistaken for evidence of talent and judgment, those who make it to the top of the pyramid are not the best: they are the luckiest. An additional undesirable side effect of this way of assessing talent is that, in many companies, astute executives devote considerable energy to positioning themselves for their next assignment. Their goal: find a spot where their results are likely to be impressive. Being good matters; but being in the right place at the right time matters more.

The antidote to this problem is, once again, a sound decision architecture. Companies that evaluate decisions on their merits, not on their results, are more likely to select the best leaders. If, as discussed in chapter 13, a good decision is a decision well made—not necessarily one that produces the optimal outcome— then judgment and skill, not luck, will be rewarded.

The upshot is clear: good people, of course, are more likely to make good decisions. But a healthy decision architecture will also help you attract, engage, and promote the best people.

A NEW MODEL OF LEADERSHIP

If you choose to embark on the journey to design a decision architecture for your team or your company, there is one last thing you may need to change: yourself. Or, more accurately, your self-image and the image you project as a decision maker.

A decision maker is never just someone who makes decisions: she must also inspire others to act on those decisions. She must be a leader. However, leadership is in the eyes of those who observe it: there is no such thing as a leader without followers. This means that for someone to be a leader, *others* must believe she is one.

Since the act of decision-making is viewed—correctly—as an important component of a leader's role, the way a person decides plays a large part in projecting leadership. Therefore, if you are in a leadership position, it makes a lot of sense for you to conform to the expectations that *others* have about what "leadership" looks like. As the saying goes: "If you want to be a leader, act like one."

But what does it mean, exactly, to act like a leader? Our answer to this question is largely informed by a stereotype. As psychologist Gary Klein puts it, "Society's epitome of credibility is John Wayne, who sizes up a situation and says, 'Here's what I'm going to do'— and you follow him." This "cowboy" model of leadership has real consequences. Leaders are largely selected for their experience and business judgment, and they are expected to rely on it, at least in part, when making decisions. They are expected to convey self-assurance when making a choice; we do not want to see them hesitate as they carefully weigh the pros and cons of multiple options. And once a decision is made, a stereotypical leader must be 100 percent confident in the success of the plan: this unshakable optimism is contagious and inspires others to give their best effort.

As we have seen throughout this book, there are serious problems with this stereotype. A leader who conforms to it is likely to fall headlong into some of the worst decision-making traps: the "John Wayne" leader proudly relies on his experience and intuition. He never displays doubt or invites criticism. He suppresses dissent and encourages groupthink without even being aware of it. And he exudes overconfidence every step of the way.

You may have noted that many of the decision-making techniques offered in this book are at odds with this traditional stereotype of leadership. Recall, for instance, the idea of encouraging the expression of nuanced viewpoints, or of role-modeling a willingness to change your mind. Not exactly the fearless cowboy! And for good reason: if a leader who conforms to the stereotype is, in fact, a poor decision maker, good decision-making practices must conflict with the stereotype.

To a certain degree, this problem can be addressed by separating the decision phase from the execution phase. "Discord plus deadline," says Eric Schmidt—once the decision is made, discord is over. "Disagree and commit," state Amazon's Leadership Principles: challenge decisions, sure, but "once a decision is determined . . . commit wholly."

This is sensible on paper. But it means that the same person who carefully nurtures dialogue, welcomes divergence, and thinks probabilistically about success should suddenly, once the decision is made, become an enthusiastic cheerleader who doesn't let doubt enter his mind. Sound difficult? It is. These contradictions, these carefully crafted oxymorons, suggest that there is something fundamentally wrong in the traditional way of thinking about leadership.

If collaboration plus process is what we want, we cannot

conform to a dated stereotype of leadership. How could we be serious about collaboration if, deep down, we keep believing that a real leader is a loner who does not need any help? How would we muster any respect for process if we believe that the best decisions are made by inspired visionaries in a great flash of insight?

Instead, we must learn to associate leadership with another set of behaviors: those of the executives who genuinely value collaboration and process and who view decision architecture as a key part of their role. These leaders sincerely believe that they alone cannot possibly have all the answers. They take responsibility for the final decision, but they also orchestrate a decision process through which their team will collectively produce the best possible answer. And they know that even the best possible strategies will not always produce the desired results, but that does not diminish their passion for achieving them. This mindset is reminiscent of the combination of extreme personal humility and intense professional resolve that Jim Collins, in *Good to Great*, associates with "Level 5" leaders. Such leaders are a minority, but you may have met some.

One thing is certain: they don't look like John Wayne! To be better leaders, we must jettison the lonesome, heroic, boundlessly self-confident cowboy. We need better role models. We need leaders who have vision, courage, and a passionate group of followers—who make tough decisions and get results but who are also humble enough to rely on their team's judgment. We need leaders who have the courage and the consistency to trust the decision processes they have put in place, sometimes even when their gut suggests otherwise.

Consider Homer's Odysseus, in the episode of the Sirens. Odysseus is self-aware enough to know his own limitations: he does not assume that he will be able to resist the temptation of the Sirens' beguiling songs, which have drawn countless others to their deaths. When he asks his sailors to tie him to the mast, thus putting his own life in their hands, he shows how much faith he has in his crew. And when he instructs them to block their own ears with beeswax, he gives up the possibility of issuing them new directions: a decision architecture has been designed, and he trusts the process to produce the best possible outcome.

In the decision architecture Odysseus has designed, there is no room for his gut instincts. We do not respect him any less for it. Like him, we all want to avert the terrible mistakes triggered by our biases. If we learn to follow his example, and to forget John Wayne, we'll be well on our way to making excellent decisions.

ACKNOWLEDGMENTS

My heartfelt thanks go first and foremost to Daniel Kahneman. Danny's boundless energy, constant curiosity, exemplary scholarship, wry sense of humor, and true humility are an ongoing source of inspiration to me and to so many. Collaborating with him is a rare privilege.

I am indebted to several other thought leaders who took a chance on a newcomer to the world of academic research. Dan Lovallo was my first guide in this new world: if not for him, I would not do what I do today. Stéphanie Dameron provided much-needed guidance and encouraged me to develop and refine ideas that appeared in the first version of this book. To her go many thanks and much admiration. Collaborating with Thomas Powell, Itzhak Gilboa, and Massimo Garbuio on various research projects was a great source of inspiration. Cass Sunstein's advice and encouragement have also been invaluable.

This book relies on countless conversations with dozens of clients, friends, and partners. They all shared with me their successes, their doubts, and their decision-making tools. Although the confidentiality of our discussions prevents me from listing their names, I would like to express my deep gratitude to them. For generously sharing their time with me during my research for this book, I would also like to thank Guillaume Aubin, Xavier

Boute, Jean-François Clervoy, Gary DiCamillo, Tristan Farabet, Franck Lebouchard, Guillaume Poitrinal, Carlos Rosillo, Nicolas Rousselet, Denis Terrien, and Stéphane Treppoz.

Some of the research that led to this book was done during my years at McKinsey, and it would not have been possible without close collaboration with many colleagues there. In particular, thanks go to Michael Birshan, Renée Dye, Marja Engel, Mladen Fruk, Stephen Hall, John Horn, Bill Huyett, Conor Kehoe, Tim Koller, Devesh Mittal, Reinier Musters, Ishaan Nangia, Daniel Philbin-Bowman, Patrick Viguerie, Blair Warner, and Zane Williams. I am also grateful to Omri Benayoun, Victor Fabius, Nathalie Gonzalez, and Neil Janin for carefully reading and thoughtfully commenting on successive drafts of the manuscript.

This book would not have seen the light of day without an unusual transatlantic coalition of wonderful publishing professionals. My friends at Débats Publics prompted me to write a first version of the book in 2014. Sophie Berlin and Pauline Kipfer at Flammarion gave it a large audience. For making it possible to release the book in English, I owe an immense debt of gratitude to my agent, John Brockman. I also thank Kate Deimling for an attentive and effective translation. Finally, the amazing editorial team at Little, Brown performed the magic required to turn a manuscript into the finished product you see now. My heartfelt thanks go to Tracy Behar, Ian Straus, Pamela Marshall, and Janet Byrne for their dedication and professionalism.

APPENDIX 1:
FIVE FAMILIES OF BIASES

PATTERN-RECOGNITION BIASES

Bias	Definition	Page
Confirmation bias; story-telling	We pay more attention to facts that support our hypotheses and neglect those that would disconfirm them, particularly when our hypotheses are organized in a coherent narrative	24
Experience bias	We reason by analogy with situations from our own experience that easily come to mind	26
Champion bias	We give too much weight to the reputation of the messenger vs. the value of the information he bears	26
Attribution error	We attribute success or failure to the role of individuals and underestimate the role of circumstances and chance	37
Hindsight bias	We judge past decisions based on information that was not available at the time they were made, especially about their outcomes	100
Halo effect	We form a general impression (of a person, company, etc.) based on a few salient features and let that impression (halo) influence our assessment of unrelated features	40
Survivorship bias	We draw conclusions from samples that include successes but exclude failures	44

ACTION-ORIENTED BIASES

Bias	Definition	Page
Overplacement	We overestimate our relative abilities, i.e., how much better than others we are	64
Planning fallacy; unrealistic optimism	We do not sufficiently consider things (and combinations of things) that could derail our plans, resulting in an optimistic bias in estimates of time and cost to completion	64
Overprecision	We overestimate the degree of confidence we can have in our estimates and forecasts	67
Competitor neglect	We develop plans that overlook competitors' likely response to our actions	68

INERTIA BIASES

Bias	Definition	Page
Anchoring	When making estimates, we are influenced by available numbers, even if they are irrelevant	80
Resource inertia	We are timid in reallocating resources to reflect our stated priorities, especially when these priorities change suddenly	82
Status quo bias	We tend to avoid making a decision and to maintain the status quo by default	90
Escalation of commitment, sunk-cost fallacy	We double down on a failing course of action, notably because we do not treat the resources previously invested as sunk costs	83
Loss aversion	We feel a loss more keenly than a gain of the same amount	97
Irrational risk aversion	We refuse to take reasonable risks, fearing that, in case of failure, our choices will seem foolish in hindsight and we will be unjustly blamed	96
Uncertainty aversion	We prefer a quantified risk, even if it's high, over an unknown risk ("uncertainty" or "ambiguity")	99

SOCIAL BIASES

Bias	Definition	Page
Groupthink	In a group, we silence our doubts and side with the prevailing opinion instead of dissenting	121
Polarization	Groups tend to reach a conclusion that is more extreme than the average viewpoint of their members—and to be more confident in it	129
Information cascades	In a group, the sequence of speakers affects the outcome of the discussion, as private information is withheld and shared information emphasized	129

INTEREST BIASES

Bias	Definition	Page
Self-serving bias	We genuinely believe in viewpoints that happen to coincide with our interests, financial or otherwise (including emotional attachments)	141
Present bias	We use inconsistent discount rates when making present-future trade-offs, leading us to overweight the present (managerial myopia)	115
Omission bias	We are more indulgent with errors of omission than errors of commission, and find it morally acceptable to benefit from them	143

APPENDIX 2: 40 TECHNIQUES FOR BETTER DECISIONS

ORCHESTRATING DIALOGUE

Techniques	Page
Ensure sufficient cognitive diversity among participants	211
Make sufficient time for real discussion	212
Put dialogue on the agenda: topics "for discussion" vs. "for decision"	213
Limit the use of PowerPoint presentations; consider replacing them with written memos	215
Ban misleading analogies and similar storytelling arguments	217
Impose a cooling-off period to discourage hasty conclusions	218
Encourage nuanced viewpoints by asking each participant for his or her "balance sheet"	218
Appoint a devil's advocate	220
Ask for more than one proposal ("mandatory alternatives")	221
Ask what you would do if the current options were off the table ("vanishing options")	221
Require presenters to pitch competing views ("alternative stories")	222
Run a premortem	224
Assemble an ad hoc committee (for example, "Six Amigos")	225
Write up the list of deal breakers and review it at decision time ("memo in the CEO's drawer")	226
And don't forget to... Set an ending time for the discussion ("discord plus deadline")	228

ENCOURAGING DIVERGENCE

Techniques	Page
Cultivate a network of informal advisors	234
Get unfiltered expert opinion	235
Keep your consultants in the dark about your own hypotheses	236
Create an official role of "outside challenger"	238
Create a "red team" or set up a "war-gaming" exercise	239
Use the "wisdom of crowds" to aggregate estimates (simple averages, prediction markets) or to collect suggestions	240
Build a model to "re-anchor" a resource allocation decision	243
Use multiple analogies to fight confirmation bias	244
Change the default to fight status quo bias (for instance, portfolio reviews)	245
Use standardized frameworks and templates for recurring decisions	246
For unique decisions, define decision criteria beforehand	249
"Stress-test" key assumptions (especially worst-case scenarios)	250
Take the "outside view" based on a reference class of comparable projects	251
Update your beliefs as new data becomes available (use Bayes's Theorem if possible)	252
And don't forget to... Find ways to cultivate humility (for example, the "anti-portfolio")	256

PROMOTING AGILE DECISION-MAKING DYNAMICS

Techniques	Page
Cultivate a friendly atmosphere	261
Foster a "speak up" culture	262
Align the incentives with the common interest	263
Find ways to learn for free	264
Conduct real experiments and allow them to fail	265
Do postmortems of successes, too	268
Increase your commitments gradually, instead of making big gambles	269
Recognize the right to fail, not the right to make mistakes	270
Strategize like a Texas sharpshooter: limit outside communication about specific strategies	272
Role-model the ability to change your mind based on facts and discussion	273
Split the decision-making power between two people (or more)	274
Decide in an "inner circle" or small committee without conflicts of interest	275
And don't forget to... Make the decision and take responsibility for it—after sleeping on it	276

NOTES

GENERAL SOURCES

On behavioral psychology, decision-making, and cognitive biases in general

Ariely, Dan. *Predictably Irrational.* New York: HarperCollins, 2008.

Cialdini, Robert B. *Influence: How and Why People Agree to Things.* New York: Morrow, 1984.

Kahneman, Daniel. *Thinking, Fast and Slow.* New York: Farrar, Straus and Giroux, 2011.

Thaler, Richard H. *Misbehaving: The Making of Behavioral Economics.* New York: W. W. Norton, 2015.

On cognitive science applied to business, and especially on the effects of cognitive biases on business decision-making

Bazerman, Max H., and Don A. Moore. *Judgment in Managerial Decision Making.* Hoboken, NJ: Wiley, 2008.

Finkelstein, Sydney, Jo Whitehead, and Andrew Campbell. *Think Again: Why Good Leaders Make Bad Decisions and How to Keep It from Happening to You.* Boston: Harvard Business Review, 2008.

Heath, Chip, and Dan Heath. *Decisive: How to Make Better Choices in Life and Work.* New York: Crown Business, 2013.

Rosenzweig, Phil. *The Halo Effect . . . and the Eight Other Business Delusions That Deceive Managers.* New York: Free Press, 2007.

Sunstein, Cass R., and Reid Hastie. *Wiser: Getting Beyond Groupthink to Make Better Decisions.* Boston: Harvard Business Review, 2015.

On behavioral strategy

Lovallo, Dan, and Olivier Sibony. "The Case for Behavioral Strategy." *McKinsey Quarterly*, March 2010, 30–43.

Notes

Powell, Thomas C., Dan Lovallo, and Craig R. Fox. "Behavioral Strategy." *Strategic Management Journal* 32, no. 13 (2011): 1369–86.

Sibony, Olivier, Dan Lovallo, and Thomas C. Powell. "Behavioral Strategy and the Strategic Decision Architecture of the Firm." *California Management Review* 59, no. 3 (2017): 5–21.

On applications of behavioral psychology to public policy

Halpern, David. *Inside the Nudge Unit: How Small Changes Can Make a Big Difference.* W. H. Allen, 2015.

Thaler, Richard H., and Cass R. Sunstein. *Nudge: Improving Decisions About Health, Wealth, and Happiness.* New Haven, CT: Yale University Press, 2008.

Finally, for an introduction to theoretical perspectives on decision-making

March, James G. *Primer on Decision Making: How Decisions Happen.* New York: Free Press, 1994.

INTRODUCTION

On errors in management decisions

Carroll, Paul B., and Chunka Mui. *Billion Dollar Lessons: What You Can Learn from the Most Inexcusable Business Failures of the Last 25 Years.* New York: Portfolio/Penguin, 2008.

Finkelstein, Sydney. *Why Smart Executives Fail: And What You Can Learn from Their Mistakes.* New York: Portfolio/Penguin, 2004.

On the related issue of organizational error, not covered in this book

Hofmann, David A., and Michael Frese, eds. *Errors in Organizations.* SIOP Organizational Frontiers Series. New York: Routledge, 2011.

Perrow, Charles. *Normal Accidents: Living with High-Risk Technologies.* New York: Basic Books, 1984.

Reason, James. *Human Error.* Cambridge: Cambridge University Press, 1990.

Other

a survey of some two thousand executives: Lovallo, Dan, and Olivier Sibony. "The Case for Behavioral Strategy." *McKinsey Quarterly*, March 2010.

unconscious-bias training: Lublin, Joann S. "Bringing Hidden Biases into the Light." *Wall Street Journal*, January 9, 2014. See also Shankar Vedantam, "Radio Reply: The Mind of the Village," *The Hidden Brain*, National Public Radio, March 9, 2018, featuring Mahzarin Banaji and others.

the "Nudge" movement: Thaler, Richard H., and Cass R. Sunstein. *Nudge:*

Improving Decisions About Health, Wealth, and Happiness. New Haven, CT: Yale University Press, 2008.

"corporate behavioral science units": Güntner, Anna, Konstantin Lucks, and Julia Sperling-Magro. "Lessons from the Front Line of Corporate Nudging." *McKinsey Quarterly*, January 2019.

Keywords like *cognition, psychology:* Sibony, Olivier, Dan Lovallo, and Thomas C. Powell. "Behavioral Strategy and the Strategic Decision Architecture of the Firm." *California Management Review* 59, no. 3 (2017): 5–21.

a McKinsey survey of some eight hundred corporate board directors: Bhagat, Chinta, and Conor Kehoe. "High-Performing Boards: What's on Their Agenda?" *McKinsey Quarterly*, April 2014.

"If we're so stupid, how did we get to the moon?" Nisbett, Richard E., and Lee Ross. *Human Inference: Strategies and Shortcomings of Social Judgment.* Englewood Cliffs, NJ.: Prentice Hall, 1980.

Nisbett, Richard E., and Lee Ross. *Human Inference: Strategies and Shortcomings of Social Judgment.* Englewood Cliffs, NJ: Prentice Hall, 1980. Cited in Chip Heath, Richard P. Larrick, and Joshua Klayman. "Cognitive Repairs: How Organizational Practices Can Compensate for Individual Shortcomings." *Research in Organizational Behavior* 20, no. 1 (1998): 1–37.

CHAPTER 1

On "oil-sniffing airplanes"

Gicquel, François. "Rapport de la Cour des Comptes sur l'affaire des avions renifleurs." January 21, 1981. https://fr.wikisource.org/w/index.php?oldid=565802.

Lascoumes, Pierre. "Au nom du progrès et de la Nation: Les 'avions renifleurs.' La science entre l'escroquerie et le secret d'État." *Politix* 48, no. 12 (1999): 129–55.

Lashinsky, Adam. "How a Big Bet on Oil Went Bust." *Fortune*, March 26, 2010.

On confirmation bias

Nickerson, Raymond S. "Confirmation Bias: A Ubiquitous Phenomenon in Many Guises." *Review of General Psychology* 2, no. 2 (1998): 175–220.

Soyer, Emre, and Robin M. Hogarth. "Fooled by Experience." *Harvard Business Review*, May 2015, 73–77.

Stanovich, Keith E., and Richard F. West. "On the Relative Independence of Thinking Biases and Cognitive Ability." *Journal of Personality and Social Psychology* 94, no. 4 (2008): 672–95.

Stanovich, Keith E., Richard F. West, and Maggie E. Toplak. "Myside Bias, Rational Thinking, and Intelligence," *Current Directions in Psychological Science* 22, no. 4 (2013): 259–64.

Notes

On fake news and filter bubbles

Lazer, David M. J., et al. "The Science of Fake News." *Science* 359 (2018): 1094–96.

Kahan, Dan M., et al. "Science Curiosity and Political Information Processing," *Political Psychology* 38 (2017): 179–99.

Kraft, Patrick W., Milton Lodge, and Charles S. Taber. "Why People 'Don't Trust the Evidence': Motivated Reasoning and Scientific Beliefs." *Annals of the American Academy of Political and Social Science* 658, no. 1 (2015): 121–33.

Pariser, Eli. *The Filter Bubble: What the Internet Is Hiding from You.* London: Penguin, 2011.

Pennycook, Gordon, and David G. Rand. "Who Falls for Fake News? The Roles of Bullshit Receptivity, Overclaiming, Familiarity, and Analytic Thinking." SSRN working paper no. 3023545, 2018.

Taber, Charles S., and Milton Lodge. "Motivated Skepticism in the Evaluation of Political Beliefs." *American Journal of Political Science* 50, no. 3 (2006): 755–69.

On the forensic confirmation bias

Dror, Itiel E. "Biases in Forensic Experts." *Science* 360 (2018): 243.

Dror, Itiel E., and David Charlton. "Why Experts Make Errors." *Journal of Forensic Identification* 56, no. 4 (2006): 600–616.

On J. C. Penney

D'Innocenzio, Anne. "J. C. Penney: Can This Company Be Saved?" Associated Press in *USA Today*, April 9, 2013.

Reingold, Jennifer. "How to Fail in Business While Really, Really Trying." *Fortune*, March 20, 2014.

On the replication crisis

Ioannidis, John P. A. "Why Most Published Research Findings Are False." *PLoS Medicine* 2, no. 8 (2005): 0696–0701.

Lehrer, Jonah. "The Truth Wears Off." *The New Yorker*, December 2010.

Neal, Tess M. S., and Thomas Grisso. "The Cognitive Underpinnings of Bias in Forensic Mental Health Evaluations." *Psychology, Public Policy, and Law* 20, no. 2 (2014): 200–211.

Simmons, Joseph P., Leif D. Nelson, and Uri Simonsohn. "False-Positive Psychology: Undisclosed Flexibility in Data Collection and Analysis Allows Presenting Anything as Significant." *Psychological Science* 22, no. 11 (2011): 1359–66.

Other

Taleb, Nassim Nicholas. *The Black Swan: The Impact of the Highly Improbable*, 2d ed. New York: Random House, 2010.

CHAPTER 2

On the halo effect

Collins, Jim, and Jerry I. Porras. *Built to Last: Successful Habits of Visionary Companies*. New York: Harper & Row, 1982.

Nisbett, Richard E., and Timothy DeCamp Wilson. "The Halo Effect: Evidence for Unconscious Alteration of Judgments." *Journal of Personality and Social Psychology* 35, no. 4 (1977): 250–56.

Peters, Thomas J., and Robert H. Waterman Jr. *In Search of Excellence: Lessons from America's Best-Run Companies*. New York: Warner Books, 1984.

Rosenzweig, Phil. *The Halo Effect . . . and the Eight Other Business Delusions That Deceive Managers*. New York: Free Press, 2007.

On forced ranking

Cohan, Peter. "Why Stack Ranking Worked Better at GE Than Microsoft." *Forbes*, July 2012.

Kwoh, Leslie. "'Rank and Yank' Retains Vocal Fans." *Wall Street Journal*, January 31, 2012.

On the perils of strategic imitation

Nattermann, Philipp M. "Best Practice Does Not Equal Best Strategy." *McKinsey Quarterly*, May 2000, 22–31.

Porter, Michael E. "What Is Strategy?" *Harvard Business Review*, November–December 1996.

On survivorship bias

Brown, Stephen J., et al. "Survivorship Bias in Performance Studies." *Review of Financial Studies* 5, no. 4 (1992): 553–80.

Carhart, Mark M. "On Persistence in Mutual Fund Performance." *Journal of Finance* 52, no. 1 (1997): 57–82.

Ellenberg, Jordan. *How Not to Be Wrong: The Power of Mathematical Thinking*. London: Penguin, 2015.

CHAPTER 3

On managers and executives using intuition

Akinci, Cinla, and Eugene Sadler-Smith. "Intuition in Management Research: A Historical Review." *International Journal of Management Reviews* 14 (2012): 104–22.

Dane, Erik, and Michael G. Pratt. "Exploring Intuition and Its Role in Managerial Decision Making." *Academy of Management Review* 32, no. 1 (2007): 33–54.

Hensman, Ann, and Eugene Sadler-Smith. "Intuitive Decision Making in Banking and Finance." *European Management Journal* 29, no. 1 (2011): 51–66.

Sadler-Smith, Eugene, and Lisa A. Burke-Smalley. "What Do We Really Understand About How Managers Make Important Decisions?" *Organizational Dynamics* 9 (2014): 16.

On naturalistic decision-making

Cholle, Francis P. *The Intuitive Compass: Why the Best Decisions Balance Reason and Instinct.* Hoboken, NJ: Jossey-Bass/Wiley, 2011.

Gigerenzer, Gerd. *Gut Feelings: Short Cuts to Better Decision Making.* London: Penguin, 2008.

Gladwell, Malcolm. *Blink: The Power of Thinking Without Thinking.* New York: Little, Brown, 2005.

Klein, Gary. *Sources of Power: How People Make Decisions.* Cambridge, MA: MIT Press, 1998.

On heuristics and biases

Kahneman, Daniel. *Thinking, Fast and Slow.* New York: Farrar, Straus and Giroux, 2011.

Tversky, Amos, and Daniel Kahneman. "Belief in the Law of Small Numbers." *Psychological Bulletin* 76, no. 2 (1971): 105–10.

———. "Judgment Under Uncertainty: Heuristics and Biases." *Science* 185 (1974): 1124–31.

On the adversarial collaboration between Kahneman and Klein

Kahneman, Daniel, and Gary Klein. "Conditions for Intuitive Expertise: A Failure to Disagree." *American Psychologist* 64, no. 6 (2009): 515–26.

"Strategic Decisions: When Can You Trust Your Gut?" Interview with Daniel Kahneman and Gary Klein. *McKinsey Quarterly*, March 2010.

On the validity of expertise in various domains

Shanteau, James. "Competence in Experts: The Role of Task Characteristics." *Organizational Behavior and Human Decision Processes* 53, no. 2 (1992): 252–66.

———. "Why Task Domains (Still) Matter for Understanding Expertise." *Journal of Applied Research in Memory and Cognition* 4, no. 3 (2015): 169–75.

Tetlock, Philip E. *Expert Political Judgment: How Good Is It? How Can We Know?* Princeton, NJ: Princeton University Press, 2005.

On the (ir-)relevance of intuition in hiring decisions

Dana, Jason, Robyn Dawes, and Nathanial Peterson. "Belief in the Unstructured Interview: The Persistence of an Illusion." *Judgment and Decision Making* 8, no. 5 (2013): 512–20.

Heath, Dan, and Chip Heath. "Why It May Be Wiser to Hire People Without Meeting Them." *Fast Company*, June 1, 2009.

Moore, Don A. "How to Improve the Accuracy and Reduce the Cost of Personnel Selection." *California Management Review* 60, no. 1 (2017): 8–17.

Schmidt, Frank L., and John E. Hunter. "The Validity and Utility of Selection Methods in Personnel Psychology: Practical and Theoretical Implications of 85 Years of Research Findings." *Psychological Bulletin* 124, no. 2 (1998): 262–74.

CHAPTER 4

On overconfidence

Moore, Don A., and Paul J. Healy. "The Trouble with Overconfidence." *Psychological Review* 115, no. 2 (2008): 502–17.

Svenson, Ola. "Are We All Less Risky and More Skillful Than Our Fellow Drivers?" *Acta Psychologica* 47, no. 2 (1981): 143–48.

Thaler, Richard H., and Cass R. Sunstein. *Nudge: Improving Decisions About Health, Wealth, and Happiness.* New Haven, CT: Yale University Press, 2008.

On optimistic forecasts and the planning fallacy

Buehler, Roger, Dale Griffin, and Michael Ross. (1994). "Exploring the 'Planning Fallacy': Why People Underestimate Their Task Completion Times." *Journal of Personality and Social Psychology* 67, no. 3 (1994): 366–81.

Flyvbjerg, Bent, Mette Skamris Holm, and Soren Buhl. "Underestimating Costs in Public Works, Error or Lie?" *Journal of the American Planning Association* 68, no. 3 (Summer 2002): 279–95.

Frankel, Jeffrey A. "Over-Optimism in Forecasts by Official Budget Agencies and Its Implications." NBER working paper no. 17239, 2011.

On overprecision

Alpert, Marc, and Howard Raiffa. "A Progress Report on the Training of Probability Assessors." In *Judgment Under Uncertainty: Heuristics and Biases*, edited by Daniel Kahneman, Paul Slovic, and Amos Tversky, 294–305. Cambridge: Cambridge University Press, 1982.

Russo, J. Edward, and Paul J. H. Schoemaker. "Managing Overconfidence." *Sloan Management Review* 33, no. 2 (1992): 7–17.

On the underestimation of competition and competitor neglect

Cain, Daylian M., Don A. Moore, and Uriel Haran. "Making Sense of Overconfidence in Market Entry." *Strategic Management Journal* 36, no. 1 (2015): 1–18.

Dillon, Karen. "'I Think of My Failures as a Gift.'" *Harvard Business Review*, April 2011, 86–89.

"How Companies Respond to Competitors: A McKinsey Survey." *McKinsey Quarterly*, April 2008.

Moore, Don A., John M. Oesch, and Charlene Zietsma. "What Competition? Myopic Self-Focus in Market-Entry Decisions." *Organization Science* 18, no. 3 (2007): 440–54.

Rumelt, Richard P. *Good Strategy/Bad Strategy: The Difference and Why It Matters.* New York: Crown Business, 2011.

On evolution selecting for biases

Santos, Laurie R., and Alexandra G. Rosati. "The Evolutionary Roots of Human Decision Making," *Annual Review of Psychology* 66, no. 1 (2015): 321–47.

On the benefits of optimism

Rosenzweig, Phil. "The Benefits—and Limits—of Decision Models." *McKinsey Quarterly*, February 2014, 1–10.

———. *Left Brain, Right Stuff: How Leaders Make Winning Decisions.* New York: Public Affairs, 2014.

Other

Graser, Marc. "Epic Fail: How Blockbuster Could Have Owned Netflix." *Variety*, November 12, 2013.

CHAPTER 5

On Polaroid

Rosenbloom, Richard S., and Ellen Pruyne. "Polaroid Corporation: Digital Imaging Technology in 1997." Harvard Business School case study no. 798-013, October 1977. https://www.hbs.edu/faculty/Pages/item.aspx?num=24164.

Tripsas, Mary, and Giovanni Gavetti. "Capabilities, Cognition, and Inertia: Evidence from Digital Imaging." *Strategic Management Journal* 21, no. 10 (2000): 1147–61.

On inertia in resource allocation

Bardolet, David, Craig R. Fox, and Don Lovallo. "Corporate Capital Allocation: A Behavioral Perspective." *Strategic Management Journal* 32, no. 13 (2011): 1465–83.

Birshan, Michael, Marja Engel, and Olivier Sibony. "Avoiding the Quicksand: Ten Techniques for More Agile Corporate Resource Allocation." *McKinsey Quarterly*, October 2013, 6.

Hall, Stephen, and Conor Kehoe. "How Quickly Should a New CEO Shift Corporate Resources?" *McKinsey Quarterly*, October 2013, 1–5.

Hall, Stephen, Dan Lovallo, and Reinier Musters. "How to Put Your Money Where Your Strategy Is." *McKinsey Quarterly*, March 2012, 11.

Notes

On anchoring

Englich, Birte, Thomas Mussweiler, and Fritz Strack. "Playing Dice with Criminal Sentences: The Influence of Irrelevant Anchors on Experts' Judicial Decision Making." *Personality and Social Psychology Bulletin* 32, no. 2 (2006): 188–200.

Galinsky, Adam D., and Thomas Mussweiler. "First Offers as Anchors: The Role of Perspective-Taking and Negotiator Focus." *Journal of Personality and Social Psychology* 81, no. 4 (2001): 657–69.

Strack, Fritz, and Thomas Mussweiler. "Explaining the Enigmatic Anchoring Effect: Mechanisms of Selective Accessibility." *Journal of Personality and Social Psychology* 73, no. 3 (1997): 437–46.

Tversky, Amos, and Daniel Kahneman. "Judgment Under Uncertainty: Heuristics and Biases." *Science* 185 (1974): 1124–31.

On the escalation of commitment

Drummond, Helga. "Escalation of Commitment: When to Stay the Course." *Academy of Management Perspectives* 28, no. 4 (2014): 430–46.

Royer, Isabelle. "Why Bad Projects Are So Hard to Kill." *Harvard Business Review*, February 2003, 48–56.

Staw, Barry, M. "The Escalation of Commitment: An Update and Appraisal." In *Organizational Decision Making*, edited by Zur Shapira, 191–215. Cambridge: Cambridge University Press, 1997.

——— . "The Escalation of Commitment to a Course of Action." *Academy of Management Review* 6, no. 4 (1981): 577–87.

On GM's Saturn business

Ritson, Mark. "Why Saturn Was Destined to Fail." *Harvard Business Review*, October 2009, 2–3.

Taylor, Alex, III. "GM's Saturn Problem." *Fortune*, December 2014.

On the small number of divestitures

Feldman, Emilie, Raphael Amit, and Belen Villalonga. "Corporate Divestitures and Family Control." *Strategic Management Journal* 37, no. 3 (2014) 429–46.

Horn, John T., Dan P. Lovallo, and S. Patrick Viguerie. "Learning to Let Go: Making Better Exit Decisions." *McKinsey Quarterly*, May 2006, 64.

Lee, Donghun, and Ravi Madhavan. "Divestiture and Firm Performance: A Meta-Analysis." *Journal of Management* 36, no. 6 (February 2010): 1345–71.

On disruption

Christensen, Clayton M. *The Innovator's Dilemma: When New Technologies Cause Great Firms to Fail*. Boston: Harvard Business School Press, 1997.

On Netflix and Qwikster

Wingfield, Nick, and Brian Stelter. "How Netflix Lost 800,000 Members, and Good Will." *New York Times*, October 24, 2011.

On status quo bias

Kahneman, Daniel, Jack L. Knetsch, and Richard H. Thaler. "Anomalies: The Endowment Effect, Loss Aversion, and Status Quo Bias." *Journal of Economic Perspectives* 5, no. 1 (1991): 193–206.

Samuelson, William, and Richard Zeckhauser. "Status Quo Bias in Decision Making." *Journal of Risk and Uncertainty* 1, no. 1 (1988): 7–59.

Notes

"...admits mistakes and kills unsuccessful initiatives in a timely manner": McKinsey study of 463 executives, 2009. See "Strategic Decisions: When Can You Trust Your Gut?" Interview with Daniel Kahneman and Gary Klein. *McKinsey Quarterly*, March 2010.

a landmark study on exit decisions: Horn, John T., Dan P. Lovallo, and S. Patrick Viguerie. "Learning to Let Go: Making Better Exit Decisions." *McKinsey Quarterly*, May 2006, 64.

CHAPTER 6

On exaggerated risk aversion

Koller, Tim, Dan Lovallo, and Zane Williams. "Overcoming a Bias Against Risk." *McKinsey Quarterly*, August 2012, 15–17.

On the lack of innovation in large corporations

Armental, Maria. "U.S. Corporate Cash Piles Drop to Three-Year Low." *Wall Street Journal*, June 10, 2019.

Christensen, Clayton M., and Derek C. M. van Bever. "The Capitalist's Dilemma." *Harvard Business Review*, June 2014, 60–68.

Grocer, Stephen. "Apple's Stock Buybacks Continue to Break Records." *New York Times*, August 1, 2018.

On loss aversion

Kahneman, Daniel, and Amos Tversky. "Prospect Theory: An Analysis of Decision Under Risk." *Econometrica* 47, no. 2 (1979): 263–91.

On hindsight bias

Baron, Jonathan, and John C. Hershey. "Outcome Bias in Decision Evaluation." *Journal of Personality and Social Psychology* 54, no. 4 (1988): 569–79.

Fischhoff, Baruch. "An Early History of Hindsight Research." *Social Cognition* 25, no. 1 (2007): 10–13.

———. "Hindsight Is Not Equal to Foresight: The Effect of Outcome Knowledge on Judgment Under Uncertainty." *Journal of Experimental Psychology: Human Perception and Performance* 1, no. 3 (1975): 288–99.

Fischhoff, Baruch, and Ruth Beyth. "'I Knew It Would Happen': Remembered Probabilities of Once-Future Things." *Organizational Behavior and Human Performance* 13, no. 1 (1975): 1–16.

On the narrative bias and hindsight bias in historical research
Risi, Joseph, et al. "Predicting History." *Nature Human Behaviour* 3 (2019): 906–12.
Rosenberg, Alex. *How History Gets Things Wrong: The Neuroscience of Our Addiction to Stories*. Cambridge, MA: MIT Press, 2018.

On Churchill's rise to power in 1940
Shakespeare, Nicholas. *Six Minutes in May: How Churchill Unexpectedly Became Prime Minister*. London: Penguin Random House, 2017.

On the hindsight bias in organizations
Thaler, Richard H. *Misbehaving: The Making of Behavioral Economics*. New York: W. W. Norton, 2015.

On the paradox of timid choices and bold forecasts
Kahneman, Daniel, and Dan Lovallo. "Timid Choices and Bold Forecasts: A Cognitive Perspective on Risk Taking." *Management Science* 39, no. 1 (1993): 17–31.
March, James G., and Zur Shapira. "Managerial Perspectives on Risk and Risk Taking." *Management Science* 33, no. 11 (1987): 1404–18.

Note
"...certainly the most significant contribution of psychology to behavioral economics": Kahneman, Daniel. *Thinking, Fast and Slow*. New York: Farrar, Straus and Giroux, 2011, 360.

CHAPTER 7

On long-term capitalism
Barton, Dominic, and Mark Wiseman. "Focusing Capital on the Long Term." *McKinsey Quarterly*, December 2013.
Business Roundtable. "Statement on the Purpose of a Corporation." August 19, 2019. Available at https://opportunity.businessroundtable.org/wp-content/uploads/2020/02/BRT-Statement-on-the-Purpose-of-a-Corporation-with-Signatures-Feb2020.pdf.
Fink, Laurence D. Letter to CEOs. March 21, 2014.
George, Bill. "Bill George on Rethinking Capitalism." *McKinsey Quarterly*, December 2013.

Polman, Paul. "Business, Society, and the Future of Capitalism." *McKinsey Quarterly*, May 2014.

Porter, Michael, and Marc Kramer. "Creating Shared Value." *Harvard Business Review*, January 2011.

On managerial myopia

Asker, John, Joan Farre-Mensa, and Alexander Ljungqvist. "Corporate Investment and Stock Market Listing: A Puzzle?" *Review of Financial Studies* 28, no. 2 (February 2015): 342–90.

Graham, John R., Campbell R. Harvey, and Shiva Rajgopal. "Value Destruction and Financial Reporting Decisions." *Financial Analysts Journal* 62, no. 6 (2006): 27–39.

On earnings guidance

Buffett, Warren E., and Jamie Dimon. "Short-Termism Is Harming the Economy." *Wall Street Journal*, June 6, 2018.

Cheng, Mey, K. R. Subramanyam, and Yuan Zhang. "Earnings Guidance and Managerial Myopia." SSRN working paper, November 2005.

Hsieh, Peggy, Timothy Koller, and S. R. Rajan. "The Misguided Practice of Earnings Guidance." *McKinsey on Finance*, Spring 2006.

Palter, Rob, Werner Rehm, and Johnathan Shih. "Communicating with the Right Investors." *McKinsey Quarterly*, April 2008.

On present bias and the problem of self-control

Benhabib, Jess, Alberto Bisin, and Andrew Schotter. "Present-Bias, Quasi-Hyperbolic Discounting, and Fixed Costs." *Games and Economic Behavior* 69, no. 2 (2010): 205–23.

Frederick, Shane, George Loewenstein, and Ted O'Donoghue. "Time Discounting and Time Preference: A Critical Review." *Journal of Economic Literature* 40, no. 2 (2002): 351–401.

Laibson, David. "Golden Eggs and Hyperbolic Discounting." *Quarterly Journal of Economics* 112, no. 2 (1997): 443–77.

Loewenstein, George, and Richard H. Thaler. "Anomalies: Intertemporal Choice." *Journal of Economic Perspectives* 3, no. 4 (1989): 181–93.

Thaler, Richard H. "Some Empirical Evidence on Dynamic Inconsistency." *Economics Letters* 8, no. 3 (1981): 201–7.

Thaler, Richard H., and Hersh M. Shefrin. "An Economic Theory of Self-Control." *Journal of Political Economy* 89, no. 2 (1981): 392–406.

CHAPTER 8

On groupthink

Janis, Irving L. *Groupthink: Psychological Studies of Policy Decisions and Fiascoes.* Boston: Wadsworth, 1982.

Schlesinger, Arthur M., Jr. *A Thousand Days: John F. Kennedy in the White House.* Boston: Houghton Mifflin, 1965.

Whyte, William H. "Groupthink (Fortune 1952)." *Fortune,* July 22, 2012.

On Buffett at Coca-Cola

Quick, Becky. CNBC *Closing Bell* interview with Warren E. Buffett, April 23, 2014. https://fm.cnbc.com/applications/cnbc.com/resources/editorialfiles/2014/04/23/2014-04-23%20Warren%20Buffett%20live%20interview%20transcript.pdf.

On cascades and group polarization

Greitemeyer, Tobias, Stefan Schulz-Hardt, and Dieter Frey. "The Effects of Authentic and Contrived Dissent on Escalation of Commitment in Group Decision Making." *European Journal of Social Psychology* 39, no. 4 (June 2009): 639–47.

Heath, Chip, and Rich Gonzalez. "Interaction with Others Increases Decision Confidence but Not Decision Quality: Evidence Against Information Collection Views of Interactive Decision Making." *Organizational Behavior and Human Decision Processes* 61, no. 3 (1995): 305–26.

Hung, Angela A., and Charles R. Plott. "Information Cascades: Replication and an Extension to Majority Rule and Conformity-Rewarding Institutions." *American Economic Review* 91, no. 5 (December 2001): 1508–20.

Stasser, Garold, and William Titus. "Hidden Profiles: A Brief History." *Psychological Inquiry* 14, nos. 3–4 (2003): 304–13.

Sunstein, Cass R. "The Law of Group Polarization." *Journal of Political Philosophy* 10, no. 2 (2002): 175–95.

Sunstein, Cass R., and Reid Hastie. *Wiser: Getting Beyond Groupthink to Make Better Decisions.* Boston: Harvard Business Review Press, 2015.

Whyte, Glen. "Escalating Commitment in Individual and Group Decision Making: A Prospect Theory Approach." *Organizational Behavior and Human Decision Processes* 54, no. 3 (1993): 430–55.

Zhu, David H. "Group Polarization in Board Decisions About CEO Compensation." *Organization Science* 25, no. 2 (2013): 552–71.

CHAPTER 9

On agency theory

Bebchuk, Lucian A., and Jesse M. Fried. "Executive Compensation as an Agency Problem." *Journal of Economic Perspectives* 17, no. 3 (2003): 71–92.

Fama, Eugene F., and Michael C. Jensen. "Separation of Ownership and Control." *Journal of Law and Economics* 26, no. 2 (1983): 301–25.

Hope, Ole-Kristian, and Wayne B. Thomas. "Managerial Empire Building and Firm Disclosure." *Journal of Accounting Research* 46, no. 3 (2008): 591–626.

Jensen, Michael C., and William H. Meckling. "Theory of the Firm: Managerial Behavior, Agency Costs and Ownership Structure." *Journal of Financial Economics* 3, no. 4 (1976): 305–60.

On managerial misconduct

Bergstresser, Daniel, and Thomas Philippon. "CEO Incentives and Earnings Management." *Journal of Financial Economics* 80, no. 3 (2006): 511–29.

Greve, Henrich R., Donald Palmer, and Jo-Ellen Pozner. "Organizations Gone Wild: The Causes, Processes, and Consequences of Organizational Misconduct." *Academy of Management Annals* 4, no. 1 (2010): 53–107.

McAnally, Mary Lea, Anup Srivastava, and Connie D. Weaver. "Executive Stock Options, Missed Earnings Targets, and Earnings Management." *Accounting Review* 83, no. 1 (2008): 185–216.

On the ultimatum game

Cameron, Lisa A. "Raising the Stakes in the Ultimatum Game: Experimental Evidence from Indonesia." *Economic Inquiry* 37, no. 1 (1999): 47–59.

Güth, Werner, Rolf Schmittberger, and Bernd Schwarze. "An Experimental Analysis of Ultimatum Bargaining." *Journal of Economic Behavior & Organization* 3, no. 4 (1982): 367–88.

Kahneman, Daniel, Jack L. Knetsch, and Richard H. Thaler. (1986). "Fairness and the Assumptions of Economics." *Journal of Business* 59, S4 (1986): S285–300.

Thaler, Richard H. "Anomalies: The Ultimatum Game." *Journal of Economic Perspectives* 2, no. 4 (1988): 195–206.

On bounded ethicality and behavioral ethics

Ariely, Dan. *The (Honest) Truth About Dishonesty: How We Lie to Everyone—Especially Ourselves*. New York: HarperCollins, 2012.

Bazerman, Max H., George Loewenstein, and Don A. Moore. "Why Good Accountants Do Bad Audits." *Harvard Business Review*, November 2002.

Bazerman, Max H., and Don A. Moore. *Judgment in Managerial Decision Making*. Hoboken, NJ: Wiley, 2008.

Bazerman, Max H., and Francesca Gino. "Behavioral Ethics: Toward a Deeper Understanding of Moral Judgment and Dishonesty." *Annual Review of Law and Social Science* 8 (2012): 85–104.

Bazerman, Max H., and Ann E. Tenbrunsel. *Blind Spots: Why We Fail to Do What's Right and What to Do About It.* Princeton, NJ: Princeton University Press, 2011.

Haidt, Jonathan. "The New Synthesis in Moral Psychology." *Science* 316 (2007): 998–1002.

Harvey, Ann H., et al. "Monetary Favors and Their Influence on Neural Responses and Revealed Preference." *Journal of Neuroscience* 30, no. 28 (2010): 9597–9602.

Kluver, Jesse, Rebecca Frazier, and Jonathan Haidt. "Behavioral Ethics for Homo Economicus, Homo Heuristicus, and Homo Duplex." *Organizational Behavior and Human Decision Processes* 123, no. 2 (2014): 150–58.

On differences in judgment of commission and omission

Paharia, Neeru, et al. "Dirty Work, Clean Hands: The Moral Psychology of Indirect Agency." *Organizational Behavior and Human Decision Processes* 109, no. 2 (2009): 134–41.

Spranca, Mark, Elisa Minsk, and Jonathan Baron. "Omission and Commission in Judgment and Choice." *Journal of Experimental Social Psychology* 27, no. 1 (1991): 76–105.

On disclosure

Cain, Daylian M., George Loewenstein, and Don A. Moore. (2005). "The Dirt on Coming Clean: Perverse Effects of Disclosing Conflicts of Interest." *Journal of Legal Studies* 34, no. 1 (2005): 1–25.

Other

Smith, Adam. *The Wealth of Nations.* Edited, with an Introduction and Notes by Edwin Cannan. New York: Modern Library, 1994.

CHAPTER 10

On taxonomies of biases, and of ways to overcome them

Bazerman, Max H., and Don A. Moore. *Judgment in Managerial Decision Making.* Hoboken, NJ: Wiley, 2008.

Dobelli, Rolf. *The Art of Thinking Clearly.* Translated by Nicky Griffin. New York: HarperCollins, 2013.

Dolan, Paul, et al. "MINDSPACE: Influencing Behaviour Through Public Policy." Cabinet Office and Institute for Government, London, UK, 2010.

Finkelstein, Sydney, Jo Whitehead, and Andrew Campbell. *Think Again: Why Good Leaders Make Bad Decisions and How to Keep It from Happening to You.* Boston: Harvard Business Press, 2008.

Halpern, David. *Inside the Nudge Unit: How Small Changes Can Make a Big Difference*. New York: W. H. Allen, 2015.

Heath, Chip, and Dan Heath. *Decisive: How to Make Better Choices in Life and Work*. New York: Crown Business, 2013.

Service, Owain, et al. "EAST: Four Simple Ways to Apply Behavioural Insights." Behavioural Insights Ltd. and Nesta. April 2014.

Tversky, Amos, and Daniel Kahneman. "Judgment Under Uncertainty: Heuristics and Biases." *Science* 185 (1974): 1124–31.

On the danger of attributing all bad outcomes, in hindsight, to biases

Rosenzweig, Phil. *Left Brain, Right Stuff: How Leaders Make Winning Decisions*. New York: Public Affairs, 2014.

On the track record of acquisitions

Bruner, Robert F. "Does M&A Pay? A Survey of Evidence for the Decision-Maker." *Journal of Applied Finance* 12, no. 1 (2002): 48–68.

Cartwright, Susan, and Richard Schoenberg. "Thirty Years of Mergers and Acquisitions Research: Recent Advances and Future Opportunities." *British Journal of Management* 17, Suppl. 1 (2006).

Datta, Deepak K., George E. Pinches, and V. K. Narayanan. "Factors Influencing Wealth Creation from Mergers and Acquisitions: A Meta-Analysis." *Strategic Management Journal* 13, no. 1 (1992): 67–84.

On competitor neglect, see sources for chapter 4. On divestitures, see sources for chapter 5.

CHAPTER 11

On efforts to overcome biases

Dobelli, Rolf. *The Art of Thinking Clearly*. Translated by Nicky Griffin. New York: HarperCollins, 2013.

Finkelstein, Sydney, Jo Whitehead, and Andrew Campbell. *Think Again: Why Good Leaders Make Bad Decisions and How to Keep It From Happening to You*. Boston: Harvard Business Press, 2008.

Hammond, John S., Ralph L. Keeney, and Howard Raiffa. "The Hidden Traps in Decision Making." *Harvard Business Review*, January 2006, 47–58.

On debiasing and the bias blind spot

Fischhoff, Baruch. "Debiasing." In *Judgment Under Uncertainty: Heuristics and Biases*, edited by Daniel Kahneman, Paul Slovic, and Amos Tversky, 422–44. Cambridge: Cambridge University Press, 1982.

Milkman, Katherine L., Dolly Chugh, and Max H. Bazerman. "How Can

Decision Making Be Improved?" *Perspectives on Psychological Science* 4, no. 4 (2009): 379–83.

Morewedge, Carey K., et al. "Debiasing Decisions: Improved Decision Making with a Single Training Intervention." *Policy Insights from the Behavioral and Brain Sciences* 2, no. 1 (2015): 129–40.

Nisbett, Richard E. *Mindware: Tools for Smart Thinking.* New York: Farrar, Straus and Giroux, 2015.

Pronin, Emily, Daniel Y. Lin, and Lee Ross. "The Bias Blind Spot: Asymmetric Perceptions of Bias in Others Versus the Self." *Personality and Social Psychology Bulletin* 28, no. 3 (2002): 369–81.

Sellier, Anne-Laure, Irene Scopelliti, and Carey K. Morewedge. "Debiasing Training Transfers to Improve Decision Making in the Field." *Psychological Science* 30, no. 9 (2019): 1371–79.

Soll, Jack B., Katherine L. Milkman, and John W. Payne. "A User's Guide to Debiasing." In *The Wiley Blackwell Handbook of Judgment and Decision Making,* Vol. 2, edited by Gideon Keren and George Wu, 924–51. Chichester, UK: Wiley-Blackwell, 2016.

On the Cuban missile crisis

Kennedy, Robert F. *Thirteen Days: A Memoir of the Cuban Missile Crisis.* New York: W. W. Norton, 1969.

White, Mark. "Robert Kennedy and the Cuban Missile Crisis: A Reinterpretation." *American Diplomacy,* September 2007.

Other

McKinsey & Company. "Dan Ariely on Irrationality in the Workplace." Interview. February 2011. https://www.mckinsey.com/business-functions/ strategy-and-corporate-finance/our-insights/dan-ariely-on-irrationality-in -the-workplace#.

Preston, Caroline E., and Stanley Harris. "Psychology of Drivers in Traffic Accidents." *Journal of Applied Psychology* 49, no. 4 (1965): 284–88.

Notes

"blind to the obvious, and we are also blind to our blindness": Kahneman, Daniel. *Thinking, Fast and Slow.* New York: Farrar, Straus and Giroux, 2011, 24.

"I'm really not optimistic…": "Strategic Decisions: When Can You Trust Your Gut?" Interview with Daniel Kahneman and Gary Klein. *McKinsey Quarterly,* March 2010.

CHAPTER 12

On accidents in space exploration

Clervoy, Jean-François, private communication.

Space travel: Wikipedia, s.v. "List of Spaceflight-Related Accidents and Incidents." Accessed July 20, 2014.

On checklists

Gawande, Atul. *The Checklist Manifesto: How to Get Things Right*. New York: Metropolitan Books, 2009.

Haynes Alex B., et al. "A Surgical Safety Checklist to Reduce Morbidity and Mortality in a Global Population." *New England Journal of Medicine* 360, no. 5 (2009): 491–99.

Kahneman, Daniel, Dan Lovallo, and Olivier Sibony. "The Big Idea: Before You Make That Big Decision." *Harvard Business Review*, June 2011.

On corporate decision-making practices

Heath, Chip, Richard P. Larrick, and Joshua Klayman. "Cognitive Repairs: How Organizational Practices Can Compensate for Individual Shortcomings." *Research in Organizational Behavior* 20, no. 1 (1998): 1–37.

CHAPTER 13

On Bill Miller

McDonald, Ian. "Bill Miller Dishes on His Streak and His Strategy," *Wall Street Journal*, January 6, 2005.

Mlodinow, Leonard. *The Drunkard's Walk: How Randomness Rules Our Lives*. New York: Vintage, 2009.

On investment decisions

Garbuio, Massimo, Dan Lovallo, and Olivier Sibony. "Evidence Doesn't Argue for Itself: The Value of Disinterested Dialogue in Strategic Decision-Making." *Long Range Planning* 48, no. 6 (2015): 361–80.

Lovallo, Dan, and Olivier Sibony. "The Case for Behavioral Strategy." *McKinsey Quarterly*, March 2010, 30–43.

Other

"The Spectacular Rise and Fall of WeWork." *The Daily* podcast, *New York Times*, November 18, 2019, featuring Masayoshi Son.

CHAPTER 14

On brainstorming

Diehl, Michael, and Wolfgang Stroebe. "Productivity Loss in Brainstorming Groups: Toward the Solution of a Riddle." *Journal of Personality and Social Psychology* 53, no. 3 (1987): 497–509.

Keeney, Ralph L. "Value-Focused Brainstorming." *Decision Analysis* 9, no. 4 (2012): 303–13.

Sutton, Robert I., and Andrew Hargadon. "Brainstorming Groups in Context: Effectiveness in a Product Design Firm." *Administrative Science Quarterly* 41, no. 4 (1996): 685–718.

On cognitive diversity

Reynolds, Alison, and David Lewis. "Teams Solve Problems Faster When They're More Cognitively Diverse." *Harvard Business Review*, March 2017, 6.

Roberto, Michael A. *Why Great Leaders Don't Take Yes for an Answer*. Upper Saddle River, NJ: Pearson Education, Inc./Prentice Hall, 2005.

On PowerPoint

Bezos, Jeff. "Forum on Leadership: A Conversation with Jeff Bezos." April 20, 2018. Accessed at: https://www.youtube.com/watch?v=xu6vFIKAUxk&amp=& feature=youtu.be&amp=&t=26m31s].

——— . Letter to Amazon shareholders ["shareowners"], [April 2017]. https://www.sec.gov/Archives/edgar/data/1018724/000119312518121161 /d456916dex991.htm

Kaplan, Sarah. "Strategy and PowerPoint: An Inquiry into the Epistemic Culture and Machinery of Strategy Making." *Organization Science* 22, no. 2 (2011): 320–46.

On authentic dissent

Greitemeyer, Tobias, Stefan Schulz-Hardt, and Dieter Frey. "The Effects of Authentic and Contrived Dissent on Escalation of Commitment in Group Decision Making." *European Journal of Social Psychology* 39, no. 4 (June 2009): 639–47.

Nemeth Charlan, Keith Brown, and John Rogers. "Devil's Advocate Versus Authentic Dissent: Stimulating Quantity and Quality." *European Journal of Social Psychology* 31, no. 6 (2001): 707–20.

On multiple options

Heath, Chip, and Dan Heath. *Decisive: How to Make Better Choices in Life and Work*. New York: Crown Business, 2013.

Nutt, Paul C. "The Identification of Solution Ideas During Organizational Decision Making." *Management Science* 39, no. 9 (1993): 1071–85.

On the premortem

Klein, Gary. "Performing a Project Premortem." *Harvard Business Review*, September 2007.

Klein, Gary, Paul D. Sonkin, and Paul Johnson. "Rendering a Powerful Tool Flaccid: The Misuse of Premortems on Wall Street." 2019. Retrieved from: https://capitalallocatorspodcast.com/wp-content/uploads/Klein-Sonkin-and-Johnson-2019-The-Misuse-of-Premortems-on-Wall-Street.pdf.

On fair process

Kim, W. Chan, and Renée Mauborgne. "Fair Process Managing in the Knowledge Economy." *Harvard Business Review*, January 2003.

Sunstein, Cass R., and Reid Hastie. *Wiser: Getting Beyond Groupthink to Make Better Decisions.* Boston: Harvard Business Review Press, 2015.

Other

"How We Do It: Three Executives Reflect on Strategic Decision Making." Interview with Dan Lovallo and Olivier Sibony. *McKinsey Quarterly*, March 2010.

Schmidt, Eric. "Eric Schmidt on Business Culture, Technology, and Social Issues." *McKinsey Quarterly*, May 2011, 1–8.

CHAPTER 15

On Michael Burry

Lewis, Michael. *The Big Short: Inside the Doomsday Machine.* New York: W. W. Norton, 2010.

On the value of divergent ideas

Gino, Francesca. *Rebel Talent: Why It Pays to Break the Rules at Work and in Life.* New York: Dey Street Books, 2018.

Grant, Adam. *Originals: How Non-Conformists Change the World.* New York: Penguin, 2017.

On red teams and structured analytic techniques

Chang, Welton, et al. "Restructuring Structured Analytic Techniques in Intelligence." *Intelligence and National Security* 33, no. 3 (2018): 337–56.

U.S. Government. "A Tradecraft Primer: Structured Analytic Techniques for Improving Intelligence Analysis. March 2009." Center for the Study of Intelligence, CIA.gov, March 2009, 1–45. https://www.cia.gov/library/center-for-the-study-of-intelligence/csi-publications/books-and-monographs/Tradecraft%20Primer-apr09.pdf.

Notes

On the wisdom of crowds

Atanasov, Pavel, et al. "Distilling the Wisdom of Crowds: Prediction Markets vs. Prediction Polls." *Management Science* 63, no. 3 (March 2017): 691–706.

Galton, Francis. "Vox Populi." *Nature* 75 (1907): 450–51.

Mann, A. "The Power of Prediction Markets." *Nature* 538 (October 2016): 308–10.

Surowiecki, James. *The Wisdom of Crowds*. New York: Doubleday, 2004.

On re-anchoring

Lovallo, Dan, and Olivier Sibony. "Re-anchor your next budget meeting." *Harvard Business Review*, March 2012.

On structured analogies

Lovallo, Dan, Carmina Clarke, and Colin F. Camerer. "Robust Analogizing and the Outside View: Two Empirical Tests of Case-Based Decision Making." *Strategic Management Journal* 33, no. 5 (2012): 496–512.

Sepp, Kalev I. "Best Practices in Counterinsurgency." *Military Review*, May 2005.

On strategic decision processes

Sibony, Olivier, Dan Lovallo, and Thomas C. Powell. "Behavioral Strategy and the Strategic Decision Architecture of the Firm." *California Management Review* 59, no. 3 (2017): 5–21.

On the outside view and reference class forecasting

De Reyck, Bert, et al. "Optimism Bias Study: Recommended Adjustments to Optimism Bias Uplifts." UK Department for Transport, n.d. Available at https://assets.publishing.service.gov.uk/government/uploads/system /uploads/attachment_data/file/576976/dft-optimism-bias-study.pdf.

Flyvbjerg, Bent. "Curbing Optimism Bias and Strategic Misrepresentation in Planning: Reference Class Forecasting in Practice." *European Planning Studies* 16, no. 1 (2008): 3–21.

Flyvbjerg, Bent, Massimo Garbuio, and Dan Lovallo. "Delusion and Deception in Large Infrastructure Projects: Two Models for Explaining and Preventing Executive Disaster." *California Management Review* 51, no. 2 (2009): 170–93.

Flyvbjerg, Bent, and Allison Stewart. "Olympic Proportions: Cost and Cost Overrun at the Olympics 1960–2012." *SSRN Electronic Journal*, June 2012, 1–23.

Kahneman, Daniel. Beware the 'Inside View.'" *McKinsey Quarterly*, November 2011, 1–4.

Lovallo Dan, and Daniel Kahneman. "Delusions of Success." *Harvard Business Review*, July 2003, 56–63.

On Bayesian updating

Silver, Nate. *The Signal and the Noise: Why So Many Predictions Fail—But Some Don't*. New York: Penguin, 2012.

Tetlock, Philip E., and Dan Gardner. *Superforecasting: The Art and Science of Prediction*. New York: Broadway Books, 2016.

Other

Sorkin, Andrew Ross. "Buffett Casts a Wary Eye on Bankers." *New York Times*, March 1, 2010, citing Warren E. Buffett's annual letter to Berkshire Hathaway shareholders.

CHAPTER 16

On the risk appetite of entrepreneurs

Grant, Adam. *Originals: How Non-Conformists Change the World*. New York: Penguin, 2017.

On experiments

Halpern, David. *Inside the Nudge Unit: How Small Changes Can Make a Big Difference*. New York: W. H. Allen, 2015.

Lourenço, Joana Sousa, et al. "Behavioural Insights Applied to Policy: European Report 2016."

Ries, Eric. *The Lean Startup*. New York: Crown Business, 2011.

On the virtue of "sleeping on it"

Dijksterhuis, Ap, et al. (2006). "On Making the Right Choice: The Deliberation Without Attention Effect." *Science* 311 (2006): 1005–7.

Vul, Edward, and Harold Pashler. "Measuring the Crowd Within: Probabilistic Representations Within Individuals." *Psychological Science* 19, no. 7 (2008): 645–48.

CONCLUSION

Notes

As psychologist Gary Klein puts it...: "Strategic Decisions: When Can You Trust Your Gut?" Interview with Daniel Kahneman and Gary Klein. *McKinsey Quarterly*, March 2010.

"Level 5" leaders: Collins, Jim. *Good to Great*. New York: HarperBusiness, 2001.

INDEX

Note: Italic page numbers refer to illustrations.

Index

ABOUT THE AUTHOR

Olivier Sibony is a professor, writer, advisor, and keynote speaker specializing in the quality of strategic decision-making. He teaches Strategy and Problem Solving at HEC Paris. He is also an Associate Fellow of Saïd Business School at Oxford University. Previously, Sibony spent twenty-five years with McKinsey & Company in France and in the United States, where he was a Senior Partner.

Sibony's research centers on improving the quality of decision-making by reducing the impact of behavioral biases. He is the author of numerous articles in academic and popular publications, including "Before You Make That Big Decision," coauthored with Nobel Prize winner Daniel Kahneman and Dan Lovallo.

Sibony is a graduate of HEC Paris and holds a PhD from Université Paris-Dauphine. He is married and the father of two children. He lives in Paris.